Story Central Plus

Teacher Edition 4 with Teacher Resources

macmillan education

Virginia Marconi

Macmillan Education Limited
4 Crinan Street
London N1 9XW

Companies and representatives throughout the world

Story Central Plus Level 4 Teacher Edition ISBN 978-1-380-06116-4
Story Central Plus Level 4 Teacher Edition with Student eBook, Reader eBook, CLIL eBook, Digital Activity Book, Teacher Resource Center, and Test Generator ISBN 978-1-380-06114-0

Teacher Edition credits:
Designed by Red Phoenix Design
Page make-up by Mike Brain Graphic Design Limited and Composure
Illustrated by Steven Wood (Advocate Art)
Cover design by Wild Apple Design Ltd

Student Book credits:
Text © Angela Llanas and Libby Williams
Design and illustration © Macmillan Education Limited 2021
The authors have asserted their rights to be identified as the authors of this work in accordance with the Copyright, Designs and Patents Act 1988.

Designed by Wild Apple Design Ltd and Pronk Media, Inc
Illustrated by Aardvart p. 78; Ilias Arahovitis (Beehive Illustration) pp. 8, 92; David Belmonte (Beehive Illustration) pp. 122 -123, 124, 125; A Corazio Albierto (Sylvie Poggio Artist Agency) pp. 24 -25, 26, 27; Russ Daff (Beehive Illustration) pp. 22, 50, 79, 93; Nelson Evergreen (Bright Agency) pp. 66 -67, 68, 69; Begoña Fernández (Adovcate Art) pp 18, 19, 20, 46, 47, 48, 74, 75, 76, 102, 103, 104, 105, 130, 131, 132; Diane Le Feyer (Advocate Art) pp. 80 -81, 82, 83; Pablo Gallego (Beehive Illustration) pp. 13b, 17, 23, 27b, 31, 41b, 55b, 59, 65, 69b, 73, 83b, 87, 97b, 101, 111b, 115, 121, 125b, 129; Dante Ginerva (Advocate Art) pp. 122 -123, 124, 125; David Lopez (Bright Agency) pp. 10 -11, 12, 13; Lucia Mascciulo (Pickled Ink) pp. 94 -95, 96, 97; David Neale (Bright Agency) pp. 52 -53, 54, 55; Ria Maria Lee (The Bright Agency) pp 32, 33, 34, 60, 61, 62, 63, 88, 89, 90, 116, 117, 118; Laszlo Veres (Beehive Illustration) pp. 36, 45, 64, 71; Steven Wood (Advocate Art) pp. 4 -135 (border design and main character artwork) 4 -5, 6-7, 10, 14, 24l, 28, 38l, 42, 52l, 56, 66l, 70, 80l, 84, 94l, 98, 108l, 112, 122l, 126.
Cover design by Wild Apple Design Ltd and Roberto Martinez
Cover artwork by Steven Wood (Advocate Art)
Cover photographs by Paul Bricknell, Shutterstock/New Africa (back cover).
Picture research by Composure
The authors and publishers would like to thank the following for permission to reproduce their photographs:
Alamy Stock Photo/Alaska Stock p. 120(5), Alamy Stock Photo/All Canada Photos pp. 120(4,6), Alamy Stock Photo/amana images inc. p. 107(c), Alamy Stock Photo/Chronicle p. 85(tr), Alamy Stock Photo/CPA Media Pte Ltd p. 64(1), Alamy Stock Photo/foodfolio p. 106(8), Alamy Stock Photo/George H.H. Huey p. 120(7), Alamy Stock Photo/Granger Historical Picture Archive pp. 15(tl), 65(cl), Alamy Stock Photo/Holger Burmeister p. 113(bl), Alamy Stock Photo/imageBROKER p. 107(br), Alamy Stock Photo/IMAGEMORE Co., Ltd. p. 113(tr), Alamy Stock Photo/Images of Africa Photobank p. 43(cl), Alamy Stock Photo/ImageZoo p. 64(7), Alamy Stock Photo/Jochen Tack p. 99(cl), Alamy Stock Photo/John Michaels p. 120(8), Alamy Stock Photo/Jon Arnold Images Ltd p. 9(cm), Alamy Stock Photo/Paul Hawkett p. 120(1), Alamy Stock Photo/Purestock p. 9(cr), Alamy Stock Photo/RGB Ventures/SuperStock p. 37(tcr), Alamy Stock Photo/robertharding pp. 106(3), 107(cr), Alamy Stock Photo/Spotmatik p. 107(bm), Alamy Stock Photo/Ted Foxx p. 57(cl),Alamy Stock Photo/Wavebreak Media ltd p. 18(br), Alamy Stock Photo/Worldspec/NASA p. 37(tcl); Getty Images/Adelman-Cohen p. 37(tr), Getty Images/Aleksandr_Vorobev p. 119(tr), Getty Images/Andreyuu p. 99(tl), Getty Images/Authenticated News/Staff p. 64(4), Getty Images/Avalon_Studio p. 57(cr), Getty Images/bhofack2 p. 120(2), Getty Images/Charles Bowman p. 15(cl), Getty Images/Comstock pp. 29(tl), 57(tl), Getty Images/Con Tanasiuk p. 64(5), Getty Images/Daniel Pludowski/EyeEm p. 43(tr), Getty Images/Danita Delimont p. 106(1), Getty Images/DEA/G. DAGLI ORTI/Contributor p. 64(3), Getty Images/DEA PICTURE LIBRARY p. 71(cl), Getty Images/duncan1890 p. 71(tl), Getty Images/GlobalStock p. 127(tr), Getty Images/HannamariaH p. 106(7), Getty Images/Heide Benser p. 51(tr), Getty Images/Inti St Clair p. 21(tr), Getty Images/Jupiterimages p. 65(tl), Getty Images/kali9 p. 33(cr), Getty Images/Library of Congress/Contributor p. 15(tr), Getty Images/ljubaphoto p. 35(tr), Getty Images/Marc Ward/Stocktrek Images p. 43(cr), Getty Images/Markus Moellenberg p. 57(tr), Getty Images/Mike Ledwith p. 106(2), Getty Images/Monty Rakusen p. 99(tr), Getty Images/Pauline St.Denis p. 107(tl), Getty Images/PeopleImages p. 49(tr), Getty Images/Pete Turner p. 85(c), Getty Images/pinyoj p. 64(2), Getty Images/plusphoto/amanaimagesRF p. 106(6), Getty Images/Prykhodov p. 64(8), Getty Images/PT Images p. 107(tr), Getty Images/RainbowJoe p. 85(tl), Getty Images/spxChrome p. 29(cr), Getty Images/Stockbyte p. 29(tm), Getty Images/Stocktrek Images p. 37(tl), Getty Images/Subir Basak p. 107(bl), Getty Images/Tetra Images p. 65(cr), Getty Images/Tim Graham/Contributor p. 120(3), Getty Images/TIMOTHY A. CLARY/Staff p. 106(4); Macmillan Education Limited/Cultura Creative (RF /Alamy Stock Photo p. 77(tr), Macmillan Education Limited/GETTY pp. 64(6), 65(br), 91(cr), Macmillan Education Limited/Godong/UIG p. 106(5), Macmillan Education Limited/IMAGE 100 p. 49(tl), Macmillan Education Limited/Macmillan Publishers p. 107(cl), Macmillan Education Limited/Redmond Durrell/Alamy Stock Photo p. 133(tr), Macmillan Education Limited/robas p. 91(t).
Commissioned Photography by MMStudios pp. 16, 30, 44, 58, 72, 86, 100, 114, 128.
Prop artwork by Carla Drury

Reader credits:
Text, design and illustration © Macmillan Education Limited 2021
Written by Angela Llanas and Libby Williams
Stories adapted by Jenny Mason
The authors have asserted their rights to be identified as the authors of this work in accordance with the Copyright, Designs and Patents Act 1988.

Page design and art editing by Wild Apple Design Ltd
Storyboard layouts by Carrie Webb (Red Phoenix Design)
Reader credits: Where's Claire? illustrated by David Lopez (Bright Agency); Lulu's Sick Day illusrated by A Corazio Albierto (Sylvie Poggio Artist Agency); Planetary Checkup illustrated by Folko Streese (Beehive Illustration); The House at the End of the Road illustrated by David Neale (Bright Agency); The Secret of Key Island illustrated by Nelson Evergreen (Bright Agency); Aladdin illustrated by Diane Le Feyer (Advocate Art); Whodunit? illustrated by Lucia Mascciulo (Pickled Ink); Thor and the Stolen Hammer illustrated by David Belmonte (Beehive Illustration); Kakapo Adventure illustrated by Dante Ginerva (Advocate Art).--
Cover design by Wild Apple Design Ltd
Cover artwork: front cover, David Lopez (Bright Agency), Diane Le Feyer (Advocate Art), and Dante Ginerva (Advocate Art); back cover, A Corazio Albierto (Sylvie Poggio Artist Agency) and Folko Streese (Beehive Illustration).

Activity Book credits:
Designed by Liz Adcock
Page make-up by Carrie Webb (Red Phoenix Design) and Composure
Illustrated by A.C. Apierto (Sylvie Poggio) pp 16 -17; David Belmonte (Beehive Illustration) pp 64 -65;
Robin Boyden (Pickled Ink) pp 6, 12, 14, 22, 35, 43, 44, 46, 51, 54, 62, 68, 74, 82, 88; Nelson Evergreen
(Bright Agency) pp 40 -41; Dante Ginerva (Advocate Art) pp 72 -73; Andy Keylock (Beehive Illustration) p15;
Diane le Feyer (Advocate Art) pp 48 -49; David Lopez (Bright Agency) p8; Luci Masciullo (Pickled Ink) p56;
David Neale (Advocate Art) pp32 -33; Andrew Painter pp 9, 10, 13, 15, 18, 21, 23, 26, 29, 30, 35, 37, 39, 45, 47, 53, 55, 59, 61, 68, 69, 77, 79, 80, 83, 84, 86, 90, 93, 94, 97, 98; Jorge Santillan (Beehive Illustration) pp 7, 11, 18 -20, 27, 28, 31, 36, 38, 42, 50, 52, 54, 58, 66, 67, 70, 71, 75, 78, 80, 81, 82, 83, 85, 86, 89, 91, 92, 95, 101, 103; Folko Streese (Beehive Illustration) pp24 -25; Steven Wood (Advocate Art) pp3 -77.
Cover design by Wild Apple Design Ltd and Roberto Martinez
Cover illustration by Steven Wood (Advocate Art)
Commissioned photograph by MMStudios p. 89.

Printed and bound in Singapore

2021
80

Contents

Contents

4

Competencies

me	act	think	learn	communicate
Activities that encourage children to accept responsibility and reflect on the consequences of lifestyle choices.	Activities that develop societal understanding and identification of children's own circumstances in a wider context.	Activities that develop critical thinking skills to reflect upon, manipulate, process, and interpret information.	Activities that foster learner autonomy, and allow children to demonstrate and put into practice learning strategies.	Activities that promote interpersonal and collaborative skills, develop teamwork, and allow children to express opinions and ideas.

Philosophy

1 Language is power.

Story Central Plus empowers children to communicate effectively and develop their knowledge of the world around them through stories. The course enables children to become critical and active readers, writers, and storytellers through its strong focus on literacy development.

2 An empowered teacher empowers children and changes lives.

Story Central Plus provides teachers with all the support they need to deliver effective and inspiring lessons. Children will respond to the meaningful texts and activities, ensuring that both teachers and children feel a real sense of achievement. Children will develop the skills they need to participate fully in their lives both inside and outside the classroom.

3 The child is not a blank slate.

Children bring their culture, beliefs, and a rich inner world to the classroom. Our materials respect this and recognize that it is key to engaging and interesting children in learning English.

4 Nurturing critical and creative thinking helps children become well-rounded and innovative adults.

Story Central Plus actively encourages creative, divergent, and playful thinking, and consistently supports the acquisition of academic knowledge.

Methodology

Literacy

Reading and writing skills are developed throughout the course. Each chapter is based around a story. An extract from the story is introduced in Student Book Lesson 3, allowing opportunities to develop reading skills and encouraging children to think creatively as they analyze the language in a meaningful context, and predict story developments. The full story is given in the beautifully illustrated Reader. Use of the Reader is fully integrated and the story links together the chapter theme and target language, providing language-rich input and enabling holistic learning. Activities engage children's interest and imagination as they are encouraged to read for pleasure. After children have read the story, their writing skills are developed through personal responses and creative writing. A love of literature is further fostered by the Oral Storytelling Videos.

Critical Literacy

Story Central Plus takes children beyond understanding texts. The material and activities help them analyze and respond, as they develop the skills of questioning and interpreting the information they encounter. Children are encouraged to discuss the story's meaning and how the values expressed relate to their lives and the world around them. Children are supported in expressing their opinions through presentations, role play, and extended writing. These essential skills will empower them to use language effectively later in life.

Critical and Creative Thinking

Critical and creative thinking are actively encouraged. Children are given every opportunity to figure things out for themselves and share their ideas. Vocabulary is presented in context, requiring them to use textual and visual clues to process and deduce meaning. Prediction, reflection, and drawing conclusions all play an important part in developing an imaginative and reflective response.

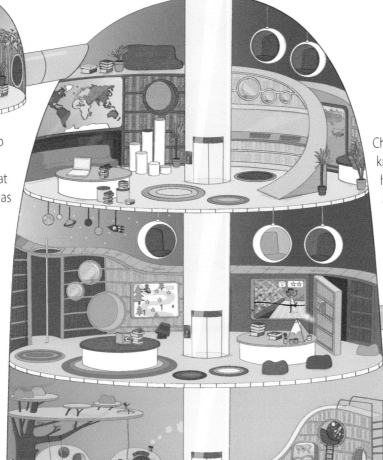

Story Central is a cool club where kids hang out with their friends and read great books. They also share ideas and stories, plan events, do homework, and drink milkshakes! In Story Central you can explore, discover, learn, research, and interact. It's the sort of place where kids really want to be!

Children will love getting to know the fun characters who hang out in Story Central. They appear in Lesson 3 and Lesson 6 in every chapter.

Level 4 Characters

Jason is a college student who works part-time in Story Central. He studies English and loves writing stories!

Felicity is an independent nine-year-old girl who likes taking the lead. She is independent and fun-loving! She loves reading.

Cheng is Felicity's best friend. He's also nine years old and he really enjoys sports. He always has a lot of good ideas!

Miguel is ten years old and loves hanging out with Felicity and Cheng at Story Central. He's really into gadgets!

Component Overview

For the Student

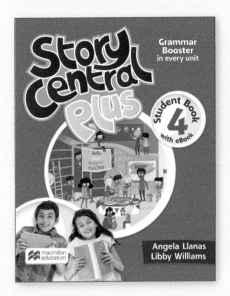

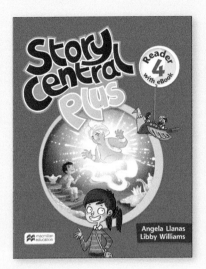

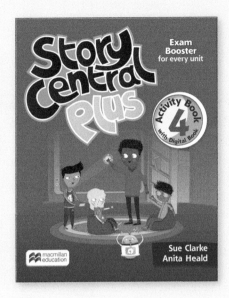

Student Book

Consists of 9 thematic chapters, featuring a story extract, literacy development, competency coverage, CLIL content, and project work. Focuses on developing critical thinking, creativity, communication, and collaboration. NEW! Grammar Booster section per chapter presents and provides further grammar practice of the target vocabulary.

Reader

Consists of 9 stories of different genres and styles. Focuses on promoting critical literacy and reading skills through developing a love of reading.

Activity Book

Consists of follow-on lessons for every Student Book lesson. Focuses on consolidating key language and skills, and developing creative use of language in writing. NEW! Exam Booster section per chapter provides Cambridge YLE practice activities.

eBooks

The Student Book has an access code which provides access to eBooks for the Student Book, Reader, and CLIL Book. The eBooks have embedded audio, video, and a set of tools to interact with the pages to provide flexibility for remote learning and give students more ways to read and learn.

The Inks Vocabulary Practice App

The Inks Apps provide a fun way for students to practice the vocabulary words they've learned for better retention. They're free and available to download from the App Store and Google Play.

Digital Activity Book

These books provide students an interactive way to practice. Students' answers are sent automatically to the gradebook so teachers and caregivers can monitor progress.

For the Teacher

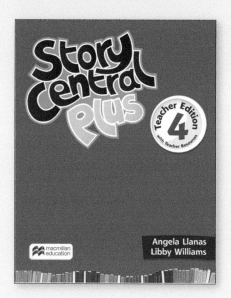

Teacher Resource Center

Consists of the class audio, and additional resources and ideas to extend lessons and learning, and give further practice of key language. Focuses on giving teachers flexibility and the means to deliver dynamic and varied lessons.

Test Generator

Pre-written tests for each chapter, mid-year, and end-of-year are available to download from the Teacher Resource Center. In addition, the Test Generator allows teachers to customize and create new tests from a bank of activities.

Teacher Edition

Consists of teaching notes for each lesson of the Student Book, Reader, and Activity Book, and suggestions on when and how to use digital components. Focuses on providing clear and concise support for lesson planning and teaching.

Oral Storytelling Videos bring the stories to life with mesmerising narration set in Story Central Plus. These are available for Chapters 1, 3, 5, 7, and 9.

Teacher Presentation Kit

Consists of the Student eBook, Digital Activity Book, Reader eBook and CLIL eBook.

Student eBook

This eBook provides a digital version of the Student Book with integrated audio, video and answer keys.

Digital Activity Book

This eBook provides an interactive version of the Activity Book that is linked to a gradebook.

Music Videos will get children dancing! They can copy the actions modeled on screen for the songs from Chapters 2, 4, 6, and 8.

Reader eBook

This eBook provides a digital version of the Reader with embedded audio and Storytelling Videos.

CLIL eBook

This eBook provides a digital version of the CLIL Book with embedded audio.

Teaching with *Story Central Plus*

Lesson 1 Vocabulary

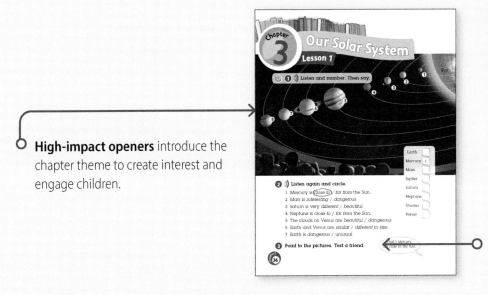

High-impact openers introduce the chapter theme to create interest and engage children.

Vocabulary is introduced through visual clues to develop **critical thinking skills**, encouraging children to deduce meaning.

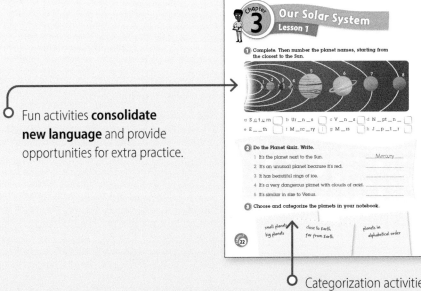

Fun activities **consolidate new language** and provide opportunities for extra practice.

Categorization activities **empower children** by giving them **choices** about how they learn.

Lesson 2 Grammar

Grammar is presented clearly and accessibly, recycling Lesson 1 vocabulary.

Grammar Central highlights new grammar structures, providing a useful reference for activities.

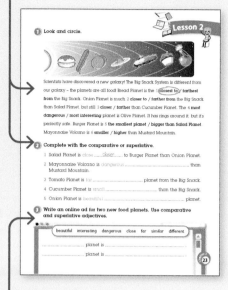

Listening activities are available to stream or download from the Teacher Resource Center and in the Student eBook.

Further grammar practice in the Activity Book consolidates language.

Writing activities provide well-supported and progressive development of writing skills.

NEW! Grammar Booster sections in the Student Book at the end of each chapter provide four pages of extra support. They include detailed grammar boxes and scaffolded practice for lessons 2 and 6, a review page that combines the grammar points in both lessons and a challenge page. These pages offer support for different language proficiency levels in the classroom. They can be assigned to individual children or the entire class.

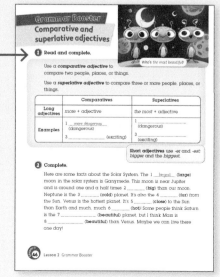

Supplementary **grammar worksheets** can be downloaded from the Teacher Resource Center to further consolidate learning in class or as homework.

Lesson 3 Reading: Story Extract

A **functional dialogue** featuring the Story Central characters teaches useful language for the classroom.

Children predict what the story is about before reading, to develop **visual literacy**.

Comprehension questions about the story extract check understanding.

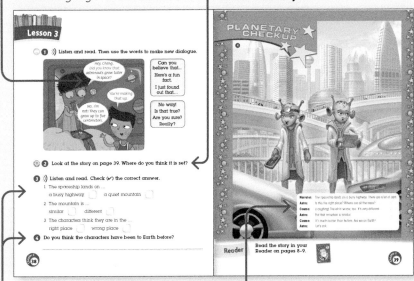

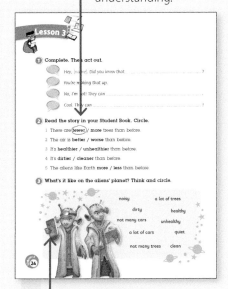

Comprehension and prediction questions develop reading skills and strategies.

The **story extract** (beginning, middle, or end) engages children but leaves plenty to the imagination.

A **prediction activity** asks children to use their **imagination** to figure out what will happen in the story.

Reader

Children read the whole story in their Reader.

A wide variety of story genres and narrative styles gives a **rich literary experience**.

Beautiful illustrations motivate children to **read for pleasure** and develop **a lifelong love of reading**.

Extensive language input allows **holistic language learning**, with the focus on overall understanding.

Lesson 4 Reading Comprehension and Critical Literacy

After reading the story in the Reader, children answer questions which help develop **reading strategies**.

The **I Can Read and Write!** feature highlights and practices text conventions.

Graphic organizer activities develop **study skills**.

Children practice the Student Book **I Can Read and Write!** text conventions.

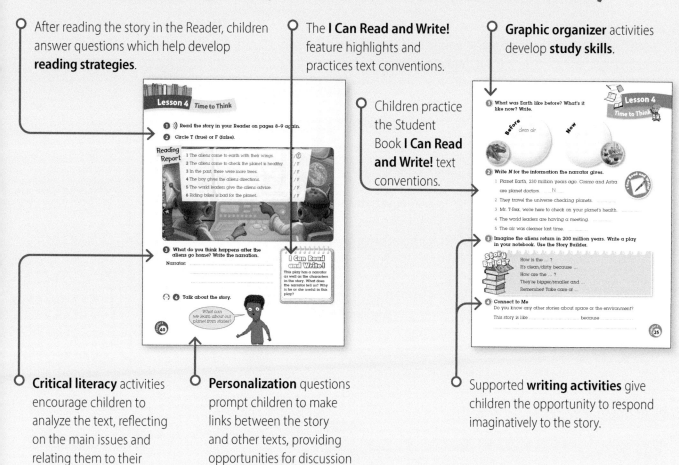

Critical literacy activities encourage children to analyze the text, reflecting on the main issues and relating them to their own lives.

Personalization questions prompt children to make links between the story and other texts, providing opportunities for discussion and self-expression.

Supported **writing activities** give children the opportunity to respond imaginatively to the story.

In the **Oral Storytelling Videos** professional storytellers act out and bring to life the Reader stories for Chapters 1, 3, 5, 7, and 9 (available in the Student eBook and the Reader eBook).

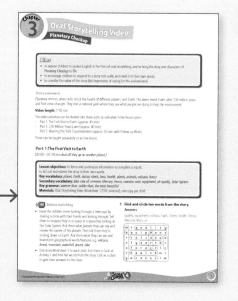

Teaching notes and worksheets for the Oral Storytelling Videos provide activity ideas for before, during, and after watching (downloadable from the Teacher Resource Center). A **Literacy Handbook** gives support and ideas for developing literacy skills with young learners.

Lesson 5 Vocabulary, Song, and Spelling

Catchy **songs** present new vocabulary in a fun, memorable, and motivating context.

Vocabulary is introduced through textual and visual clues to develop **critical thinking skills** (deduction of meaning).

Word work activities consolidate vocabulary and help develop strategies for memorizing vocabulary.

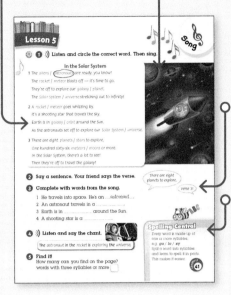

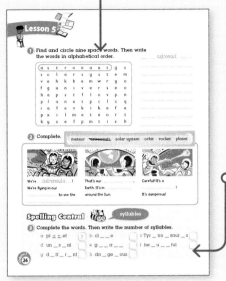

Speaking activities give practice in a meaningful context to develop fluency.

Spelling tips are covered in **Spelling Central**, with a chant and activity to give practice.

Children identify and practice the spellings from the Student Book **Spelling Central** feature.

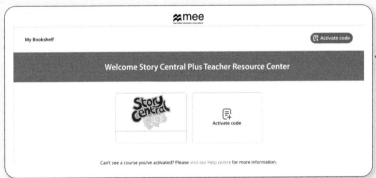

Supplementary **phonics worksheets** can be downloaded from the Teacher Resource Center to further consolidate learning in class or as homework.

Music Videos for Chapters 2, 4, 6, and 8 encourage children to move to the music and the actions consolidate the learning of the target vocabulary (available in the Student eBook).

The lively clan of The Inks on the **Student's App** provide children with motivating and challenging games to practice the chapter vocabulary from Lesson 1 and Lesson 5 outside the classroom. *The Inks* Apps are free and available on the App Store and Google Play.

Lesson 6 Grammar and Reading

The Story Central characters present new **grammar** in a lively, meaningful context which recycles the vocabulary from the chapter.

Grammar Central highlights new grammar structures and provides a useful reference.

Children are given the opportunity for controlled **written practice** of the new structures.

Grammar practice activities give staggered support.

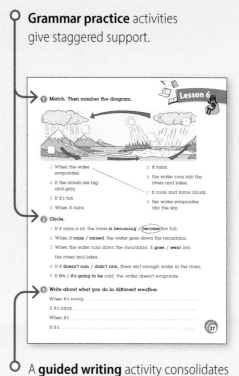

A **guided writing** activity consolidates grammar and progressively develops writing skills.

NEW! Grammar Booster sections in the Student Book at the end of each chapter provide four pages of extra support. They include detailed grammar boxes and scaffolded practice for lessons 2 and 6, a review page that combines the grammar points in both lessons and a challenge page. These pages offer support for different language proficiency levels in the classroom. They can be assigned to individual children or the entire class.

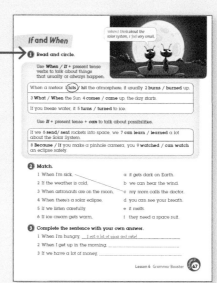

Supplementary **grammar worksheets** can be downloaded from the Teacher Resource Center to further consolidate learning in class or as homework.

Lesson 7 CLIL

The **CLIL** focus gives the opportunity to find out about other curricular areas (such as science, math, social science) through English.

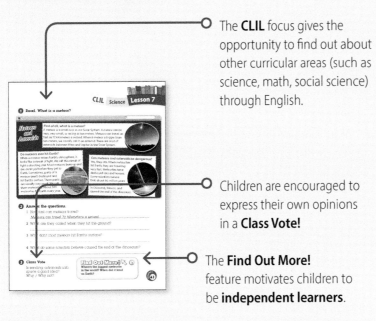

Children are encouraged to express their own opinions in a **Class Vote!**

The **Find Out More!** feature motivates children to be **independent learners**.

Children use their **Find Out More!** research to complete a mini-project extending the CLIL topic.

Lesson 8 Project

Children do a **craft experiment, or presentation** that relates to the chapter theme and Reader story.

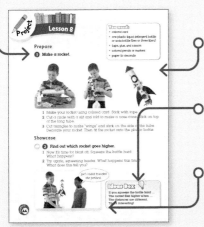

Photographs provide clear, step-by-step instructions.

An Ideas Box gives children useful language that they can use in their presentation.

Children then **present** their project to the class.

An interactive speaking task—a **fun game** for children to complete in pairs—rounds off the chapter.

The **CLIL eBook** expands the CLIL topics from the Student Book with **additional real-world content and practice activities.**

Each CLIL lesson has an optional **graphic organizer** template to help children organize their findings (downloadable from the Teacher Resource Center).

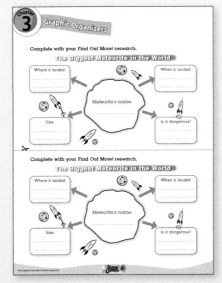

Review

The Review lesson provides **further practice and consolidation** of language from the chapter.

Children reflect on their own progress and color in the appropriate circle to record their progress (**self-evaluation**).

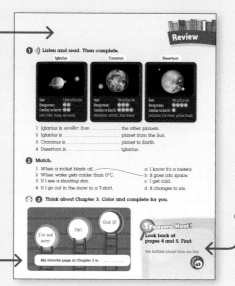

A fun **Treasure Hunt!** activity takes children back to the Welcome section (pp. 4–5) to find an item from the chapter.

New! Exam Booster sections in the Activity Book (pp. 78–104) provides **Cambridge English Young Learners Exams**-style activities practicing the language from each chapter. These help prepare for the Reading and Writing, Listening and Speaking papers of the Cambridge English Exam.

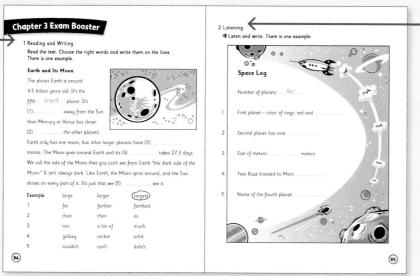

Class audio for the listening activities are in the Teacher Resource Center.

The Teacher Resource Center provides a wealth of assessment support including pre-written chapter, mid-year, and end-of-year tests. **CEYLT (Cambridge YLE)**-style speaking prompts and tips are also available.

Festivals worksheets and teaching notes to be used during the year bring the world outside into the classroom and help to foster an understanding of different cultures.

Teacher Edition Overview

Chapter Overview

An **Overview** at the start of every chapter provides a quick reference point to show what is covered.
The **Competency Focus** shows where competencies are developed throughout the chapter.
The **Digital Overview** shows the variety of digital resources available for the chapter.

Student Book and Activity Book Lessons

Each lesson opens with the lesson objectives, key language, and any materials required.

A **Warmer** activity introduces children to the lesson topic, activating prior knowledge, and getting the children energized!

Reduced pages for the **Student Book** and the **Activity Book** give easy reference to the components being used.

Optional activities allow you to extend lessons and offer opportunities for further practice and personalization.

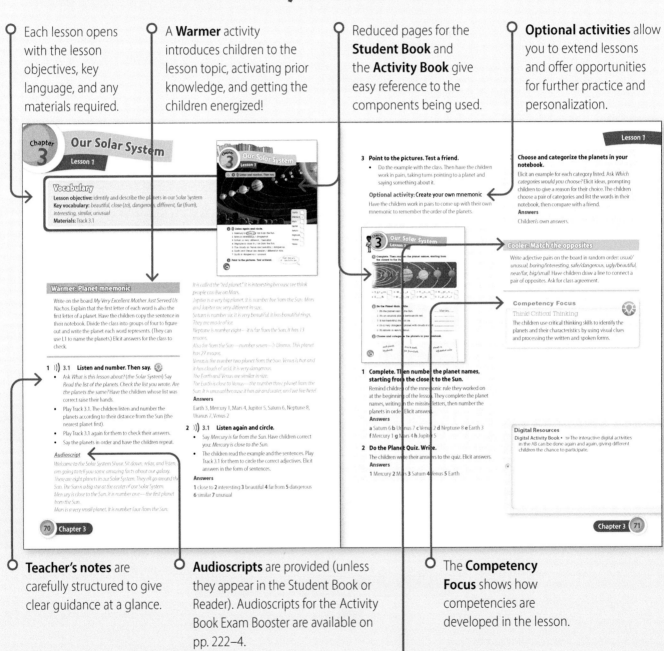

Teacher's notes are carefully structured to give clear guidance at a glance.

Audioscripts are provided (unless they appear in the Student Book or Reader). Audioscripts for the Activity Book Exam Booster are available on pp. 222–4.

The **Competency Focus** shows how competencies are developed in the lesson.

A **Cooler** activity allows children to review language learned in a fun context.

Reader

The **Reader** lesson contains a range of additional activities that teachers can use as they please. Teachers can get children to read the Reader story at home or in class.

Story Time helps you get the most out of the Reader component, helping teachers become more effective storytellers in the classroom.

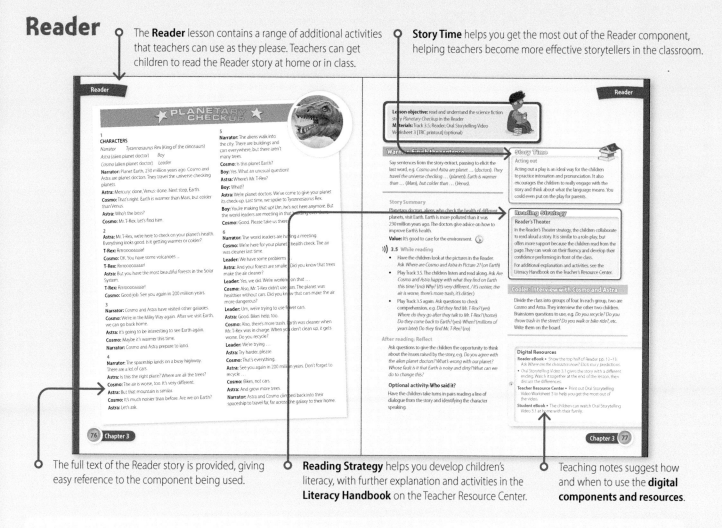

The full text of the Reader story is provided, giving easy reference to the component being used.

Reading Strategy helps you develop children's literacy, with further explanation and activities in the **Literacy Handbook** on the Teacher Resource Center.

Teaching notes suggest how and when to use the **digital components and resources**.

Games Bank

Below are details of popular and easy-to-use games that can be played in different lessons to engage, stimulate and motivate.

Bingo

Draw a grid with nine squares on the board and have the children copy it into their notebooks. The children add a vocabulary item to each square. Call out items. The children cross them off if they have them. When all are crossed off, they shout *Bingo!*

I Spy

Divide the children into two teams. Have a child from the first team look around the class and secretly choose one object. They say *I spy with my little eye something beginning with (C)!* The other team guesses the object. Teams take turns.

Ready, Set, Draw!

Divide the children into teams. Secretly give a child from each team a word to draw.

The first team to identify the word correctly wins a point.

Simon Says

Have the children stand. Say actions for them to mime. They can only mime when you say *Simon says (swim)*. If you say just *Swim*, they stand still. If a child does the wrong mime, they sit down. The last child standing is the winner.

Spelling Bee

Divide the class into two teams. Say a word. The children from each team take turns writing it on the board. Each correctly spelled word wins a point.

The Chain Game

Have the class stand. Start off a chain, e.g. *I went to the store and I bought apples.*

Each child repeats the chain so far and adds an item, e.g. *I went to the store and I bought apples and oranges.* If a child makes a mistake or can't think of an item, they sit down. The last child standing wins.

The Shark Game

Draw on the board six steps leading down to water. On the top step, draw a stick person. In the water, draw a shark. Think of a word and draw a line to represent each letter. The children take turns calling out a letter. If it's correct, write the letter on the corresponding line. If it's wrong, erase the stick person and move him down one step, closer to the shark. If the children guess the word correctly, the class wins a point.

Story Central

Lesson objectives: remember Story Central characters; sing the course song
Key language: *welcome, characters, costume, poems, mysteries, history, violin*
Materials: Tracks 0.2 and 0.3; a whistle or other noisemaker (Warmer)

Warmer: Play "The Hello Game"

Set out four chairs in a circle, facing out. Ask six children to come to the front of the class. Shake hands with one and say *Hello, my name is* … Have the children introduce themselves to each other in the same way. Blow the whistle. Everyone runs to find a chair. The two children who do not get one go back to their desk. Choose two different children to replace them. Repeat several times.

1))) 0.2   Listen and sing.

- Have the children look at the picture. Ask *Who can you see?* Elicit the character names. (*Felicity, Cheng, Miguel, Jason*) Point to the word for *hello* in different languages.
- Play Track 0.2. The children listen to the song and read along.
- Play Track 0.2 again for the children to sing along.

Optional activity: Show me …

Have the children look at the picture. Say *Show me a child eating pizza* for them to hold up their book and point to the appropriate part of the picture. They then work in pairs, taking turns prompting with *Show me* … and finding the detail in the picture.

1 Complete for you and a friend. Then share your answers with the class.

The children answer the questions for themselves. They then ask and answer the questions in pairs. Ask pairs to ask and answer for the class.

Answers

Children's own answers.

2))) 0.3 Who is it? Write.

Play Track 0.3 twice. (See p. 22 for audioscript.) The children listen out for what the Story Central characters do. They write the name of the character who says each sentence. Elicit answers.

Answers

1 Miguel **2** Felicity **3** Miguel **4** Cheng **5** Felicity

Cooler: Sing and do

))) Track 0.2

Agree on actions for the song. Play Track 0.2 twice for the children to sing along and do the actions.

Digital Resources

Student eBook, Digital Activity Book • All SB and AB pages can be shown on the board. Use them for "heads-up" teaching and reference throughout the lesson. For "heads-up" teaching activities, ask the children to close their book so that you have their full attention.

• You can access the tools in the tool bar along the top of the screen, e.g. *Timer*, *Highlighter*. The audio, answer keys and videos can be accessed by buttons next to the corresponding activities.

The Big Book Fair

Lesson objectives: review vocabulary and grammar from *Story Central Plus* 3
Key language: *comic books, cookies, ice cream stand, island, lamp, planet, science books*
Materials: Track 0.3

Warmer: Play "The Telephone Game"

Play the game with *Story Central is a lot of fun.* and *Every day is a special day in Story Central.* (see Games Bank p. 19).

1 Look and write the number of the correct book.

- Have the children look at the books, read the topics, and write the number of the correct book.
- Elicit answers.

Answers

a story about a lamp 5; a story about an island 3; a story about the planets 2

2))) 0.3 Listen and write C (Cheng), M (Miguel), or F (Felicity).

- Have the children look at the pictures and identify the characters. Ask *What's Cheng/Felicity/Miguel doing?*
- Play Track 0.3 The children listen and read along. Then they complete the grid.

- Play Track 0.3 again. Ask *Why didn't Cheng buy any science books? (because he didn't like any) Who bought some cookies? (Cheng) Who made them? (Felicity and her mom) What are they going to do with the money? (buy movies and books for Story Central)*

Audioscript

Miguel: Hi, Jason.

Jason: Are you having fun at our big book fair, Miguel?

Miguel: Yes, it's great. Look! I bought some old comic books. I'm going to look at the science book stand now. Did you buy any science books, Cheng?

Cheng: I looked at the science book stand, but I didn't like any of the books.

Jason: There's a stand for new books, too. We have lots of interesting new stories this year, and we're all going to read them at Story Central.

Miguel: Yes, I saw those. Hey, where did you buy those cookies, Cheng?

Cheng: From the ice cream and cookie stand. Felicity made them with her mom. She's going to sell them and buy new books and movies for Story Central with the money.

Miguel: How much are the cookies? I have $10.

Cheng: Oh, you can buy lots with $10!
Miguel: Great! I'm going to buy some cookies and ice cream.
Jason: Oh, and tell Felicity what books and movies you want for the Story Central library.

Answers

	did	going to
buy some old comic books	M	
look at the science book stand	C	M
buy cookies	C	M
make cookies	F	
buy new books for Story Central		F
buy ice cream		M

3   Write about you.

- Elicit ideas for each prompt.
- Have the children write about their favorite books and movies, then swap with a friend to compare.

Optional activity: In the past, in the future

Say sentences about what you did during your vacation and are going to do soon. For sentences in the past, the children turn to face the back of the class; for sentences about the future, they put both arms in the air in front of them.

4   Find a friend with two answers the same as you in Activity 3.

The children mingle and ask questions to find another child who shares at least two answers from Activity 3. When they find them, they sit together. Elicit answers. Have children raise their hand if they wrote the same thing.

5   Complete with words you know in English.

The children write words in each category. They can do this in pairs as a race. Elicit answers. Challenge the class to get ten different words in each category.

Answers

Children's own answers.

Divide the class into groups of six. Model the game. Say *I'm going to make a cake.* Have a child say *The teacher is going to make a cake and* (e.g.) *I'm going to play soccer.* The next child repeats the whole sequence, then adds a new detail. Have the children play the game in groups in this way. If a child makes a mistake or cannot think of a detail to add, the chain starts again.

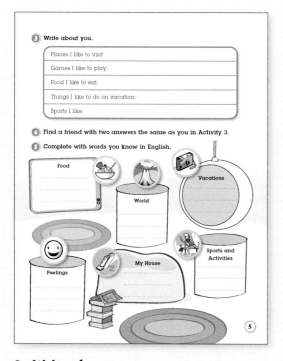

3   Write about you.

The children write about things they like.

Answers

Children's own answers.

Digital Resources

Student eBook • Encourage the children to imagine they are a Story Central character and think up responses to the questions in SB Activity 3. Have children use *Pen* to write in a detail each.

Around the World
Overview

The children will:

- use critical thinking skills to identify countries and their languages.
- talk about what there was/wasn't in a country.
- read, understand, and act out a story.
- talk about the rides at an amusement park.
- compare quantities.
- find out about ferris wheels.
- plan an amusement park.

Key Vocabulary

Countries: Canada, Egypt, France, Germany, Japan, Mexico
Languages: Arabic, English, French, German, Japanese, Spanish
Amusement park rides: amusement park, carousel, ferris wheel, roller coaster, slide, swing, zip line

Key Grammar

- Was there (a swimming pool at your hotel)? Yes, there was.
- Were there (many people)? Yes. There were (people from Germany, Japan, and Egypt).
- There aren't many (children on the swings). There isn't much (time left).
- I need a few (ideas). We always have a lot of (ideas).

Reading Skills

Story: *Where's Claire?*
Genre: modern adventure story

Literacy Development

- predict story content from title and pictures
- interpret and personalize the theme of the story
- add description to your writing

Functional Language

- Try this. I'm …
- That looks like fun!

Spelling

Compound nouns

CLIL: History—The ferris wheel

The children find out about the ferris wheel.

Competency Focus

The children will:

use critical thinking skills to identify countries and their languages. (Lesson 1)

predict the content of a story. (Lesson 3)

identify and talk about park rides. (Lesson 5)

---

apply new grammar to previously learned vocabulary. (Lesson 2)

talk about what there is in an amusement park. (Lesson 6)

---

work in pairs to act out a dialogue. (Lesson 3)

present their amusement park to the class. (Lesson 8)

---

personalize the story by thinking about how they might act in a similar situation. (Lesson 4)

evaluate their own progress in the chapter. (Review)

---

develop cultural understanding by finding out more about amusement parks. (Lesson 7)

Digital Overview

Teacher Presentation

Student eBook and Digital Activity Book

- Oral Storytelling Video 1.1: *Where's Claire?*
- Interactive versions of AB activities
- Integrated audio and answer key for all activities

Teacher resources for planning, lesson delivery, and homework

Teacher Resource Center

- Class Planner Chapter 1
- Worksheets to print out (including notes and answers):
  - Grammar Worksheet 1A: Was there …? Were there …?
  - Grammar Worksheet 1B: many, much, a few, a lot of
  - Phonics Worksheet 1
  - Oral Storytelling Video Worksheet 1: *Where's Claire?*
  - CLIL Graphic Organizer 1
  - Test Chapter 1
- Test Generator
- Literacy Handbook

Watch the Oral Storytelling Video

Children's resources for consolidation and practice at home

Student eBook and Reader eBook

- Oral Storytelling Video 1.1: *Where's Claire?*

The Inks Student's App

Vocabulary games: Countries/languages and amusement park rides

Vocabulary

Lesson objective: identify and say countries and their languages
Key vocabulary: *Egypt, Canada, France, Germany, Japan, Mexico;*
Arabic, English, French, German, Japanese, Spanish
Materials: Track 1.1

Warmer: English across the world

Have the children in pairs write a list of countries where English is spoken (*the USA, the UK* (*England, Scotland, Wales, Northern Ireland*), *Canada, Australia, New Zealand,* etc.) and list as many cities as they can for each country. Elicit answers.

1))) 1.1 Listen and number. Then say.

- Have the children look at the pictures. Ask *Which building is most interesting?* Elicit ideas.
- Play Track 1.1 twice for the children to listen and number the houses. Elicit the answers.
- Say the new words for the children to repeat.

Audioscript

Man: Welcome to the International Fun Park. Here, you can visit houses from around the world. Find the houses on the map.
Woman: First, enjoy beautiful France. It's next to the entrance, and number one on the map. There are a lot of apartments in this big house. Can you see the Eiffel Tower? In France, they speak French.
Man: House number 2 is from Germany. It's a black and white house with a lot of windows. They speak German in Germany.
Woman: Next to Germany is the house from Canada. It's number 3 on the map. There is a lot of snow, but it is warm inside the house. In Canada, there are two languages: English and French.
Man: House number 4 is from Japan. It's on an island in a lake. The house is very tall and it has a lot of roofs! Can you guess what
language they speak in Japan? That's right, Japanese!
Woman: Look for the desert next. This is Egypt, number 5. This house is white because the Sun is very hot. People speak many languages in Egypt, but the main language is Arabic.
Man: The final house, number 6, is a house from Mexico. It's yellow and orange and it's very old. They speak many languages in Mexico, too, but the main language in Mexico is Spanish.

Answers

Japanese house 4, Egyptian house 5, Mexican house 6, Canadian house 3, German house 2, French house 1

2))) 1.1 Listen again and check (✔) the languages of each country.

- Say *In France they speak English.* Elicit the correct version. (*In France they speak French.*)
- Play Track 1.1 again. The children listen and check the correct language for each country. Say each country to elicit the language spoken there.

Answers

1 French **2** German **3** English/French **4** Japanese **5** Arabic **6** Spanish

3 Point to the pictures. Test a friend.

- Have two children read the example aloud.
- Divide your class into pairs. The children take turns pointing to a house in the picture in Activity 1 and saying where it is, and responding with a sentence on the language they speak there (without looking at their book).

4 Write the names of other countries you know and their languages.

- Elicit other countries the children know and write them on the board, e.g. *USA, China, Australia, India, Italy, Brazil,* etc.
- The children copy them in their notebook and write the language people speak in each country. They can do this individually or in small groups. Encourage them to add more countries/languages. Elicit answers.

Answers

Children's own answers.

Optional activity: Country, city, language

In pairs, the children take turns saying a country and responding with a city there and the language spoken.

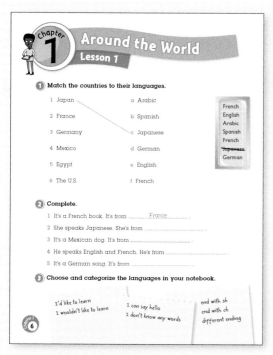

1 Write the languages.

The children write the language for each country using the words supplied. Elicit answers.

Answers

1 English, French **2** French **3** German **4** Spanish **5** Arabic **6** Japanese

2 Complete.

The children complete the sentences by writing in the correct country. Elicit answers.

Answers

1 France **2** Japan **3** Mexico **4** Canada **5** Germany

3 Choose and categorize the languages in your notebook.

Remind the children that organizing vocabulary into categories makes it easier to learn. Elicit an example for each category listed. Ask *Which categories would you choose?* Elicit ideas, prompting children to give a reason for their choice. The children choose a pair of categories and list the words in their notebook, then compare with a friend.

Answers

Children's own answers.

Cooler: What about you?

Say *I can speak English and Spanish. What about you?* Have a child answer, then pose the question to another child. Divide the class into groups of six to do the activity. Have them repeat with *My mother/father/sister/brother can speak French. What about yours?*

Competency Focus

The children use critical thinking skills to identify the countries and their languages by using visual clues and processing the written and spoken forms.

Digital Resources

- **Student eBook, Digital Activity Book** • All SB and AB pages can be shown on the board. Use them for "heads-up" teaching and reference throughout the lesson.
- TIP All audio is accessible within the SB/AB pages: choose the audio buttons next to the corresponding activities.
- **Digital Activity Book** • Use the AB page to give feedback on activities, using the built-in interactive activities or answer keys, as appropriate.

Grammar

Lesson objectives: ask and answer about past vacations

Key grammar: *Was there (a swimming pool at your hotel)? Yes, there was. Were there (many people)? Yes. There were (people from Germany, Japan, and Egypt).*

Secondary language: *amusement park, competition, rides, vacation, winner*

Materials: Track 1.2; Grammar Worksheet 1A [TRC printout] (optional)

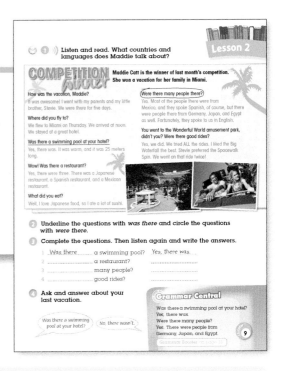

Warmer: Play "The Shark Game"

Play the game with *Japanese* and *Arabic* (see Games Bank p. 19).

1))) 1.2 Listen and read. What countries and languages does Maddie talk about?

- Have the children look at the pictures in the travel magazine. Pre-teach *amusement park* and *rides.*

- Play Track 1.2. The children listen and read along. Ask *What countries and languages does Maddie talk about?* (Mexico, Germany, Japan, Egypt, Spanish, English)

- Play Track 1.2 again. Ask *Where did Maddie go on vacation?* (Miami) *Who did she go with?* (her family) *How big was the swimming pool?* (25 meters long) *How many restaurants were there?* (three)

2 Underline the questions with *was there* and circle the questions with *were there.*

- Have a child read the examples in the text in Activity 1. The children underline questions with *was there* and circle questions with *were there.* Elicit the questions.

Answers

Underlined: Was there a swimming pool at your hotel?
Was there a restaurant?

Circled: Were there many people there?
Were there good rides?

Grammar Central

Was there a swimming pool at your hotel? ...

Have the children look at the patterns. Elicit the difference between *Was there ...?* and *Were there ...?* (singular, plural) Ask what the questions would be in the present tense. (*Is there ...? Are there ...?*) Prompt with nouns to elicit questions in the past, e.g. *a lot of people.* (*Were there a lot of people?*)

For extra practice, try the **Grammar Booster** section in the Student Book (p. 18).

Answers p. 18

Activity 1: **2** there was **3** Was there **4** there wasn't **5** Were there **6** there were **7** Were there **8** there weren't

Activity 2: **2** there were **3** Was there **4** there were **5** Were there **6** there weren't **7** Was there **8** there wasn't

3))) 1.2 Complete the questions. Then listen again and write the answers.

- The children complete the questions.

- Play Track 1.2 again. The children listen and write.

Answers

1 Was there; Yes, there was.
2 Was there; Yes, there were three.
3 Were there; Yes, there were.
4 Were there; Yes, there were.

4 Ask and answer about your last vacation.

- Model the dialogue with a child. Have the children work in pairs, taking turns asking and answering questions about their last vacation. Monitor and make notes of problems and good use of language to look at with the class.

Optional activity: A memory game

Give the children one minute to look at Student Book pp. 6–7 carefully. They then close their book and take turns asking and answering questions using *There was/were*.

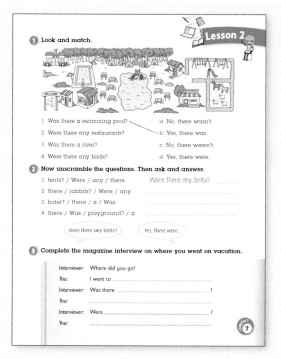

1 Look and match.

The children look at the picture and match the questions and answers. Elicit responses.

Answers

1 b 2 d 3 a 4 c

2 Now unscramble the questions. Then ask and answer.

The children unscramble the questions. Elicit questions. Have two children read the example aloud. Divide the class into pairs to take turns asking the questions and answering using the information in the picture.

Answers

1 Were there any tents? **2** Were there any rabbits?
3 Was there a hotel? **4** Was there a playground?

3 Complete the magazine interview on where you went on vacation.

The children complete the interview with vocabulary from the lesson. Have children practice their interview and act it out for the class.

Answers

Children's own answers.

Cooler: Play "The Chain Game"

Have the children imagine they were all at the same place during their last vacation. Say *At the hotel, there was a big swimming pool.* Have a child say *At the hotel, there was a big swimming pool and* (e.g.) *there were three restaurants.* The next child repeats the whole sequence, then adds a new detail. Have the children play the game in groups in this way. If a child makes a mistake or cannot think of a detail to add, the chain starts again.

Competency Focus

Learn

The children develop learning strategies by recognizing and applying language patterns. They show their understanding of previously acquired vocabulary and use it in a new context.

Digital Resources

Student eBook • For the TE Optional activity, first show SB pp. 6–7 and have children use *Pen* to circle features they can then refer to in the memory game.

Digital Activity Book • Use the digital interactive activities to check AB answers.

Teacher Resource Center • Print out Grammar Worksheet 1A for extra practice after SB Activity 2.

Reading: Story Extract

Lesson objectives: commenting positively on an activity; predict story content from title and pictures; read the extract from *Where's Claire?* (beginning)

Functional language: *Try this. I'm … That looks like fun!*

Secondary language: *carousel, costumes, ferris wheel, roller coaster, slide*

Materials: Tracks 1.3 and 1.4

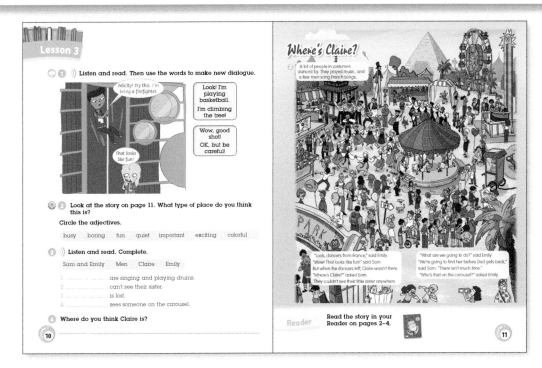

Warmer: Amusement parks

Draw a ferris wheel on the board. Ask *Where do you find this?* Elicit *amusement park* (or pre-teach, as necessary) and write it on the board. Ask *Do you like going to amusement parks? When did you last go to one? Who with? What did you like the most?* Have a class discussion.

Functional language

1))) 1.3   Listen and read. Then act out.

- Have the children look at the picture. Ask *What is Cheng pretending to be?* (*a firefighter*)

- Play Track 1.3. The children listen and read along. Ask *Does Felicity like what Cheng is doing?* (*yes*)

- Play Track 1.3 again, pausing for the children to listen.

- Have them create similar dialogues in pairs using other jobs they know, e.g. *vet, police officer, cleaner, doctor, chef,* etc.

Before reading

2   Look at the story. What type of place do you think this is? Circle the adjectives.

- Have the children look at the picture and the story title. Ask *Where are all these people?* (*amusement park*) *What are they doing?* (*dancing, walking, buying popcorn,* etc.)

- Ask the children to circle the adjectives that describe the amusement park. Elicit answers.

Answers

busy, fun, exciting, colorful

3))) 1.4   Listen and read. Complete.

- Play Track 1.4. The children listen and read along.

- Play Track 1.4 again and have the children complete the sentences using the words supplied. Elicit answers.

Answers

1 Men **2** Sam and Emily **3** Claire **4** Emily

4 Where do you think Claire is?

- Ask *Can the children see their sister?* (no) *Is Claire on the carousel?* (no) *Can you see Claire?*

- Have the children write where they think Claire is. Elicit ideas including reasons but do not confirm. Say they will have to read the story to find out.

Answers

Children's own answers.

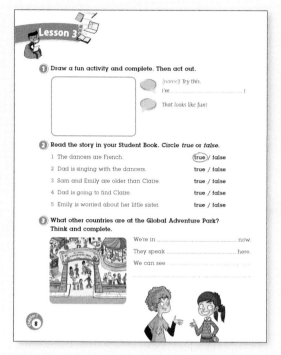

1 Draw a fun activity and complete. Then act out.

Divide the class into pairs to draw a fun activity and complete the dialogue, then act it out. Have pairs act out for the class.

Answers

Children's own answers.

2 Read the story in your Student Book. Circle *true* or *false*.

Read the example and elicit why the answer is true. (*Emily says "dancers from France!"*) The children read the Student Book story extract again and circle true or false for each sentence. Elicit answers, including the correct versions of the false statements.

Answers

1 true **2** false **3** true **4** false **5** true

3 What other countries are at the Global Adventure Park? Think and complete.

Elicit ideas on what other countries there are at the Global Adventure Park. The children write their own ideas. Elicit responses.

Answers

Children's own answers.

Cooler: Play "Finish the Word"

Divide the class into two teams. Start spelling a word (e.g. *carousel, roller coaster, slide, dancers*). When children think they know it, they raise their hand and say it and spell it. If they say and spell the correct word before you finish spelling it, they get one point for their team. If they say the wrong word or spell it incorrectly, they lose a point.

Competency Focus

Collaborate and Communicate

The children act out an authentic dialogue together, putting into practice the functional language.

Think! Critical Thinking

The children apply reading skills (exploiting pictures and text clues) to understand the story.

Digital Resources

Student eBook, Digital Activity Book • Hover over each icon in the tool bar to reveal the function of each button.

- TIP With the answer key you can choose to show the answers all at once or one by one.

Where's Claire?

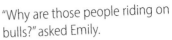

1

This is Dad.

This is Sam.

This is Emily.

And this is Claire.

They're going to visit Global Adventure Park. It's a big amusement park with a lot of rides. All the rides are from different countries. Walking around the park is like traveling around the world.

"I'm going to get popcorn," Dad said to Sam and Emily. "Stay here and watch Claire."

2

A lot of people in costumes danced by. They played music, and a few men sang French songs.

"Look, dancers from France," said Emily.

"Wow! That looks like fun!" said Sam.

But when the dancers left, Claire wasn't there.

"Where's Claire?" asked Sam.

They couldn't see their little sister anywhere.

"What are we going to do?" said Emily.

"We're going to find her before Dad gets back," said Sam. "There isn't much time."

"Who's that on the carousel?" asked Emily.

3

The carousel had a lot of painted horses. There weren't many children there.

A woman wearing a German dress came over.

"Welcome to Germany. Who are you looking for?"

"Our little sister. Was she here?" said Sam.

"I don't think so," said the woman.

"Look, is that her on the slide?" asked Emily.

4

"I guess we're in Egypt now," said Sam.

"Yes, the writing is Arabic," said Emily.

Sam and Emily went down the slide, but Claire wasn't there.

"Where's Claire?" asked Sam.

"Oh, no! Is that her on the ferris wheel?" asked Emily.

5

"Why are those people riding on bulls?" asked Emily.

"We're in Mexico now. Some people are speaking Spanish," said Sam.

Then Emily saw a few footprints in the Japanese sand garden.

"Who made those footprints?" she asked.

"I think we're going to find Claire in Japan," said Sam.

6

"What's that?" Sam asked the man in Japanese clothes.

"That's a Chinese dragon roller coaster. In China, dragons are good luck," said the man.

"They're lucky for us too! Look who's riding on the dragon!" said Sam.

"It's Claire!" they both shouted at once.

7

"Where have you been?" said Sam.

"I went all around the world!" said Claire.

"What are we going to tell Dad?" asked Emily.

8

Just then, Dad arrived with the popcorn.

"Sorry, was I long?" he asked. "What do you want to do first? China looks like fun."

"We're tired" said Sam and Emily. "Can we go home now?"

"好!" said Claire.

Lesson objective: read and understand the modern adventure story *Where's Claire?* in the Reader
Materials: Track 1.5; Reader; Oral Storytelling Video Worksheet 1 [TRC printout] (optional)

Warmer: Review the story extract

Have the children identify the story characters. Ask *What's Claire/Emily/Sam wearing? Where's Dad?*

Story Summary

Claire visits an international theme amusement park with her sister, Emily, and brother, Sam. When their dad goes to buy popcorn, Claire gets lost. Sam and Emily search the park, traveling though different "countries." Eventually, they find Claire in China.

Value: keep close to your family.

))) **1.5   While reading**

- Have the children look at the pictures in the Reader. Ask them to point to Claire in each picture.

- Play Track 1.5. The children listen and read along. Ask *Which countries do the children visit?*

- Play Track 1.5 again. Ask questions to check comprehension, e.g. *Where are Claire and her family?* (*at the Global Adventure Park*) *What are the people in France doing?* (*dancing*) *Is Clare in Germany?* (*no*) *Where do they find Claire?* (*in China*) *Why are the children tired?* (*They visited a lot of countries.*)

After reading: Reflect

- Ask questions to give the children the opportunity to think about the issues raised by the story, e.g. *Do you think Claire was naughty? Why/Why not? What about Emily and Sam? Was it their fault that Claire was lost? Why didn't they tell their dad? Were they worried?*

Optional activity: A point of view

Write on the board *Dad, Claire, Emily, Sam* and *worried, fun, patient, excited, nice, happy, naughty.* Elicit adjectives to describe each character. Divide the class into four groups. Have each group choose a character and tell the story from their point of view. Ask groups to tell the class their version.

Story Time

Creating the right atmosphere

Creating the right atmosphere can motivate the children for reading. Ask them to sit in a horseshoe shape around you. Make sure they have their Reader on their lap, and read along as you play the CD or read the story aloud.

Reading Strategy

Drawing Conclusions

The ability to draw conclusions is important when reading any text, but particularly for stories, where the underlying message might not be obvious. A good reader draws conclusions based on facts extracted from the text as well as on their personal experience and knowledge.

For additional explanation and activities, see the Literacy Handbook on the Teacher's Resource Center.

Cooler: At the Global Adventure Park

Have the children look at pp. 4–5 of their Reader. Describe people in the pictures in detail, e.g. *A girl is looking at some houses and there's a teddy bear on the ground next to her.* Have the children race to find each person and call out *Here!* when they have found them.

Digital Resources

Reader eBook • Show Reader pp. 4–5 on the board to do the Cooler activity. Have children use *Pen* to circle the people when they find them.

• Oral Storytelling Video 1.1 gives the story with a different ending. Watch it together at the end of the lesson, then discuss the differences.

Teacher Resource Center • Print out Oral Storytelling Video Worksheet 1 to help you get the most out of the video.

Student eBook • The children can watch Oral Storytelling Video 1.1 at home.

Reading Comprehension and Critical Literacy

Lesson objectives: write descriptive text; relate the story to personal experiences

Materials: Track 1.5; Reader; Oral Storytelling Video Worksheet 1 [TRC printout] (optional)

Lesson 4 Time to Think

1.)) Read the story in your Reader on pages 2–4 again.

2. Number the events from the story in order.

Reading Report

a Sam and Emily went to Germany. ☐

b Sam and Emily found Claire in China. ☐

c Dad came back with the popcorn. ☐

d Sam and Emily saw that Claire wasn't there ☐

e Sam and Emily went to a pyramid in Egypt. ☐

f Dad took Sam, Emily, and Claire to the amusement park. ☐

g Dad went to buy popcorn. ☐

3. Look back at Picture 3. Help Sam and Emily find Claire. Write some clues for them.

There are people from ....

They are ....

I can see ....

Claire is ....

I Can Read and Write!

Use the pictures for ideas to add description to your writing. Write about the colors, clothes, nationalities, and what the characters are doing.

4. Talk about the story.

Have you ever been lost in a busy place? What did you do?

12

Note: Please ensure that your class has read the Reader story before you do this lesson.

Warmer: Play "Ready, Set, Draw"

Play the game using *popcorn, ferris wheel, carousel, slide, roller coaster* (see Games Bank p. 19).

1))) 1.5 Read the story in your Reader.

- Have the children read the story. (Alternatively, play Track 1.5 and have them read along.) Elicit whether they were correct in their predictions in Lesson 3 Activity 4.

- Check comprehension by asking *Why were Sam and Emily worried?* (*They couldn't find Claire.*) *Were they happy at the end of the story?* (*Yes—but very tired!*) *What language is Claire speaking at the end?* (*Chinese*) Ask the children to guess what Claire is saying. (*OK*)

2 Number the events from the story in order.

- Have the children put the sentences in order, then compare answers in pairs. Elicit the sentences in the correct order.

Answers

a 4 b 6 c 7 d 3 e 5 f 1 g 2

I Can Read and Write!

Have the children look at Picture 1 in the story. Ask a few questions to elicit descriptions, e.g. *What color is the pyramid? What's next to the carousel? What's the woman in … doing?* The children then continue in this way, taking turns asking and answering in pairs.

3 Look back at Picture 3. Help Sam and Emily find Claire. Write some clues for them.

- Remind the children that pictures are very useful information sources and they should always study them carefully to help understand a story. To focus on this reading strategy, ask them to look at Picture 3 and describe it in as much detail as possible.

- They then complete the sentences. Elicit answers.

Answers (suggested)

There are people from Germany. They are drinking, eating, and listening to a band. I can see a pyramid slide in the Egypt zone. Claire is sliding down the slide.

4 Talk about the story.

- Have the children read Jason's question and raise their hand if they (or their brothers or sisters) have been lost. Ask *What did you do? What did your parents say when you found them?*

- Have children say what they should do if they are lost.

Optional activity: Who said it?

Read out dialogue from the story to elicit who said it.

1 Complete the information about Claire's trip.

The children complete the summary of Claire's trip using the words supplied. Elicit answers.

Answers

France, danced; Germany; Arabic; Mexico; Japan, walked; China

2 Look at Germany in the Global Adventure Park. Write the letters. Complete.

The children practice the **I Can Read and Write!** feature by looking at the picture of Germany in their Reader. Elicit the topic of the missing word in each sentence first. Then the children write the correct letters and complete the sentences with details from the story. Elicit answers.

Answers

1 d 2 a 3 c 4 b

1 white 2 national dress/costume 3 eating and drinking 4 pretty/nice/small, etc.

3 Imagine you visited the Global Adventure Park. Write an email to your friend in your notebook. Use the Story Builder.

Use the **Story Builder** prompts to elicit ideas. The children write an email in their notebook, then swap with a friend to check. Have children read their email for the class.

Answers

Children's own answers.

4 Connect to Me

Elicit ideas on stories with descriptions of different countries (e.g. *Around the World in Eighty Days*) before the children write their own response. Elicit responses.

Answers

Children's own answers.

Cooler: Continue the story

))) 1.5

Tell the children to listen carefully because you are going to stop the recording so they can continue the story. Play Track 1.6, pausing every so often to elicit what happens next.

Competency Focus

Me: Critical Literacy

The children use critical thinking skills to reflect on the theme of the story and relate it to their personal experience.

Digital Resources

Reader eBook • Divide the class into teams. Teams take turns saying an item for another team to circle using *Pen*, e.g. the characters, *cat, monkey, ice cream, balloon*. If correct, they win one point. Use *Add personal note* to keep the score.

• If you haven't already, watch Oral Storytelling Video 1.1 (version of the story with a different ending).

Teacher Resource Center • If you haven't already, print out Oral Storytelling Video Worksheet 1 to do the support activities.

Vocabulary, Song, and Spelling

Lesson objectives: identify and talk about park rides;
practice compound nouns

Key vocabulary: *amusement park, carousel, ferris wheel, roller coaster, slide, swing, zip line*

Secondary language: *playground, popcorn*

Materials: Tracks 1.6 and 1.7; red and blue pens; Phonics Worksheet 1 [TRC printout] (optional)

Warmer: Pre-teach vocabulary

Point to the picture in Student Book Activity 1 to pre-teach the vocabulary. Agree on a mime for each word. Say the words in random order for the children to mime.

1))) 1.6   Listen and number. Then sing.

- Play Track 1.6 twice. The children listen and number the words to match the pictures of the rides. Elicit answers.

- Play Track 1.6 again for the children to sing along and mime the rides.

Answers

amusement park 6, swing 2, slide 3, carousel 4,
roller coaster 5, ferris wheel 1, zip line 7

2   Talk about rides you like and don't like. Say why.

- Read the example. Elicit more positive and negative adjectives that could be used with this model and write them on the board, e.g. *cool, amazing, exciting, fantastic, the best; frightened, nervous, bored, sick/dizzy*. Give another example, e.g. *I like to go on the roller coaster. It's amazing!*

- Divide the class into pairs. The children take turns talking about the rides in the song, using the adjectives on the board or their own ideas. Invite children to say their sentences to the class.

Optional activity: Missing vowels

Write the key vocabulary on the board with the vowels missing. Children come to the board to fill in a vowel. The class confirms.

3   Plan your day at the amusement park. Write.

- Read the example and add another sentence, e.g. *Then, I'm going to go on the slide.*

- Give the children time to write at least three sentences in their notebook, using *First, Then,* and *going to.* They swap with a friend to check. Elicit answers.

Answers

Children's own answers.

Spelling Central

Compound nouns

Elicit examples of one-word compound nouns, e.g. *waterfall, sunglasses,* and two-word compound nouns, e.g. *school uniform, picnic area.* Point out that the children need to memorize whether compound nouns are written as one or two words.

4))) 1.7   Listen and say the chant.

- Play Track 1.7. The children listen and read along. Elicit the compound nouns.

- Play Track 1.7 again, pausing for the children to repeat.

5 Find it!

- Set a time limit for the children to find compound nouns on the page. Elicit answers.
- Elicit any other compound nouns they know.

Answers

7—amusement park, roller coaster, ferris wheel, zip line, popcorn, playground, everyone

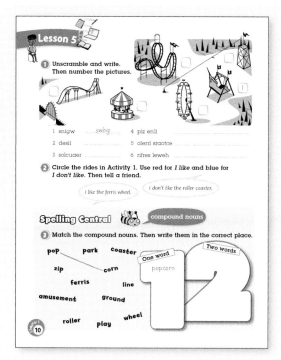

1 Unscramble and write. Then number the pictures.

The children unscramble and write the words. Then they write the number of each word by the correct picture. Elicit answers.

Answers

1 swing **2** slide **3** carousel **4** zip line **5** roller coaster **6** ferris wheel

5, 4, 2, 3, 6, 1

2 Circle the rides in Activity 1. Use red for *I like* and blue for *I don't like*. Then tell a friend.

The children use red and blue pens to circle the pictures depending on their preferences. Then they talk about their likes and dislikes in pairs.

Answers

Children's own answers.

3 Match the compound nouns. Then write them in the correct place.

To practice the **Spelling Central** feature, the children match the pairs of words to make compound nouns, using a single line if one word and a double line for two-word answers. Then they write the word in the correct number (in 1 if one word, in 2 if two words). Elicit answers by having children write them on the board.

Answers

One word: popcorn, playground
Two words: amusement park, ferris wheel, zip line, roller coaster

Cooler: Sing loudly, sing quietly ...

 1.6

Play the song for the children to sing along. Start loud in each verse, gradually reducing the volume. Have the children sing more quietly to match the volume, so for the last lines they are singing just above a whisper.

Competency Focus

Think! Critical Thinking

The children use critical thinking skills to identify written and spoken forms of new words, and match each word with its visual representation.

Digital Resources

Student eBook • For the Spelling Central activity, children show the compound words on the page using *Highlighter* to identify one-word compounds, and *Pen* to circle two-word compounds.

Teacher Resource Center • For phonics practice, print out Phonics Worksheet 1.

Grammar and Reading

Lesson objective: talk about quantities

Key grammar: *There aren't many (children on the swings).*
There isn't much (time left). I need a few (ideas). We always
have a lot of (ideas).

Secondary language: *citizen, competition, roller coaster,*
slide, swing

Materials: Track 1.8; Grammar Worksheet 1B [TRC printout]
(optional)

Warmer: Play "Word Ping-Pong"

Divide the class into two teams. Any child can call
out a word related to an amusement park as a
prompt. The other team has to respond with another
amusement park word. If they repeat a word or take longer
than five seconds, the other team wins a point. The team
with the most points wins.

1))) **1.8   Listen and read. What's Jason's story
about?**

- Have the children look at the story. Ask *What is Miguel
  talking about in Picture 4?* (*an amusement park/swings/
  roller coaster/slides*) *What do people at Story Central
  like to do?* Elicit ideas.

- Play Track 1.8. The children listen and read along. Ask
  What's Jason's story about? (*children from different
  countries who are at an amusement park*)

- Play Track 1.8 again. Ask *Why is Jason writing a story?*
  (*for a competition*) *Does he win?* (*yes*) *What do they
  want to do to celebrate?* (*go to an amusement park*)

Grammar Central

There aren't many children on the swings. ...

Have the children look at the patterns. Elicit that *many*,
a lot of, and *a few* are used with plural verbs and nouns,
e.g. *There are/aren't a lot of books.* Ask how *much* is
different. (*singular verb and noun, e.g. There isn't much
time.*) Elicit sentences about the class, e.g. *There are a lot of
girls in the class. There aren't many computers in this class.*

For extra practice, try the **Grammar Booster** section in the
Student Book (pp. 19–21).

Answers p. 19

Activity 1: **2** a lot of **3** isn't much **4** a lot of **5** aren't many **6** a
lot of **7** a few

Activity 2: **2** aren't many **3** a few **4** many **5** much

Activity 3: Children's own answers.

p. 20

Activity 1: **2** many **3** a few **4** much **5** were **6** a few **7** looked
8 many **9** a few **10** sat **11** many **12** Was there

Activity 2: Children's own answers.

p. 21

Activity 1: **2** many **3** a few **4** much **5** were **6** a few **7** looked
8 many **9** a few **10** sat **11** many **12** Was there

Activity 2: Children's own answers.

2 Look at the story. Complete.

- Read the example sentence. Have the children look at the pictures and ask *How many pens are there?* (*three*)
- The children look at the picture and complete the sentences using the words supplied. Elicit answers.

Answers

1 a few **2** a lot of **3** aren't many **4** isn't much

Optional activity: Play "The Spelling Game"

Divide the class into two teams. Give each team a piece of paper. Say a new vocabulary word, e.g. *ferris wheel, roller coaster, zip line, amusement park*. The children on each team take turns writing a letter until the word is complete. When you have done all the words, the teams swap and check each other's spelling.

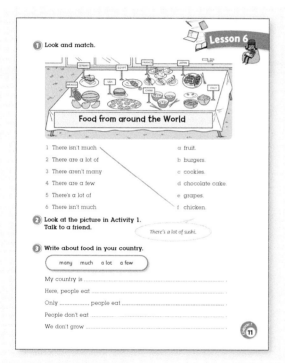

3 Write about food in your country.

Use the sentence openings to elicit ideas about national food in the children's country. Then they complete the sentences using the words supplied. Have children read their sentences for the class.

Answers

Children's own answers.

Cooler: Play "Consequences"

Play the game using *Who was at the amusement park? What ride did they ride first? Who did they meet? What did they say to that person? What did that person do? What did the children do?* (see Games Bank p. 19).

Competency Focus

Learn

The children develop learning strategies by recognizing and applying language patterns in different contexts.

1 Look and match.

The children look at the picture and match the sentence halves. Elicit answers.

Answers

1 f **2** c **3** b **4** e **5** a **6** d

2 Look at the picture in Activity 1. Talk to a friend.

The children take turns making different sentences about the picture in Activity 1. Ask pairs to tell the class their sentences.

Digital Resources

Student eBook • Have children use *Highlighter* to identify *many, much, a few,* and *a lot of* in the SB Activity 1 text.

Teacher Resource Center • For extra grammar practice, print out Grammar Worksheet 1B.

CLIL: Math—The ferris wheel

Lesson objective: find out about the history of the ferris wheel
Materials: CLIL Graphic Organizer 1 [TRC printout] (optional)

CLIL History Lesson 7

1 Read. Who was George W. Ferris?

The Ferris Wheel

George W. Ferris lived in Pittsburgh in Pennsylvania. He was an engineer and built bridges.

In 1893, there was a World's Fair in Chicago. People came from different countries to share new ideas. The organizers of the World's Fair in Chicago wanted to show the visitors a lot of exciting things. Gustave Eiffel built the Eiffel Tower for the World's Fair in Paris in 1889. That was very exciting! What could Chicago do?

Then George W. Ferris heard about the problem. He designed the world's first ferris wheel for the fair. It was 80.5m high. There were 36 wooden cars on the wheel. Each car held 60 people.

Everyone was very excited about Ferris's wheel. The ride cost 50 cents and lasted around 20 minutes. Around 38,000 people went on the wheel every day! Ferris wheels are still popular in amusement parks today.

2 **Read and correct.**
1 Ferris made the first ferris wheel in 1889.
  Ferris made the first ferris wheel in 1893.
2 He made it for the World's Fair in France.

3 There were 16 wooden cars on the wheel.

4 There are no ferris wheels today.

3 **Class Vote**
Are ferris wheels scary?
Why / Why not?

Find Out More! ↖
Choose carousel or playground slide.
Who invented it and when?

15

Write groups of four words on the board, using key vocabulary from Lessons 1 and 5. One of the words should not fit into the group, e.g. *Canada, French, Egypt, Mexico* or *run, jump, dance, rollercoaster.* Elicit the odd one out and why.

1 Read. Who was George W. Ferris?

- The children read the first paragraph. Ask *Who was George W. Ferris?* (*the engineer who designed the ferris wheel*)
- The children read the rest of the text. Ask *How many people could sit in each car?* (*60*) *How much did the ride cost?* (*50 cents*) *How many people went on the ferris wheel every day?* (*38,000*)

2 Correct the sentences.

- Have the child read the example and point to the corresponding part in the text.
- The children correct the sentences, scanning the text to find the information. Elicit answers.

Answers

1 Ferris made the first ferris wheel in 1893. **2** He made it for the World's Fair in Chicago. **3** There were 36 wooden cars on the wheel. **4** Ferris wheels are still popular today.

3 Class Vote

- Ask *Who likes riding on a ferris wheel?* Elicit answers. Then ask *Are ferris wheels scary?* Give the class a minute to think, then take a vote with a show of hands.
- Elicit answers and reasons why it can be scary, e.g. *it's very high, it moves a lot, it's windy, people shout a lot,* etc.

Find Out More! ↖
Have the children choose a ride to research: carousel or playground slide. If necessary, explain what they are. Invite them to give reasons for their choice. Suggest appropriate resources, e.g. Internet, library books, etc. The children will need to complete this research before doing the follow-up activity in the Activity Book. (It could be set as homework.)

Optional activity: Invent a new ride for an amusement park

Divide the class into groups of four. Have each group discuss and invent a new ride for an amusement park. They draw the ride and present it to the class, using *There are/aren't* and adjectives such as *exciting, awesome,* etc. to describe it. They also say where it is and what there is/isn't around it. Have a class vote on the best ride.

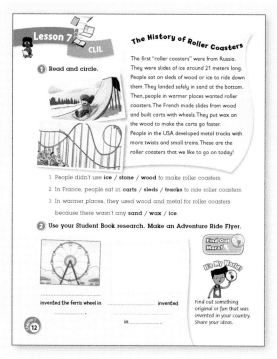

1 Read and circle.

The children read the article, then circle the correct option from three to complete the sentences summarizing it. Elicit answers. Ask *Where were the first roller coasters from?* (*Russia*) *What did people sit on?* (*They sat on sleds of wood or ice.*) *Why did the French put wax on the wood carts?* (*to make them go faster*) *Who developed metal tracks?* (*the Americans*)

Answers

1 stone **2** carts **3** ice

2 Use your Student Book research. Make an Adventure Ride Flyer.

Divide the class into groups of four. Have the children pool the information they learned from their research in the Student Book and the Activity Book. They draw their researched ride and complete the sentences individually. Have children show their drawings and read their sentences to the class.

Answers

Children's own answers.

It's My World!

Encourage the children to do some further research about a fun invention made in their country. Share information as a class, either now or in the next lesson.

Cooler: On the ferris wheel

Have the children draw a big ferris wheel with ten cars. In each car, they write a word related to amusement parks. They then mingle and show each other their ferris wheels and words. Elicit words. Were there any words which only one person wrote?

Competency Focus

Act

The children carry out research to find out more about a ride at an amusement park. This helps them expand their learning and relate it to their world, both inside and outside the classroom.

Digital Resources

Student eBook • Display the SB page on the board to do Activity 1 points 1 and 2, for an alternative "heads-up" introduction to the topic. This helps the children engage.

Student eBook, Digital Activity Book • TIP Store ideas in *Add personal note* for easy access during the lesson.

Teacher Resource Center • Print out CLIL Graphic Organizer 1 for the children to use in collating their Find Out More! research.

CLIL eBook • The children can use the CLIL eBook to expand their knowledge of the lesson topic.

Project

Lesson objectives: review language from Chapter 1; complete a craft project; research, plan, and present an amusement park

Materials: a large sheet of posterboard, colored pencils or markers, amusement park maps, scissors, glue; two game pieces and a coin for each pair

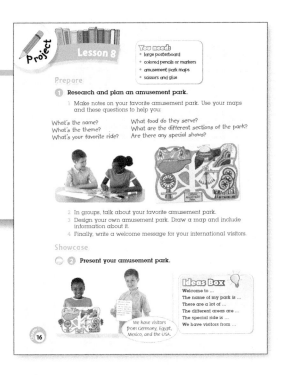

Warmer: Play "Vocabulary Review"

Play the game with *Egypt, France, Arabic, English, Spanish, amusement park, swing, roller coaster, ferris wheel, zip line* (see Games Bank p. 19).

Prepare

1 Research and plan an amusement park.

- Distribute the materials. Read through the instructions together and ensure the children are clear on what to do.

- Have the children make notes on their favorite amusement park, using the questions as prompts. Then they discuss the features of their favorite amusement parks in groups.

- They design their amusement parks individually. Then they write a welcome message for visitors, using the **Ideas Box** for support. Give support as necessary.

Alternative craft activity

An easier project is to simply draw and color the map of the amusement park, and to write the names of the rides, restaurants, and sections, then prepare a welcome message for visitors, using the **Ideas Box** for support.

Showcase

2 Present your amusement park.

- Explain to the groups that they will present their amusement park to the class.

- The groups practice their welcome message, with each member saying a line.

- Have the groups do their presentation.

Optional activity: Let's go to the amusement park!

Have the groups display their amusement parks around the classroom for the class to browse and choose their favorite. Have a class vote on the amusement park they would most like to visit.

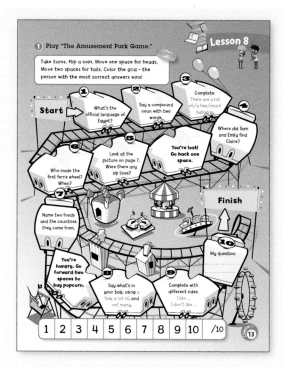

Competency Focus

Collaborate and Communicate

By working together, the children consolidate their understanding of the language learned in a way which they will find fun and engaging. They also demonstrate their ability to work with friends and use interpersonal skills.

1 Play "The Amusement Park Game."

Have the children write a new question in the blank space. Divide the class into pairs and give each pair a coin (or something else they can flip, e.g. an eraser with 1 and 2 written on opposite sides). Explain that they play the game on one shared book, but color the squares at the bottom of the page in their own book when they get a question correct. If they land on an unnumbered space, they follow the instructions. The child with the most correct answers wins.

Answers

1 Arabic **2** *any one of:* roller coaster, ferris wheel, zip line, amusement park **3** a few **4** on the Chinese dragon roller coaster **5** No, there weren't. **6** George Ferris, 1893
7–10 Children's own answers.

Cooler: Play "Word Steps"

Write *Arabic* on the board. Have the children use the last letter to start a new word and form steps, e.g. *Arabic— carousel—look—kayak*. Play as a class or in groups, starting with a new word from Chapter 1.

Digital Resources

Student eBook • For the craft activity, display the SB page and point to the pictures, stage by stage, as you talk the class through the process.

Digital Activity Book • You can use *Timer* for the AB Activity 1 game. Set a time. The child who has most correct answers when the time is up wins.

Language Review

Lesson objective: review language from Chapter 1
Materials: Tracks 1.6, 1.9 and AB 1.1

Warmer: Play "The Telephone Game"

Play the game with *There aren't many children on the swings.* and *A lot of children want to go on the slide.* (see Games Bank p. 19).

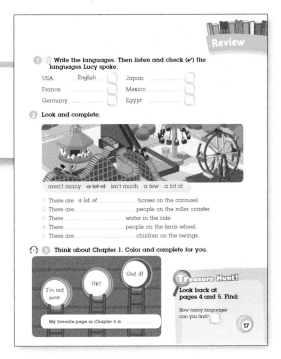

1))) **1.9 Write the languages. Then listen and check (✔) the languages Lucy spoke.**

- Have the children write the language for each country. Elicit answers.
- Play Track 1.9 twice. The children listen and write a check by each language Lucy spoke. Elicit answers.

Audioscript

Dan: Hi, Lucy. How was your International Languages Day at school?

Lucy: It was great! I spoke a few different languages.

Dan: Were there a lot of French students?

Lucy: Yes, there were—I spoke a lot of French.

Dan: How about students from Germany?

Lucy: Well, there weren't many German students, so I didn't speak German.

Dan: Were there students from other countries?

Lucy: Yes, there were. There were two students from Japan.

Dan: Did you speak Japanese, then?

Lucy: No, they spoke to me in English—I was surprised! But there was a student from Mexico ... so I spoke some Spanish.

Dan: Wow, that's a lot of languages! Was there any unusual food?

Lucy: Well, I'm not sure. I saw some Arabic food, but there wasn't much food left at the end.

Answers

Languages: English, French, German, Japanese, Spanish, Arabic

Lucy spoke: French, English, Spanish

2 Look and complete.

- Ask a child to read the example. Have the children look at the picture and complete the sentences using the words supplied. Then they check answers in pairs. Elicit answers.

Answers

1 a lot of **2** a few **3** isn't much **4** aren't many **5** a lot of

3 Think about Chapter 1. Color and complete for you.

- Have the children look back at Chapter 1. Elicit their favorite parts. The children then color the circle which represents how they feel about their own progress (self-evaluation).
- Have the children complete the sentence about their favorite page. Elicit responses.

Treasure Hunt!

Have the children look at pp. 4–5 and count the languages. Elicit the answer. (*four—English, Spanish, French, Japanese*)

Cooler: Sing and mime

))) **1.6**

Agree on actions for the different rides. Play Track 1.6 for the children to sing along and mime.

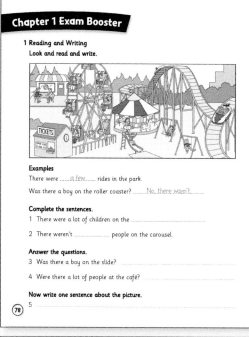

Chapter 1 Exam Booster

1 Reading and Writing
Look and read and write.

Examples

There were ......a few...... rides in the park.

Was there a boy on the roller coaster? ......No, there wasn't......

Complete the sentences.

1 There were a lot of children on the ....

2 There weren't .... people on the carousel.

Answer the questions.

3 Was there a boy on the slide? ....

4 Were there a lot of people at the café? ....

Now write one sentence about the picture.

5 ....

(78)

2 Listening

Listen and draw lines. There is one example.

Tom   Vicky   Paul   Daisy

Lucy   Jane   Ben

(79)

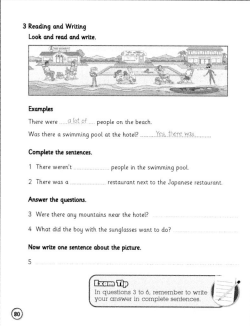

3 Reading and Writing.
Look and read and write.

Examples

There were ......a lot of...... people on the beach.

Was there a swimming pool at the hotel? ......Yes, there was......

Complete the sentences.

1 There weren't .... people in the swimming pool.

2 There was a .... restaurant next to the Japanese restaurant.

Answer the questions.

3 Were there any mountains near the hotel? ....

4 What did the boy with the sunglasses want to do? ....

Now write one sentence about the picture.

5 ....

Exam Tip
In questions 3 to 6, remember to write your answer in complete sentences.

(80)

1 Reading and Writing. Look and read and write.

The children use the picture to complete and then answer each sentence. Check answers.

Answers

1 Ferris Wheel **2** many **3** Yes, there was. **4** Yes, there were. **5** Children's own answers.

2))) AB 1.1 Listening. Listen and draw lines. There is one example.

Play Track AB 1.1 twice. The children listen and match the names to the books pictured. Check answers.

Answers (Audioscript on p. 19)

Lines between: Tom—*The Adventures of Hans;* Vicky—*Mi Casa;* Lucy—*Recipes;* Paul—*La Neige/The Snow;* Ben—*The Cairo Mystery*

3 Read and Writing. Look and read and write.

The children look at the picture and complete the sentences, then answer the questions. Check answers.

Answers

1 many **2** French **3** Yes, there were. **4** He wanted to go kayaking. **5** Children's own answers.

Competency Focus

Me: Self-evaluation

The children reflect on the chapter and express their opinions about their own progress.

Digital Resources

Teacher Resource Center • Print out Test Chapter 1 to use at the end of this lesson. The Test Generator also allows you to create customized tests.

Digital Activity Book • For the Exam Booster activities on the AB page, choose the audio button on the page to access the recordings.

Student's App • Encourage the children to play the games on their smartphone/tablet as a fun way to review the chapter vocabulary. (*The Inks* Apps are free and available on the App Store and Google Play)

Chapter 2 — At the Doctor's Overview

The children will:

- use critical thinking skills to identify common illnesses.
- give advice to somebody who is sick using *should* and *shouldn't*.
- read, understand, and act out a story.
- talk about injuries and first-aid.
- talk about what they could/couldn't do when they were sick.
- find out about strange medicines and cures.
- make a first-aid kit.

Key Vocabulary

Common illnesses: backache, cold, cough, earache, fever, headache, sore throat, stomach ache

Accidents and injuries: bandage, broken leg, burn, crutches, cut, medicine, pain, shot

Key Grammar

- You should (stay at home for three days). You shouldn't (go to school).
- Could you (walk)? I could (walk). I couldn't (play soccer or baseball for a long time).

Reading Skills

Story: *Lulu's Sick Day*
Genre: cautionary tale

Literacy Development

- predict story content from title and pictures
- interpret and personalize the theme of the story
- find rhyming words

Functional Language

- Is something wrong?
- That's too bad! Would you like … ?

Spelling

The spellings *ir*, *ur*, *er* for the sound *ir*

CLIL: Social sciences—Strange medicines

The children find out about strange medicines.

Competency Focus

The children will:

use critical thinking skills to identify illnesses. (Lesson 1)	apply new grammar to previously learned vocabulary. (Lesson 2)	work in pairs to act out a dialogue. (Lesson 3)	personalize the story by thinking about how other people help them feel better when they are sick. (Lesson 4)	develop a wider understanding of food that can be used as medicine. (Lesson 7)
predict the content of a story. (Lesson 3)	talk about past abilities. (Lesson 6)	act out a patient–doctor dialogue for the class. (Lesson 8)		
identify and talk about injuries and first-aid. (Lesson 5)			evaluate their own progress in the chapter. (Review)	

Digital Overview

Teacher Presentation

Student eBook and Digital Activity Book

- Music Video 2.1 (2.2): *Oh, No! What Happened?*
- Interactive versions of AB activities
- Integrated audio and answer key for all activities

Teacher resources for planning, lesson delivery, and homework

Teacher Resource Center

- Class Planner Chapter 2
- Worksheets to print out (including notes and answers):
  - Grammar Worksheet 2A: You should/shouldn't …
  - Grammar Worksheet 2B: Could you …? I could/couldn't …
  - Phonics Worksheet 2
  - CLIL Graphic Organizer 2
  - Festival Worksheet: Thanksgiving
  - Test Chapter 2
- Test Generator
- Literacy Handbook

Watch the Music Video

Children's resources for consolidation and practice at home

Student eBook

- Music Video 2.1 (2.2): *Oh, No! What Happened?*

The Inks Student's App

Vocabulary games: Common illnesses and accidents/injuries

Vocabulary

Lesson objective: identify and talk about common sicknesses
Key vocabulary: *backache, cold, cough, earache, fever, headache, sore throat, stomach ache*
Materials: Track 2.1

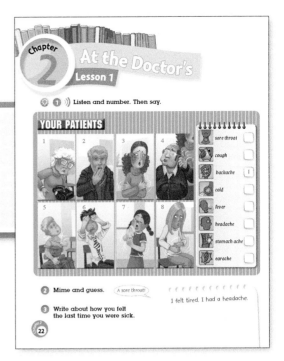

Warmer: Play "Simon Says"

Play the game with parts of the body, e.g. (*Simon says*) *touch your neck/head/ears/back/stomach/(left/right) arm/ leg/nose/mouth/eyes.* (see Games Bank p. 19).

1))) 2.1 Listen and number. Then say.

- Have the children look at the pictures in the game. Ask *Where are these people?* (*at the doctor's*) *Why are they there?* (*They don't feel well.*) (They may need to use L1.)
- Play Track 2.1 twice. The children listen and point.
- They write the number of each patient pictured by the word for the problem. Elicit answers.
- Say the new words for the children to repeat.

Audioscript

Boy: Hey, come and help me play this game. There are lots of patients at the doctor's today. Let's figure out what's wrong with them.
Girl: Sure. Let's start with the old lady. The one with the curly, white hair. I think she has a backache. Can you see? She's holding her back.
Boy: Oh, yes. Can you see the old man with the gray beard and mustache? It looks like he has a cough. He's covering his mouth.
Girl: The man wearing the brown jacket? I can see him. And look at the tall, thin woman. I think she has a fever. She's hot and cold at the same time.

Boy: And look at the short man with glasses. He has an earache. He has his hand over his ear.
Girl: Oh, no. And the little boy with the teddy bear has a sore throat.
Boy: Yes, I think you're correct. He's touching his neck. Can you see the boy wearing a school uniform? He has a headache.
Girl: Yes, he's holding his head with two hands, right? And there's a little girl with a cold. She's wearing the red T-shirt. Her nose is the same color as her T-shirt!
Boy: Oh, yes. And can you see the girl with the long, blond hair? I think she has a stomach ache.
Girl: Oh, yes, she's sitting down and holding her stomach. What a busy day at the doctor's! How are you today?
Boy: I'm fine, thank you!

Answers

sore throat 5, cough 2, backache 1, cold 7, fever 3, headache 6, stomach ache 8, earache 4

2 Mime and guess.

- Mime having a sore throat to elicit *A sore throat!* The first child to guess correctly then mimes another health problem.
- Divide the class into small groups. The children take turns miming and guessing.

3 Write about how you felt the last time you were sick.

- Ask *When was the last time you were sick? How did you feel? Did you have to see the doctor?* Have children talk about their experience to the class.

- Read the example. The children write about their experience in their notebook. Give support as necessary. They compare with a friend. Ask children to tell the class about their friend's experience.

Answers

Children's own answers.

Optional activity: Matching

Divide the board in two. Write in random order the words for sickness on the left and for the parts of the body on the right: *sore throat—neck, backache—back, earache—ear, stomach ache—stomach, fever—body, cold—body, headache—head, cough—throat.* Have the children match them. Elicit answers.

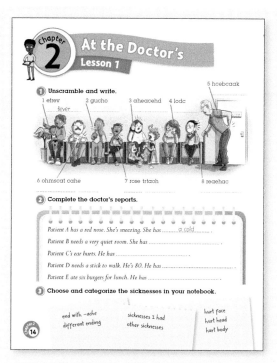

1 Unscramble and write.

The children unscramble and write the picture labels.

Answers

1 fever 2 cough 3 headache 4 cold 5 backache
6 stomach ache 7 sore throat 8 earache

2 Complete the doctor's reports.

The children read the patient histories and write the sickness. Elicit answers.

Answers

A a cold B a headache C an earache D a backache
E a stomach ache

3 Choose and categorize the sicknesses in your notebook.

Remind the children that organizing vocabulary into categories makes it easier to learn. Elicit an example for each category listed. Ask *Which categories would you choose?* Elicit ideas, prompting children to give a reason for their choice. The children choose a pair of categories and list the words in their notebook, then compare with a friend.

Answers

Children's own answers.

Cooler: Play "Tic-Tac-Toe"

Play the game with *sore throat, cough, backache, cold, fever, headache, stomach ache, earache, doctor,* doing a mime for each word to elicit a correct sentence with the word (see Games Bank p. 19).

Competency Focus

Think! Critical Thinking

The children use critical thinking skills to understand the vocabulary by using visual clues and processing the written and spoken forms.

Digital Resources

Student eBook • Play "Kim's Game" with the new vocabulary. Use *Timer* to give the class one minute to memorize the items, then one minute to recall them.

- Say the sicknesses pictured in SB Activity 1 in random order. Children use *Pen* to circle each one.

Grammar

Lesson objective: give advice when someone is sick
Key grammar: *You should (stay at home for three days). You shouldn't (go to school).*
Secondary language: *catch an illness, medicine, sneeze, tissue, toothache*
Materials: Track 2.2; Grammar Worksheet 2A [TRC printout] (optional); small pieces of paper with vocabulary, bag (optional)

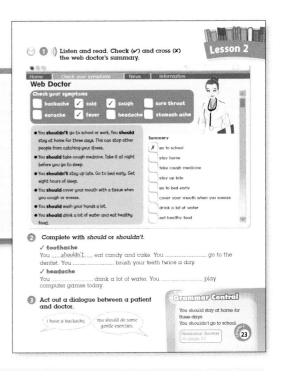

Warmer: Unscramble the words

Write on the board scrambled versions of *sore throat, cough, backache, cold, fever, headache, stomach ache, earache.* Working in pairs, the children write the words. They swap with another pair to check.

1)) **2.2** **Listen and read. Check (✔) and cross (✗) the web doctor's summary.**

- Have the children look at the web doctor's website. Pre-teach *symptoms, medicine, sneeze, toothache.*
- Play Track 2.2. The children follow and check or cross the advice in the Summary list. Elicit answers.
- Play Track 2.2 again. Ask further questions, e.g. *What are the symptoms?* (cold, cough, and fever) *What should people do when they cough or sneeze?* (cover their mouth with a tissue, and then throw the tissue away)

Answers

✔   stay home, take cough medicine, go to bed early, cover your mouth when you sneeze, drink a lot of water, eat healthy food

✗   go to school, stay up late

Grammar Central

You should stay at home for three days. …

Have the children look at the patterns. Elicit when we use *should/shouldn't.* (*to give advice*) Give examples of problems/situations and elicit advice, e.g. *It's my mom's birthday!* (*You should buy her a present.*) *I'm really tired!* (*You shouldn't play tennis. You should go to bed early tonight.*), etc. Pay attention to the silent *l* in *should/shouldn't.*

For extra practice, try the **Grammar Booster** section in the Student Book (p. 32)

Answers p. 32

Activity 1: **2** shouldn't **3** should **4** shouldn't **5** should **6** shouldn't

Activity 2: **2** should cover **3** shouldn't eat **4** should call **5** shouldn't run **6** should study

2 Complete with *should* or *shouldn't.*

- Elicit the two sicknesses. (*toothache* and *headache*) Have the children complete the advice individually, then compare answers in pairs.
- Elicit answers in the form of completed sentences.

Answers

Toothache: shouldn't, should, should
Headache: should, shouldn't

3 Act out a dialogue between a patient and doctor.

- Have two children read out the example.
- Divide the class into pairs. They take turns being the doctor and patient. Encourage them to adapt the example dialogue using sicknesses from Lesson 1 and new ideas for advice.
- Invite pairs to act out for the class.

Optional activity: What should I do?

Divide the class into two teams. Write the Lesson 1 vocabulary items on separate pieces of paper and put them in a bag. A child from each team takes a piece of paper and reads it. Their team then has to provide as many sentences as possible giving advice, e.g. *stomach ache—You shouldn't eat chocolate*. Teams win one point for each correct sentence. Accept all plausible sentences.

1 Circle.

The children circle *should* or *shouldn't* to complete what the doctor says. Elicit answers.

Answers

1 should **2** should **3** shouldn't **4** should **5** shouldn't
6 should

2 Complete with *should* or *shouldn't*. Then act out.

The children complete the mini-dialogues using *should* or *shouldn't*. Elicit answers. Divide the class into pairs. The children act out the mini-dialogues, taking turns asking for and giving advice.

Answers

1 shouldn't **2** should **3** shouldn't **4** shouldn't **5** should

3 Write some advice for the Web Doctor website.

The children look at the symptoms checked and write advice for the patient. Have children read out their advice.

Answers

Children's own answers.

Cooler: Advice for children

Draw a picture of a grumpy boy and girl on the board. Say *They aren't very good children*. Elicit advice on how they could be better children, e.g. *You should listen to your teacher*. At the end, draw a smile on the boy and girl and say *They're good children now! Thanks!*

Competency Focus

Learn

The children develop learning strategies by recognizing and applying language patterns. They show their understanding of previously acquired vocabulary and use it in a new context.

Digital Resources

Student eBook • Use *Highlighter* to focus on the grammar structures in the SB Grammar Central Box.

- After completing SB Activity 1, elicit advice for each answer prompt, e.g. *You shouldn't go to school*.

Teacher Resource Center • For extra grammar practice, print out Grammar Worksheet 2A.

Reading: Story Extract

Lesson objectives: sympathize with a sick person; predict story content from title and pictures; read the extract from *Lulu's Sick Day* (beginning)

Functional language: *Is something wrong? That's too bad! Would you like … ?*

Secondary language: *caring, fake, misery, nasty, painful, shot*

Materials: Tracks 2.3 and 2.4

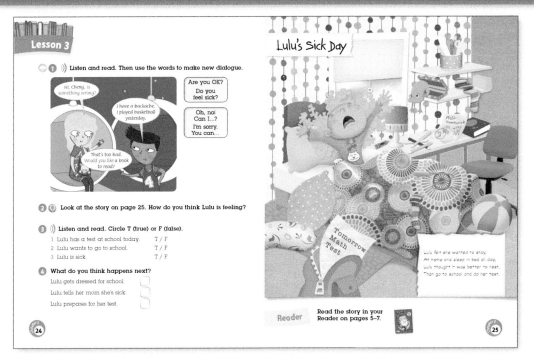

Warmer: Play "Ready, Set, Draw"

Play the game with vocabulary from Lesson 1 (see Games Bank p. 19).

Functional language

1))) **2.3   Listen and read. Then act out.**

- Have the children look at the picture. Ask *What's wrong with Cheng?* Elicit ideas.

- Play Track 2.3. The children listen and read along. Check whether the children were right.

- Play Track 2.3 again, pausing for the children to repeat.

- Have them act out the dialogue in pairs. Encourage them to replace *backache* with different sicknesses and *I played basketball* with different reasons.

Before reading

2   Look at the story. How do you think Lulu is feeling?

- Have the children look at the picture. Elicit the title of the story: *Lulu's Sick Day.* Ask *Where's Lulu?* (*in her room*) *How do you think she's feeling?* Elicit ideas and reasons.

3))) **2.4   Listen and read. Circle T (true) or F (false).**

- The children read the sentences.

- Play Track 2.4 twice. The children listen and read along. They circle T (true) or F (false) for each sentence.

- Elicit answers, including the correct version of the false sentences.

- Ask *Did Lulu want to go to school?* (*no*) *Why not?* (*because she had a test*)

Answers

1 T 2 F 3 F

4 What do you think happens next?

- Have the children think and check one of the three options. Elicit ideas including reasons but do not confirm. Say they will have to read the story to find out.

Answers

Children's own answers.

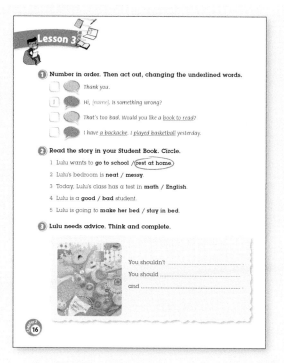

Cooler: Play "Jump the Line"

Play the game with *You shouldn't wash your hands. You should drink a lot of water. People with a cough shouldn't take cough medicine. You should get eight hours of sleep., etc.* (see Games Bank p. 19).

Competency Focus

Collaborate and Communicate

The children act out an authentic dialogue together, putting into practice the functional language.

Think! Critical Thinking

The children apply reading skills (exploiting pictures and text clues) to understand the story.

1 Number in order. Then act out, changing the underlined words.

Divide the class into pairs to number the lines of dialogue in order, then act it out, changing the underlined words. Have pairs act out for the class.

Answers

4, 1, 3, 2

2 Read the story in your Student Book. Circle.

The children read the Student Book story extract again. They answer the questions by circling the correct option in each pair. Elicit answers.

Answers

1 rest at home **2** messy **3** math **4** bad **5** stay in bed

3 Lulu needs advice. Think and complete.

Elicit ideas for advice to give Lulu. The children complete the sentences. Invite children to read their advice to the class.

Answers

Children's own answers.

Digital Resources

Student eBook • To give feedback on AB Activity 3, have children complete the interactive digital activity or use *Pen*.

- TIP Choose the audio button on the SB page to access recordings for listening activities.

Lulu's Sick Day

1
Lulu felt she wanted to stay,
At home and sleep in bed all day,
Lulu thought it was better to rest,
Than go to school and do her test.

2
"Is something wrong?" her mother said.
"Why are you lying here in bed?"
Lulu gave a tired croak,
"I'm sorry, Mom, I have a sore throat.
"I really think I have a cold."
This was the lie that Lulu told.
"That's too bad! You shouldn't go to school,"
Her mother said. "Let's keep you cool."

3
"I'll bring you drinks and food in bed,
So you can rest your painful head.
Should I bring something for your stomach?
Would you like some bread and honey?"
Lulu thought this was the best,
Much better than a nasty test.
She knew she really shouldn't lie,
But still she gave a great big sigh.
"Should I bring a cup of tea?
Would you like some soup, maybe?
I'll run a bath, nice and deep.
Then perhaps you'll have a sleep."

4
"Would you like a magazine?
Should I rub some smelly cream?
And would you like some books to read?"
"Yes, please, I would," Lulu agreed.
Lulu thought this was the best,
Much better than a nasty test.
She knew she really shouldn't lie.
Again she gave a great big sigh.

5
Her caring mom at last could see,
What caused her daughter's misery.
As Lulu gave another groan,
Mom went to get the telephone.
"Doc," she said, "Lulu's in pain."
The Doctor went on to explain.
"I think," he said, "because she's hot,
She needs the biggest kind of shot."

6
Now suddenly Lulu was better.
She pulled on her skirt, and then her sweater.
"I think that I should go to school,
I really shouldn't break that rule."
Poor Lulu learned, on that same day,
Lying to mom will never pay.
And you should never try to fake,
A sore throat or a stomach ache.

Lesson objective: read and understand the cautionary tale *Lulu's Sick Day* in the Reader
Materials: Track 2.5; Reader

Warmer: Clap and stamp

Have the children stand up. Say true/false sentences about the story extract, e.g. *Lulu is in her room.* (*T*) *Lulu wants to go to school.* (*F*) The children clap their hands if the sentence is true and stamp their feet if it is false. If they make a mistake, they sit down. The last child standing wins.

Story Summary

Lulu, a schoolgirl, lies to her mom and pretends to be sick. She stays at home to avoid taking a test at school. When the doctor says she needs a shot, Lulu decides that lying is not the best option.

Value: Be honest.

2.5 While reading

- Have the children look at the pictures in the Reader. Ask *Is Lulu having a nice time?* (*yes*)

- Play Track 2.5. The children listen and read along. Ask *What's wrong with Lulu?* (*nothing*)

- Play Track 2.5 again. Ask questions to check comprehension, e.g. *Is Lulu telling the truth?* (*no*) *How does her mom take care of her?* (*She brings her drinks, food, magazines, and books.*) *Why does Lulu decide to go to school in the end?* (*She doesn't want to have a shot.*)

After reading: Reflect

Ask *What do you think about Lulu? Was she naughty? How did Lulu's mom feel in the end? Have you ever stayed home from school because you had a test?*

Optional activity: Act out

Divide the class into pairs. The pairs choose a scene from the story and recreate a dialogue, e.g. between Lulu and her mom or between Lulu's mom and the doctor. Alternatively, they can make up a conversation between Lulu and a friend in which Lulu tells her what she has done. Have pairs practice their dialogues, then act them out for the class.

Story Time

Exploiting rhythm

A rhyming poem is ideal to get the children interested in poetry and rhymes. Make the children conscious of the cadence of the poem. Play the last verses on the CD again, and have them follow the intonation by clapping on the stressed syllables.

Reading Strategy

Rhyming Words

Poems and stories that use rhyme are popular with children. In English, rhyming texts give the opportunity to notice and contrast spelling patterns and help the children improve their pronunciation and intonation.

For additional explanation and activities, see the Literacy Handbook on the Teacher's Resource Center.

Cooler: Who said that?

Have the children work in pairs. They take turns reading a line of dialogue from the story and identifying the character speaking.

Digital Resources

Reader eBook • Ask the children to recall their predictions for what happens to Lulu. Ask *What happens to Lulu?* Show Picture 5. The children raise their hand to answer as soon as they have an idea.

- For the Cooler, have children use *Pen* to circle the character speaking each time.

Reading Comprehension and Critical Literacy

Lesson objectives: focus on rhyming words; relate the story to personal experiences

Materials: Track 2.5; Reader

Note: Please ensure that your class has read the Reader story before you do this lesson.

Warmer: Play "Finish the Word"

Divide the class into two teams. Start spelling a word (e.g. *headache, stomach ache, shot, cough, backache*). When children think they know it, they raise their hand and say it and spell it. If they say and spell the correct word before you finish spelling it, they get one point for their team. If they make a mistake, they lose a point.

1))) 2.5 Read the story in your Reader.

- Have the children read the story. (Alternatively, play Track 2.5 and have them read along.) Elicit whether they were correct in their predictions in Lesson 3 Activity 4.

- Check comprehension by asking *Why was Lulu naughty?* (*She pretended to be sick because didn't want to take the test.*) *What did she do in the end?* (*She went to school.*)

2 Circle all the correct answers.

- The children read the sentences and choose the correct endings. Explain that there may be more than one answer to each question.

- Elicit answers.

Answers

1 a, b **2** a, b **3** a, b **4** a, c

I Can Read and Write!

Have the children read the text on p. 8 of the Reader. Elicit the rhyming words, e.g. *stay—day, rest—test*. Then the children work in pairs, taking turns saying a word from the story and responding with the rhyming word.

3 How does Lulu feel at the end of the story? Complete the poem.

- Ask *How does Lulu feel at the end of the story?* Elicit ideas, e.g. *sorry, sad, bad*, etc.

- Have the children work in pairs to complete the poem using the words supplied. Point out that it has to rhyme. Read the poem as a class.

Answers

sorry, bad, sick, fine, careful, happy

4 Talk about the story.

- Have the children read Jason's question, and answer it. Ask *Were you very sick? Did you go to the doctor's? Did the doctor come to see you? What did your mom do? What did your friends do? Did they visit you?*

Optional activity: Play "Find the Rhymes"

Write on the board, jumbling the order: *two/who, show/no, tea/tree, here/we're, hair/where, I/fly, they/play, meet/eat, bread/said, eight/straight*. Divide the class into two teams. Have one child from each team come to the front. Read out a sentence with one of the words in it. Teams take turns finding and circling the word and the word that rhymes with it. The team with the most circles wins.

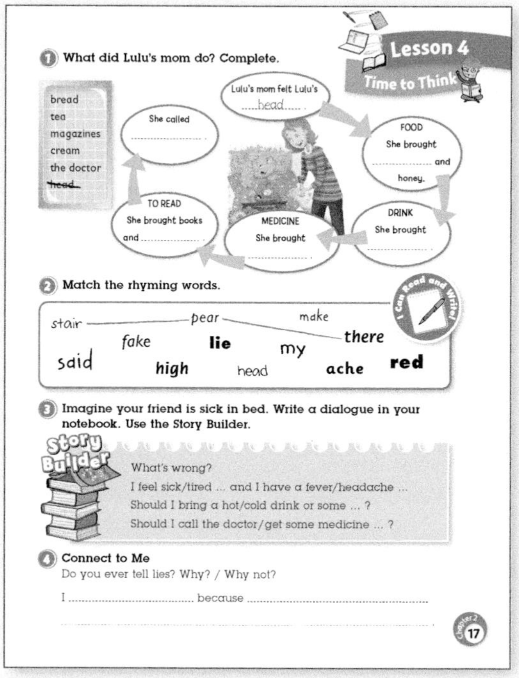

The workbook page shows:

Lesson 4 — Time to Think

1 What did Lulu's mom do? Complete.

bread
tea
magazines
cream
the doctor
head

Lulu's mom felt Lulu's ......head......

She called ......

FOOD She brought ...... and honey.

TO READ She brought books and ......

MEDICINE She brought ......

DRINK She brought ......

2 Match the rhyming words.

stair — pear — make
fake — lie — there
said — high — my — ache — red
head

I Can Read and Write!

3 Imagine your friend is sick in bed. Write a dialogue in your notebook. Use the Story Builder.

Story Builder
What's wrong?
I feel sick/tired ... and I have a fever/headache ...
Should I bring a hot/cold drink or some ... ?
Should I call the doctor/get some medicine ... ?

4 Connect to Me
Do you ever tell lies? Why? / Why not?
I .... because ....

17

Cooler: Play "Disappearing Text"

Write a sentence on the board, e.g. *You should cover your mouth with a tissue when you cough.* Have the children read it aloud. Erase a word and have the children read the whole sentence again. Continue erasing words until the children are saying the sentence without any prompts.

Competency Focus

Me: Critical Literacy

The children use critical literacy skills to reflect on the theme of the story and relate it to their personal experience.

1 What did Lulu's mom do? Complete.

The children complete the sentences using the words supplied. Elicit answers.

Answers

head, bread, tea, cream, magazines, the doctor

2 Match the rhyming words.

Ask the children what they notice about words with the same sounds. (*They are not always spelled the same way.*) The children practice the **I Can Read and Write!** feature by matching the rhyming words. Elicit answers.

Answers

stair/pear/there, said/red/head, high/lie/my, fake/make/ache

3 Imagine your friend is sick in bed. Write a dialogue in your notebook. Use the Story Builder.

Use the **Story Builder** prompts to elicit ideas. The children write a dialogue in their notebook, then swap with a friend to check. Have pairs read their dialogues for the class.

Answers

Children's own answers.

4 Connect to Me

Elicit ideas on telling/not telling lies (e.g. *tell lies to be polite/not hurt someone's feelings; not tell lies to avoid problems*) before the children write their own response. Elicit responses.

Answers

Children's own answers.

Digital Resources

Presentation Kit • TIP You can move the answer key pop-up window around the screen to have the activity and the answers side by side.

Vocabulary, Song, and Spelling

Lesson objectives: identify and talk about injuries and first-aid; practice spelling words with *ir, ur, er*

Key vocabulary: *bandage, broken leg, burn, crutches, cut, medicine, pain, shot*

Secondary language: *bit, chased, dragon, snake*

Materials: Tracks 2.6 and 2.7; red, blue, and green pens/pencils; Phonics Worksheet 2 [TRC printout] (optional)

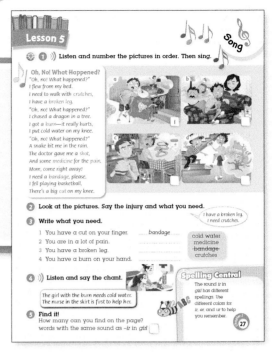

Warmer: Pre-teach vocabulary

Point to the picture in Student Book Activity 1 to pre-teach the vocabulary. Then point and say the wrong word to elicit the correct one.

1))) 2.6 Listen and number the pictures in order. Then sing.

- Have the children look at the highlighted words in the song.
- Play Track 2.6. The children listen and number the pictures in order. Elicit answers.
- Play Track 2.6 again for the children to sing along and mime the injuries.

Answers

a 1 b 4 c 3 d 2

2 Look at the pictures. Say the injury and what you need.

- Read the example. In pairs, the children take turns saying an injury and what they need. The child listening can mime offering the medicine/cure.
- Invite children to say their sentences for the class.

3 Write what you need.

- Have a child read the example. The children read the situations and write the correct cure using the words supplied.
- Elicit answers.

Answers

1 bandage 2 medicine 3 crutches 4 cold water

Spelling Central

ir, er, ur words

Say *girl, her,* and *burn* for the children to repeat. Elicit that the pronunciation is the same. Have them circle the words in the chant: *ir* in red, *er* in blue, and *ur* in green.

4))) 2.7 Listen and say the chant.

- Have the children look at the picture. Ask *What can you see?*
- Play Track 2.7. Elicit the *ir, er,* and *ur* words.
- Play Track 2.7 again, pausing for the children to repeat.

5 Find it!

- Set a time limit for the children to find *ir, er,* and *ur* words on the page. Elicit answers.
- Elicit any other *ir, er,* and *ur* words they know.

Answers

7—burn, hurts, water, nurse, skirt, first, her

Optional activity: Dictation

Have the children dictate simple sentences about ailments to each other, e.g. *I have a broken leg. I need crutches.* After each pair of sentences, the children can check each other's spelling and then continue.

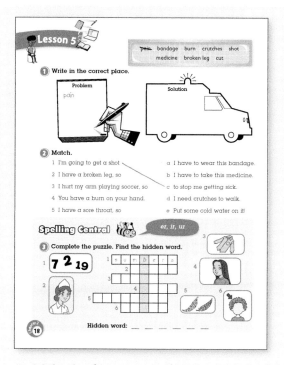

Cooler: Play "Tic-Tac-Toe"

Play the game with teams taking turns to spell an *er, ir,* or *ur* word correctly to win a square (see Games Bank p. 19).

Competency Focus

Think! Critical Thinking

The children use critical thinking skills to identify written and spoken forms of new words, and match each word with its visual representation.

1 Write in the correct place.

The children write the words supplied in the correct category: *Problem* or *Solution.* Elicit answers.

Answers

Problem: pain, burn, broken leg, cut

Solution: bandage, crutches, shot, medicine

2 Match.

The children match the sentences. Elicit anwers.

Answers

1 c 2 d 3 a 4 e 5 b

3 Complete the puzzle. Find the hidden word.

To practice the **Spelling Central** feature, the children look at the pictures and complete the puzzle. Then they find and write the hidden word. Elicit answers, asking children to spell each word.

Answers

1 numbers 2 nurse 3 shirt 4 girl 5 feathers 6 curly

Hidden word: burger

Digital Resources

Student eBook • Choose the karaoke version of Music Video 2.1 (2.2) and encourage the children to dance and sing along, using the lyrics on screen. Associating movements with words makes them more memorable. Pause for the children to continue dancing and singing.

• Encourage the children to share Music Video 2.1 (2.2) at home with their family.

Teacher Resource Center • For phonics practice, print out Phonics Worksheet 2.

Grammar and Reading

Lesson objective: talk about what they could/couldn't do when they were sick

Key grammar: *Could you (walk)? I could (walk). I couldn't (play soccer or baseball for a long time).*

Secondary language: *baseball, computer games, soccer, wing*

Materials: Tracks 2.6 and 2.8; Grammar Worksheet 2B [TRC printout] (optional)

Warmer: Say the next word

))) **2.6**

Play Track 2.6, pausing at random points in the song. Have children tell you how the song continues.

---

1))) **2.8** **Listen and read. What's wrong with the bird?**

- Have the children look at the pictures. Ask *What's Felicity doing?* (*reading a book*)

- Play Track 2.8. The children listen and read along. Ask *What's wrong with the bird?* (*It has a broken wing./ It flew into a window.*)

- Play Track 2.8 again. Ask further questions, e.g. *Where do they put the bird?* (*in a box*) *Does the vet see it?* (*no*) *Why?* (*because it can fly again in the end*) *Who couldn't play soccer?* (*Cheng*) *Why?* (*he broke his leg*)

2 **Complete the vet's report card.**

- Have the children look at the picture. Ask *What's Mr. Croc?* (*a crocodile*) *What's wrong with Mr. Croc?* (*He has a broken leg and a broken tail.*)

- Read the examples. The children complete the report card, then compare answers in pairs. Elicit answers.

Answers

Could; Could; Could; Could; couldn't; could; couldn't; could

Grammar Central

Could you walk? ...

Have the children look at the patterns. Ask *When do you use could and couldn't?* (*to talk about ability in the past*) Ask *Could Cheng walk?* (*Yes, he could.*) *Could he play soccer?* (*No, he couldn't.*) Have the children continue this activity in pairs.

For extra practice, try **Grammar Booster** section in the Student Book (pp. 33–35).

Answers p. 33

Activity 1: **2** couldn't **3** Could **4** could **5** Could **6** couldn't

Activity 2: **2** Could **3** could **4** Could **5** couldn't **6** could **7** could **8** couldn't

p. 34

Activity 1: **2** couldn't **3** could **4** shouldn't **5** should **6** should **7** should

Activity 2: **2** Could **3** could **4** should **5** shouldn't **6** Should

p. 35

Activity 1: **2** couldn't **3** couldn't **4** Could **5** going to **6** could **7** could **8** shouldn't **9** should **10** shouldn't **11** a lot of

Activity 2: Children's own answers.

Optional activity: Make a chain

Divide the class into groups of six. Say *When I was five years old, I could read. What could you do?* Have the first child in each group answer, turn to the next child on the right, and ask the question. When all the children have spoken, start a new round saying *When I was five years old, I couldn't play the piano. What couldn't you do?*

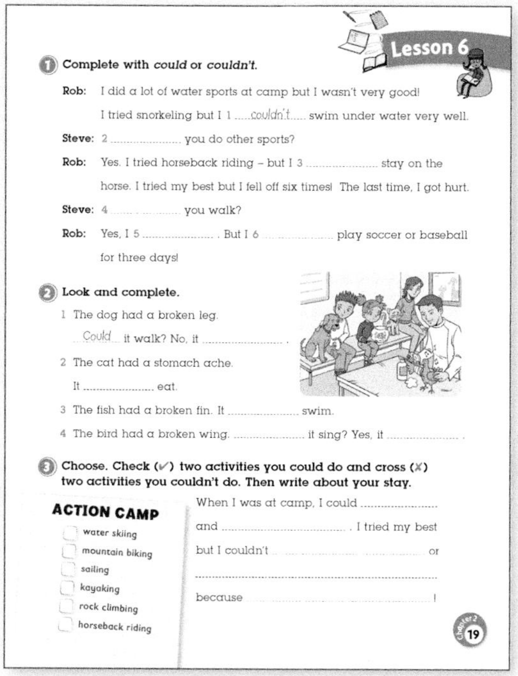

Cooler: Play "The Shark Game"

Play the game using *I broke my right arm once.* and *Cheng couldn't play soccer or baseball for a long time.* Draw a line for each word and explain the sentence is about the Story Central story (see Games Bank p. 19).

Competency Focus

Learn

The children develop learning strategies by recognizing and applying language patterns in different contexts.

(Student Book page excerpt)

Lesson 6

1 Complete with *could* or *couldn't*.

Rob: I did a lot of water sports at camp but I wasn't very good! I tried snorkeling but I 1 __couldn't__ swim under water very well.

Steve: 2 _____ you do other sports?

Rob: Yes. I tried horseback riding – but I 3 _____ stay on the horse. I tried my best but I fell off six times! The last time, I got hurt.

Steve: 4 _____ you walk?

Rob: Yes, I 5 _____ . But I 6 _____ play soccer or baseball for three days!

2 Look and complete.

1 The dog had a broken leg. __Could__ it walk? No, it _____ .

2 The cat had a stomach ache. It _____ eat.

3 The fish had a broken fin. It _____ swim.

4 The bird had a broken wing. _____ it sing? Yes, it _____ .

3 Choose. Check (✔) two activities you could do and cross (✗) two activities you couldn't do. Then write about your stay.

ACTION CAMP
- water skiing
- mountain biking
- sailing
- kayaking
- rock climbing
- horseback riding

When I was at camp, I could _____ and _____ . I tried my best but I couldn't _____ or _____ because _____ .

19

---

1 Complete with *could* or *couldn't*.

The children complete the dialogue. Elicit answers.

Answers

1 couldn't 2 Could 3 couldn't 4 Could 5 could 6 couldn't

2 Look and complete.

The children look at the picture and complete the sentences. Elicit answers.

Answers

1 Could, couldn't 2 couldn't 3 couldn't 4 Could, could

3 Choose. Check (✔) two activities you could do and cross (✗) two activities you couldn't do. Then write about your stay.

Say *Imagine you went to Action Camp last year. What could you do? What couldn't you do?* Have the children check and cross activities in the list. They complete the text about their stay, then compare answers in pairs.

Answers

Children's own answers.

Digital Resources

Student eBook • Display the SB page on the board. Read through the story one picture at a time. Ask questions to check comprehension as you go.

• Have children use *Highlighter* to identify the *Could you …?* questions and *could/couldn't* sentences in SB Activity 1.

Teacher Resource Center • For extra grammar practice, print out Grammar Worksheet 2B.

CLIL: Social sciences—Strange medicines

Lesson objective: find out about strange medicines
Materials: CLIL Graphic Organizer 2 [TRC printout] (optional)

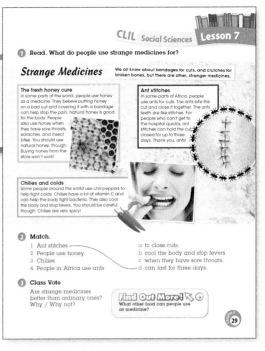

Warmer: How do you cure a cold?

Ask *What did Lulu's mom do when she said she was sick?* (*She brought her drinks, food, magazines, and books.*) Then ask *What does your mom give you when you have a cold?* Elicit both medicines and natural remedies, such as honey and lemon.

1 Read. What do people use strange medicines for?

- Have the children look at the pictures. Ask *What can you see?*

- The children read the text. Ask *What do people use honey for?* (cuts, sore throat, earache, and insect bites) *Which part of the ants closes the cut?* (teeth) *What do chilies fight?* (colds, bacteria, and fevers)

- Ask *Would you try any of these strange medicines?*

2 Match.

- Read the example. The children match the sentence halves, referring to the text.

- Elicit answers.

Answers

1 d 2 c 3 b 4 a

Optional activity: Natural medicines

Have the children make a list of all the natural medicines they have taken when they were sick, e.g. yogurt/cinnamon/chamomile for an upset stomach, etc. Have them compare their list with a friend. Have them read their lists for the class to comment on.

3 Class Vote

- Elicit a few ordinary medicines, e.g. *pills, syrup, creams,* etc. Then ask *Are strange medicines better than ordinary ones?* Have children vote "yes" by raising both hands and "no" by putting their hands on their head.

- Count the votes and elicit reasons why (*they don't have side effects, they're cheap, they're easy to get*) and why not (*some health problems need strong medicines, sometimes they don't work*).

Find Out More!

Ask the children to research other foods that can be used as medicines. Suggest appropriate resources, e.g. Internet, library books, parents/grandparents, etc. The children will need to complete this research before doing the follow-up activity in the Activity Book. (It could be set as homework.)

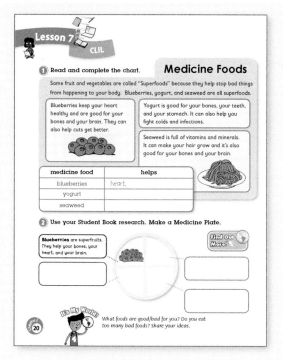

Play the game with *backache, cold, cough, earache, fever, headache, sore throat, stomach ache, bandage, broken leg, burn, crutches, cut, medicine, pain, shot* (see Games Bank p. 19).

Competency Focus

Act

The children carry out research to find out more about natural medicines. This helps them expand their learning and relate it to their world, both inside and outside the classroom.

1 Read and complete the chart.

The children read the text and complete the chart. Elicit answers.

Answers

blueberries: heart, bones, brain; help cuts get better

yogurt: bones, teeth, stomach; helps fight colds/infections

seaweed: hair, bones, brain

2 Use your Student Book research. Make a Medicine Plate.

Divide the class into groups of four. Have the children pool the information learned from their research in the Student Book and the Activity Book. They make their Medicine Plate and complete the labels individually. Have children show their plates and talk about them to the class.

Answers

Children's own answers.

It's My World!

The children discuss in small groups what good/bad food they eat and whether they eat too many bad foods. Elicit answers.

Digital Resources

Presentation Kit • For AB Activity 2 feedback, have children use *Pen* to write and draw answers. Elicit who else used the same information with a show of hands.

• TIP You can set a time limit using *Timer* to make any activity more competitive and fun. Use it here for AB Activity 1.

Teacher Resource Center • Print out CLIL Graphic Organizer 2 for the children to use in collating their Find Out More! research.

CLIL eBook • The children can use the CLIL eBook to expand their knowledge of the lesson topic.

Project

Lesson objectives: review language from Chapter 2; make a first-aid kit; act out a patient–doctor dialogue

Materials: posterboard, colored pencils or markers, glue/stapler, scissors, paper to draw items for first-aid kit; health problem cards (optional); two game pieces and a coin for each pair

Warmer: Play "Vocabulary Review"

Play the game with *sore throat, cough, backache, fever, stomach ache, earache, bandage, crutches, pain, shot* (see Games Bank p. 19).

Prepare

1 Make a first-aid kit.

- Brainstorm items for a first-aid kit (e.g. bandages, band aids, hand gel, medicine, wipes, aspirin, etc.).
- Distribute the materials. Read through the instructions together and ensure the children are clear on what to do.
- The children make their first-aid kits and the objects to put inside. Give support as necessary.

Alternative craft activity

An easier project is for the children to draw and decorate a first-aid kit, showing all the elements they want to put inside it.

Showcase

2 Pretend you're a doctor.

- Have two children read the example dialogue. Divide the class into pairs.
- The children practice a patient–doctor dialogue using the **Ideas Box** for support.
- Ask children to act out their dialogues for the class.

Optional activity: In the waiting room

Prepare cards, each with a different health problem written on it (from Lesson 1 or 5). Give five children a card each. Have them stand at the front of the class and mime having this problem until you say *Stop!* They freeze in position. The class identifies each problem and suggests solutions. Repeat with different children and cards.

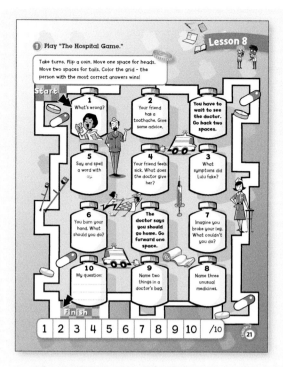

1 Play "The Hospital Game."

See p. 43 for instructions on how to play the game.
Answers

1 He has a cold. **2** You should go to the dentist. / You shouldn't eat candy. **3** a cold and a sore throat
4 medicine **5** *any one of:* say, away, today, etc.
6 You should put it under cold water. **7** I couldn't walk/run/play soccer, etc. **8** *any three of:* honey, chilies, ants, blueberries, yogurt, seaweed **9** medicine, bandages **10** Children's own answer.

Cooler: Understand silent speech

Write key vocabulary from Chapter 2 on the board. Tell the children to listen carefully. When you have their full attention, mouth a word silently for the children to identify just by watching the movement of your mouth. The first child to guess correctly takes your place.

Competency Focus

Collaborate and Communicate

By working together, the children consolidate their understanding of the language learned in a way which they will find fun and engaging. They also demonstrate their ability to work with friends and use interpersonal skills.

Digital Resources

Student eBook • Use *Timer* to give the children one minute to study the Ideas Box. Then minimize the page. Elicit the sentence openings one at a time, asking a different child to complete each one.

Language Review

Lesson objective: review language from Chapter 2
Materials: Tracks 2.9, AB 2.1 and AB 2.2

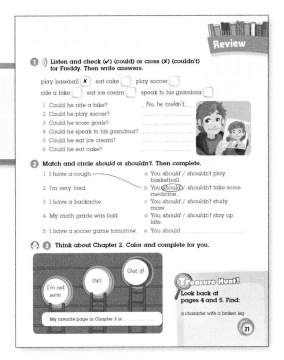

Warmer: That's too bad …

Write on the board *That's too bad …* Elicit problems/
situations, e.g. *I have a sore throat. I failed my test.* The
children take turns in pairs telling their problems and
responding *That's too bad …* + a suggestion.

1))) 2.9 Listen and check (✔) (could) or cross (✗) (couldn't) for Freddy. Then write answers.

- Play Track 2.9. The children listen and check or cross the activities. Elicit answers.
- The children write answers to the questions using the check/cross information. Elicit answers.

Audioscript

Marty: Ha, ha! Look at that picture. Is that you?
Freddy: Yes. I was only four. This was my first bike. I couldn't ride my bike well. I couldn't stay on it!
Marty: But, could you play soccer?
Freddy: Oh, yes! I could kick the ball really well and I could score goals!
Marty: Well, I could play baseball when I was four—my dad taught me.
Freddy: I remember that vacation. I was at my grandma's house. I was sick and I had a sore throat. I couldn't speak for two weeks.
Marty: Ha, ha! That was good for your family.
Freddy: No, it was really bad. I couldn't eat much. I could only eat ice cream.
Marty: That doesn't sound so bad!

Answers

✔ play soccer, eat ice cream
✗ play baseball, eat cake, ride a bike, speak to his grandma

1 No, he couldn't. **2** Yes, he could. **3** Yes, he could.
4 No, he couldn't. **5** Yes, he could. **6** No, he couldn't.

2 Match and circle *should* or *shouldn't*. Then complete.

- The children match the problems with the advice and circle *should* or *shouldn't*. Point out that in answer **e**, they have to complete the advice with their own ideas.
- Invite children to read out a problem and piece of advice.

Answers

1 b, should **2** d, shouldn't **3** a, shouldn't **4** c, should
5 e + children's own answers

3 Think about Chapter 2. Color and complete for you.

- Children color the circle which represents how they feel about their own progress (self-evaluation).
- Have the children complete the sentence.

Treasure Hunt!

Have the children look at pp. 4–5 to find a character with a broken leg.

Cooler: Play "Monkey"

Divide the class into two teams (A and B), who stand up facing each other. Have the first child in Team A begin reading the story. When you shout *Monkey!*, the reading switches over to the first child on Team B. Continue in this way.

Chapter 2 Exam Booster

1 Reading and Writing

Look and read. Choose the correct words and write them on the lines. There is one example.

Example			
headache	bandage	crutches	burn
shot	doctor	fever	earache

Example

You have this when your head hurts. ......headache......

Questions

1 The person you visit when you're sick. ....

2 You put this on if you hurt your arm or leg. ....

3 You use these when you can't walk very well. ....

4 You get this when you touch something that is too hot. ....

5 A doctor gives you this to stop you from getting sick. ....

⑧

2 Listening

Listen to the phone calls. What's wrong? Write a letter in each box. There is one example.

1 Mr. Brown [E]   2 Mrs. Robson [ ]

3 Johnny [ ]   4 Mr. Davis [ ]

5 Julie [ ]   6 Paul [ ]

A   B   C   D

E   F   G   H

⑧

3 Listening

Listen to Sally talking to her friends and family about their problems. Which problem did each person have? Write a letter in each box. There is one example.

1 Ben [C]   2 Kim [ ]

3 Grandpa [ ]   4 Lily [ ]

5 Peter [ ]   6 Aunt Jane [ ]

A   B   C   D

E   F   G   H

Exam Tip
Check your answers carefully when you listen again.

⑧

---

1 Reading and Writing. Look and read. Choose the correct words and write them on the lines. There is one example.

The children write the items described. Check answers.

Answers

1 doctor 2 bandage 3 crutches 4 burn 5 shot

2))) AB 2.1 Listening. Listen to the phone calls. What's wrong? Write a letter in each box. There is one example.

Play Track AB 2.1 twice. The children listen and match.

Answers (Audioscript on p. 222)

Mrs Robson A Johnny G Mr Davis C Julie H Paul B

3))) AB 2.2 Listening. Listen to Sally talking to her friends and family about their problems. Which problem did each person have? Write a letter in each box.

Play AB Track 2.2. The children listen and match.

Answers (Audioscript on p. 222)

Kim B Grandpa H Lily E Peter D Aunt Jane F

Competency Focus

Me: Self-evaluation

The children reflect on the chapter and express their opinions about their own progress.

Digital Resources

Teacher Resource Center • Print out Test Chapter 2 to use at the end of this lesson. The Test Generator also allows you to create customized tests.

• Print out Festival Worksheet: Thanksgiving to expand the children's knowledge of US celebrations.

Our Solar System Overview

The children will:

- use critical thinking skills to identify the planets and their characteristics.
- compare the planets in our Solar System.
- read, understand, and act out a story.
- talk about the Solar System and space.
- talk about scientific truths.
- find out about meteors and asteroids.
- make a rocket.

Key Vocabulary

Adjectives for planets: beautiful, close (to), dangerous, different, far (from), interesting, similar, unusual

Space: alien, astronaut, galaxy, meteor, moon, orbit, planet, rocket, Solar System, star, universe

Key Grammar

- (Mars) is smaller than (Earth).
- (Earth) is more interesting than (the other seven planets).
- (Neptune) is the farthest from (the Sun).
- (Saturn) is the most beautiful (planet).
- When the moon goes in front of the Sun, there is an eclipse.
- If you look at the Sun, it can damage your eyes.

Reading Skills

Story: *Planetary Checkup*
Genre: science fiction

Literacy Development

- predict story content from title and pictures
- interpret and personalize the theme of the story
- think about the role of the narrator in the play

Functional Language

- Did you know that …?
- You're making that up.
- No, I'm not!

Spelling

Split long words into syllables

CLIL: Science—Meteors and asteroids

The children find out about meteors and asteroids.

Competency Focus

The children will:

use critical thinking skills to identify the planets in our Solar System. (Lesson 1)

predict the content of a story. (Lesson 3)

identify and talk about the Solar System and space. (Lesson 5)

apply new grammar to previously learned vocabulary. (Lesson 2)

talk about scientific truths. (Lesson 6)

work in pairs to act out a dialogue. (Lesson 3)

experiment with a rocket and draw conclusions. (Lesson 8)

personalize the story by summarizing what they learned about our planet. (Lesson 4)

evaluate their own progress in the chapter. (Review)

develop a wider understanding of space. (Lesson 7)

Digital Overview

Teacher Presentation
Student eBook and Digital Activity Book

- Oral Storytelling Video 3.1: *Planetary Checkup*
- Interactive versions of AB activities
- Integrated audio and answer key for all activities

Teacher resources for planning, lesson delivery, and homework
Teacher Resource Center

- Class Planner Chapter 3
- Worksheets to print out (including notes and answers):
  - Grammar Worksheet 3A: smaller than, more interesting than
  - Grammar Worksheet 3B: When the moon goes ... If you look ...
  - Oral Storytelling Video Worksheet 3: *Planetary Checkup*
  - Phonics Worksheet 3
  - CLIL Graphic Organizer 3
  - Festival Worksheet: Christmas
  - Test Chapter 3
- Test Generator
- Speaking Assessment: Cambridge English Young Learners Exams

Watch the Oral Storytelling Video

- Literacy Handbook

Children's resources for consolidation and practice at home
Student eBook and Reader eBook

- Oral Storytelling Video 3.1: *Planetary Checkup*

The Inks Student's App
Vocabulary games: Adjectives for planets and space

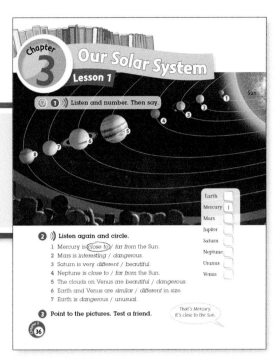

Vocabulary

Lesson objective: identify and describe the planets in our Solar System
Key vocabulary: *beautiful, close (to), dangerous, different, far (from), interesting, similar, unusual*
Materials: Track 3.1

Warmer: Planet mnemonic

Write on the board *My Very Excellent Mother Just Served Us Nachos.* Explain that the first letter of each word is also the first letter of a planet. Have the children copy the sentence in their notebook. Divide the class into groups of four to figure out and write the planet each word represents. (They can use L1 to name the planets.) Elicit answers for the class to check.

1)))) 3.1 Listen and number. Then say.

- Ask *What is this lesson about?* (*the Solar System*) Say *Read the list of the planets. Check the list you wrote. Are the planets the same?* Have the children whose list was correct raise their hands.
- Play Track 3.1. The children listen and number the planets according to their distance from the Sun (the nearest planet first).
- Play Track 3.1 again for them to check their answers.
- Say the planets in order and have the children repeat.

Audioscript

Welcome to the Solar System Show. Sit down, relax, and listen. I am going to tell you some amazing facts about our galaxy. There are eight planets in our Solar System. They all go around the Sun. The Sun is a big star at the center of our Solar System. Mercury is close to the Sun. It is number one—the first planet from the Sun.
Mars is a very small planet. It is number four from the Sun.

It is called the "red planet." It is interesting because we think people can live on Mars.
Jupiter is a very big planet. It is number five from the Sun. Mars and Jupiter are very different in size.
Saturn is number six. It is very beautiful. It has beautiful rings. They are made of ice.
Neptune is number eight—it is far from the Sun. It has 13 moons.
Also far from the Sun—number seven—is Uranus. This planet has 27 moons.
Venus is the number two planet from the Sun. Venus is hot and it has clouds of acid. It is very dangerous.
The Earth and Venus are similar in size.
The Earth is close to Venus—the number three planet from the Sun. It is unusual because it has air and water, and we live here!

Answers

Earth 3, Mercury 1, Mars 4, Jupiter 5, Saturn 6, Neptune 8, Uranus 7, Venus 2

2)))) 3.1 Listen again and circle.

- Say *Mercury is far from the Sun.* Have children correct you: *Mercury is close to the Sun.*
- The children read the example and the sentences. Play Track 3.1 for them to circle the correct adjectives. Elicit answers in the form of sentences.

Answers

1 close to **2** interesting **3** beautiful **4** far from **5** dangerous **6** similar **7** unusual

3 Point to the pictures. Test a friend.

- Do the example with the class. Then have the children work in pairs, taking turns pointing to a planet and saying something about it.

Optional activity: Create your own mnemonic

Have the children work in pairs to come up with their own mnemonic to remember the order of the planets.

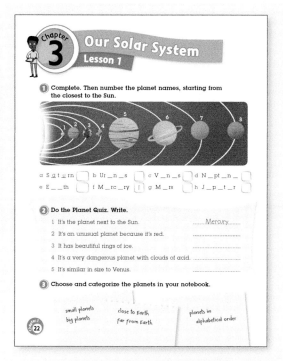

1 Complete. Then number the planet names, starting from the closest to the Sun.

Remind children of the mnemonic rule they worked on at the beginning of the lesson. They complete the planet names, writing in the missing letters, then number the planets in order. Elicit answers.

Answers

a Saturn 6 b Uranus 7 c Venus 2 d Neptune 8 e Earth 3 f Mercury 1 g Mars 4 h Jupiter 5

2 Do the Planet Quiz. Write.

The children write their answers to the quiz. Elicit answers.
Answers

1 Mercury 2 Mars 3 Saturn 4 Venus 5 Earth

3 Choose and categorize the planets in your notebook.

Elicit an example for each category listed. Ask *Which categories would you choose?* Elicit ideas, prompting children to give a reason for their choice. The children choose a pair of categories and list the words in their notebook, then compare with a friend.
Answers

Children's own answers.

Cooler: Match the opposites

Write adjective pairs on the board in random order: *usual/unusual, boring/interesting, safe/dangerous, ugly/beautiful, near/far, big/small.* Have children draw a line to connect a pair of opposites. Ask for class agreement.

Competency Focus

Think! Critical Thinking

The children use critical thinking skills to identify the planets and their characteristics by using visual clues and processing the written and spoken forms.

Digital Resources

Digital Activity Book • TIP The interactive digital activities in the AB can be done again and again, giving different children the chance to participate.

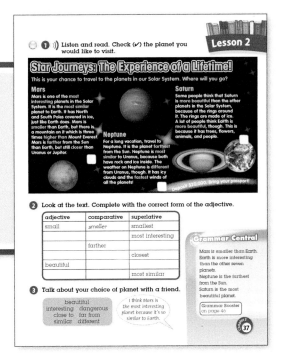

Grammar

Lesson objective: compare the planets in our Solar System

Key grammar: *(Mars) is smaller than (Earth). (Earth) is more interesting than (the other seven planets). (Neptune) is the farthest from (the Sun). (Saturn) is the most beautiful (planet).*

Secondary language: *icy, pole, similar, wind*

Materials: Track 3.2; Grammar Worksheet 3A [TRC printout] (optional); three sets of cards with the planet names from Lesson 1 (Warmer)

Warmer: Play "Order the Planets"

Divide the class into three groups. Give each group a set of cards with the planet names on them. Explain that each group has two minutes to order the planets: Group 1 in order from the Sun; Group 2 alphabetically; Group 3 in order of size. Elicit answers.

1))) 3.2 Listen and read. Check (✔) the planet you would like to visit.

- Pre-teach *pole*. Play Track 3.2. The children listen and read along. They check the planet they would like to travel to. Elicit answers with reasons, e.g. *I'd like to visit Saturn because it's beautiful.*

- Play Track 3.2 again. Ask further questions, e.g. *Which is smaller: Mars or Earth? (Mars is smaller than Earth.) Which is the planet farthest from the Sun? (Neptune) Which is the planet closest to the Sun? (Mercury)*

Answers

Children's own answers.

2 Look at the text. Complete with the correct form of the adjective.

- Have the children look at the adjectives in bold in the text and look at the example. Elicit what we add to *small* to form the comparative and superlative. (–er and –est) Repeat with adjectives of two or more syllables, using *interesting*. (more and most + *adjective*)

- The children complete the grid. Elicit answers, asking children to write them on the board.

Answers

small—smaller—smallest
interesting—more interesting—most interesting
far—farther—farthest
close—closer—closest
beautiful—more beautiful—most beautiful
similar—more similar—most similar

Grammar Central

Mars is smaller than Earth. ...

Have the children look at the patterns. Elicit when we use comparative adjectives (*to compare two people/places/things*) and superlative adjectives (*to talk about one person/place/thing in a group of three or more*). Divide the class in two. Call out other adjectives for one part of the class to say the comparative form and the other the superlative. Have them say a sentence using the correct form.

For extra practice, try **Grammar Booster** section in the Student Book (p. 46)

Answers p. 46

Activity 1: **2** the most dangerous **3** more exciting **4** the most exciting

Activity 2: **2** bigger **3** coldest **4** farthest **5** closer **6** hotter **7** most beautiful **8** more beautiful

3 Make sentences about places you know.

- Read the example and elicit a few more.

- Divide the class into pairs. The children take turns talking about a place they know. They use the comparative and superlative form of the adjectives supplied, and give a reason.

Optional activity: Comparative adjectives

Divide the board in two sections with headings –er and more, and write separately big, short, excited, surprised, long, different, thin, tall, straight, hot, cool, clean. Have the children write the comparative forms of the adjectives in the correct column in their notebook. Elicit answers.

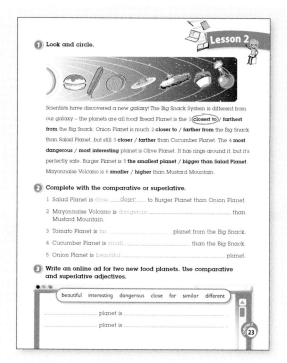

1 Look and circle.

Point out the Big Snack (as the Sun at the center of the system). Elicit the planets in the Big Snack System. (Bread Planet, Cucumber Planet, Onion Planet, Olive Planet, Burger Planet, Salad Planet, Tomato Planet) Ask Which planet is Mayonnaise Volcano on? (Tomato Planet) Elicit which of the options are comparatives and which are superlatives. Then the children look at the picture and circle the correct words to complete the text. Elicit answers.

Answers

1 closest to **2** closer to **3** farther **4** most interesting
5 bigger than Salad Planet **6** higher

2 Complete with the comparative or superlative.

The children complete the sentences about the Big Snack galaxy using the correct form of the adjectives supplied. Elicit answers.

Answers

1 closer **2** more dangerous **3** the farthest **4** smaller
5 the most beautiful

3 Write an online ad for two new food planets. Use comparative and superlative adjectives.

Brainstorm words for new food planets, e.g. yogurt, strawberry, cheese, etc. The children write about their two planets using comparative and superlative forms of the adjectives supplied. They swap with a friend to check. Invite children to read their ad to the class.

Answers

Children's own answers.

Cooler: Make a wordsearch

Show how to make a wordsearch by drawing a 10 by 10 grid on the board. There should be space for one letter in each square. Insert a few words in the comparative and the superlative, some horizontally and some vertically, with some intersecting. Have the children draw their grids in their notebook, and write in six comparative or superlative adjectives, then fill in the empty spaces with random letters. Then they swap and do a friend's wordsearch. Monitor and check spelling.

Competency Focus

Learn

The children develop learning strategies by recognizing and applying language patterns. They show their understanding of previously acquired vocabulary and use it in a new context.

Digital Resources

Student eBook • Use Add personal note for extra review of the comparative and superlative. Write an adjective and have two children write the comparative and superlative forms. Repeat with different adjectives and children.

Teacher Resource Center • For extra grammar practice, print out Grammar Worksheet 3A.

Reading: Story Extract

Lesson objectives: express disbelief; predict story content from title and pictures; read the extract from the story *Planetary Checkup* (middle)

Functional language: *Did you know that …? You're making that up. No, I'm not!*

Secondary language: *boss, galaxy, highway, leader, mountain, recycle, volcano*

Materials: Tracks 3.3 and 3.4

Warmer: Play "Tic-Tac-Toe"

Play the game with *near, far, dangerous, unusual, interesting, beautiful, similar, different, ugly* (see Games Bank p. 19). To win a square, a child has to say a sentence using the word.

Functional language

1))) 3.3 Listen and read. Then act out.

- Ask *Where are Cheng and Jason sitting?* (*on trees*)
- Play Track 3.3. The children listen and read along. Ask *Is Jason telling the truth?* (*yes*)
- Play Track 3.3 again, pausing for the children to repeat.
- Have the children act out the dialogue in pairs. Encourage them to use different interesting facts. Invite pairs to act it out for the class.

Before reading

2 Look at the story. Where do you think it is set?

- Elicit the story title. (*Planetary Checkup*) Have the children look at the picture. Ask *Where do you think it is set?* (*on Earth*)
- Ask *What can you see in the picture?* (*two aliens, a mountain*, etc.) Elicit ideas on what the story might be about.

3))) 3.4 Listen and read. Check (✔) the correct answer.

- Ask the children to read the sentences and options.
- Play Track 3.4 twice. The children listen and read along. They draw a check mark by each correct ending.
- Elicit answers.
- Ask *What can't the aliens see?* (*trees*) *Why is it noisy?* (*There are a lot of cars.*)

Answers

1 a busy highway **2** similar **3** wrong place

4 Do you think the characters have been to Earth before?

Have the children think and write down their answers. Elicit ideas including reasons but do not confirm. Say they will have to read the story to find out.

Answers

Children's own answers.

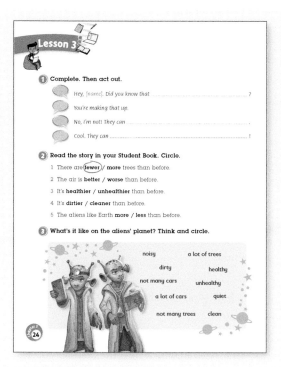

Have the children draw the next scene in the story. Prompt as necessary: *Do they meet a person or an animal? How does the person/animal react? What do the aliens say to them? Does the person answer back? / What does the animal do?* Children show their pictures and say what happens.

Competency Focus

Collaborate and Communicate

The children act out an authentic dialogue together, putting into practice the functional language.

Think! Critical Thinking

The children apply reading skills (exploiting pictures and text clues) to understand the story.

1 Complete. Then act out.

Divide the class into pairs to complete and act out the dialogue. Have pairs act out for the class.

Answers

Children's own answers.

2 Read the story in your Student Book. Circle.

The children read the Student Book story extract again. They answer the questions by circling the correct option in each pair. Elicit answers.

Answers

1 fewer 2 worse 3 unhealthier 4 dirtier 5 less

3 What's it like on the aliens' planet? Think and circle.

The children imagine the aliens' planet and circle the words/phrases that describe it. Elicit answers.

Answers

Children's own answers.

Digital Resources

Student eBook, Digital Activity Book, Reader eBook, CLIL eBook • Do not be afraid to turn off the screen! Children benefit from variety of pace and focus and sometimes you will want to work just with books or without prompts. Work the digital materials into your teaching in the way that suits you best.

★ PLANETARY ★ CHECKUP

1

CHARACTERS

Narrator   *Tyrannosaurus Rex* (King of the dinosaurs)

Astra (alien planet doctor)   *Boy*

Cosmo (alien planet doctor)   *Leader*

Narrator: Planet Earth, 230 million years ago. Cosmo and Astra are planet doctors. They travel the universe checking planets.

Astra: Mercury: done, Venus: done. Next stop, Earth.

Cosmo: That's right. Earth is warmer than Mars, but colder than Venus.

Astra: Who's the boss?

Cosmo: Mr. T-Rex. Let's find him.

2

Astra: Mr. T-Rex, we're here to check on your planet's health. Everything looks good. Is it getting warmer or colder?

T-Rex: Rrrrooooaaaar!

Cosmo: OK. You have some volcanoes ...

T-Rex: Rrrrooooaaaar!

Astra: But you have the most beautiful forests in the Solar System.

T-Rex: Rrrrooooaaaar!

Cosmo: Good job. See you again in 200 million years.

3

Narrator: Cosmo and Astra have visited other galaxies.

Cosmo: We're in the Milky Way again. After we visit Earth, we can go back home.

Astra: It's going to be interesting to see Earth again.

Cosmo: Maybe it's warmer this time.

Narrator: Cosmo and Astra prepare to land.

4

Narrator: The spaceship lands on a busy highway. There are a lot of cars.

Astra: Is this the right place? Where are all the trees?

Cosmo: The air is worse, too. It's very different.

Astra: But that mountain is similar.

Cosmo: It's much noisier than before. Are we on Earth?

Astra: Let's ask.

5

Narrator: The aliens walk into the city. There are buildings and cars everywhere, but there aren't many trees.

Cosmo: Is this planet Earth?

Boy: Yes. What an unusual question!

Astra: Where's Mr. T-Rex?

Boy: What!?

Astra: We're planet doctors. We've come to give your planet its check-up. Last time, we spoke to Tyrannosaurus Rex.

Boy: You're making that up! Um, he's not here anymore. But the world leaders are meeting in that building over there.

Cosmo: Good. Please take us there.

6

Narrator: The world leaders are having a meeting.

Cosmo: We're here for your planet's health check. The air was cleaner last time.

Leader: We have some problems ...

Astra: And your forests are smaller. Did you know that trees make the air cleaner?

Leader: Yes, we did. We're working on that ...

Cosmo: Also, Mr. T-Rex didn't use cars. The planet was healthier without cars. Did you know that cars make the air more dangerous?

Leader: Um, we're trying to use fewer cars.

Astra: Good. Bikes help, too.

Cosmo: Also, there's more trash. Earth was cleaner when Mr. T-Rex was in charge. When you don't clean up, it gets worse. Do you recycle?

Leader: We're trying ...

Astra: Try harder, please.

Cosmo: That's everything.

Astra: See you again in 200 million years. Don't forget to recycle ...

Cosmo: Bikes, not cars.

Astra: And grow more trees.

Narrator: Astra and Cosmo climbed back into their spaceship to travel far, far across the galaxy to their home.

Lesson objective: read and understand the science fiction story *Planetary Checkup* in the Reader
Materials: Track 3.5; Reader; Oral Storytelling Video Worksheet 3 [TRC printout] (optional)

Warmer: Finish the sentence

Say sentences from the story extract, pausing to elicit the last word, e.g. *Cosmo and Astra are planet ... (doctors). They travel the universe checking ... (planets). Earth is warmer than ... (Mars), but colder than ... (Venus).*

Story Summary

Planetary doctors, aliens who check the health of different planets, visit Earth. Earth is more polluted than it was 230 million years ago. The doctors give advice on how to improve Earth's health.

Value: It's good to care for the environment.

))) 3.5 While reading

- Have the children look at the pictures in the Reader. Ask *Where are Cosmo and Astra in Picture 2?* (on Earth)

- Play Track 3.5. The children listen and read along. Ask *Are Cosmo and Astra happy with what they find on Earth this time?* (no) *Why?* (*It's very different. / It's noisier, the air is worse, there's more trash, it's dirtier.*)

- Play Track 3.5 again. Ask questions to check comprehension, e.g. *Did they find Mr. T-Rex?* (yes) *Where do they go after they talk to Mr. T-Rex?* (home) *Do they come back to Earth?* (yes) *When?* (millions of years later) *Do they find Mr. T-Rex?* (no)

After reading: Reflect

Ask questions to give the children the opportunity to think about the issues raised by the story, e.g. *Do you agree with the alien planet doctors? What's wrong with our planet? Whose fault is it that Earth is noisy and dirty? What can we do to change this?*

Optional activity: Who said it?

Have the children take turns in pairs reading a line of dialogue from the story and identifying the character speaking.

Story Time

Acting out

Acting out a play is an ideal way for the children to practice intonation and pronunciation. It also encourages the children to really engage with the story and think about what the language means. You could even put on the play for parents.

Reading Strategy

Reader's Theater

In the Reader's Theater strategy, the children collaborate to read aloud a story. It is similar to a role-play, but offers more support because the children read from the page. They can work on their fluency and develop their confidence performing in front of the class.

For additional explanation and activities, see the Literacy Handbook on the Teacher's Resource Center.

Cooler: Interview with Cosmo and Astra

Divide the class into groups of four. In each group, two are Cosmo and Astra. They interview the other two children. Brainstorm questions to use, e.g. *Do you recycle? Do you throw trash in the street? Do you walk or bike ride?*, etc. Write them on the board.

Digital Resources

Reader eBook • Show the top half of Reader pp. 12–13. Ask *Where are the characters now?* Elicit story predictions.

- Oral Storytelling Video 3.1 gives the story with a different ending. Watch it together at the end of the lesson, then discuss the differences.

Teacher Resource Center • Print out Oral Storytelling Video Worksheet 3 to help you get the most out of the video.

Student eBook • The children can watch Oral Storytelling Video 3.1 at home with their family.

Reading Comprehension and Critical Literacy

Lesson objectives: learn about the role of the narrator in a story; relate the story to personal experiences

Materials: Track 3.5; Reader; Oral Storytelling Video Worksheet 3 [TRC printout] (optional)

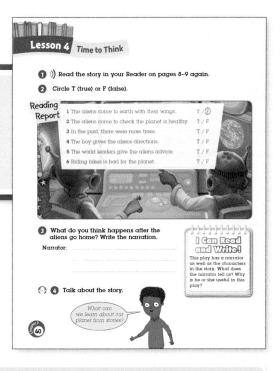

Note: Please ensure that your class has read the Reader story before you do this lesson.

Warmer: Play "I Spy ..."

Model the activity. Choose a picture from the Reader story and say *I spy with my little eye something beginning with "a" in Picture (four).* Have the children play the game in groups, each time choosing a different picture.

1))) 3.5 Read the story in your Reader.

- Have the children read the story. (Alternatively, play Track 3.5 and have them read along.) Elicit whether they were correct in their predictions in Lesson 3 Activity 4.
- Check comprehension by asking *Do Cosmo and Astra want to protect Earth?* (yes) *What do they want people to do?* (grow more trees, use fewer cars, recycle)

2 Circle T (true) or F (false).

- Have the children work in pairs. They circle T (true) or F (false) for each sentence.
- Elicit answers, including the correct version of the false sentences.

Answers

1 F 2 T 3 T 4 T 5 F 6 F

I Can Read and Write!

Have the children look at the story. Ask *Is the narrator part of the action in the story?* (no) *What information does the narrator give us?* (where the characters are, when the story takes place, etc.) Ask *Why is it useful to have a narrator?* (because the characters don't say all of the information)

3 What do you think happens after the aliens go home? Write the narration.

- Elicit ideas on what happens after the aliens go home.
- Have the children write their narration. Have children read their texts to the class.

Answers

Children's own answers.

4 Talk about the story.

- Have the children read Jason's question, and talk about what they learned about Earth from the story, e.g. about the state of Earth in the past and now, what we can do to make things better, etc.

Optional activity: Save our planet

Have the children work in groups of four, writing five simple things they can do to change the situation on Earth. Have each group report to the class. Elicit and write some rules that the class agrees on.

Cooler: Act out your play

Divide the class into groups and have them act out their plays from Activity Book Activity 3 for the class. Have a vote on the most interesting play.

Competency Focus

Me: Critical Literacy

The children use critical literacy skills to reflect on the theme of the story and relate it to their personal experience.

---

1 **What was Earth like before? What's it like now? Write.**

The children write notes comparing Earth before and now. Elicit ideas.

Answers

Before: clean air, cool, quiet, a lot of trees

Now: dirty air, warmer, a lot of cars, noisy, few trees

2 **Write *N* for the information the narrator gives.**

The children practice the **I Can Read and Write!** feature by writing N by the sentences given by the narrator. Elicit answers.

Answers

N *by* 1, 2, 4

3 **Imagine the aliens return in 200 million years. Write a play in your notebook. Use the Story Builder.**

Use the **Story Builder** prompts to elicit ideas. The children write a play in their notebook, then swap with a friend to check.

Answers

Children's own answers.

4 **Connect to Me**

Elicit ideas on stories about space or the environment (e.g. *The Time Machine*) before the children write their own response. Elicit responses.

Answers

Children's own answers.

Digital Resources

Digital Activity Book • Use the AB page to give feedback on activities, using the interactive digital activities or the answer keys.

Student eBook, Digital Activity Book • TIP Give children the opportunity to be your assistant! Ask a child to be responsible for choosing the relevant buttons (e.g. to go to the next activity or the answer key).

Student eBook, Reader eBook • If you haven't already, show Oral Storytelling Video 3.1.

Teacher Resource Center • If you haven't already, print out Oral Storytelling Video Worksheet 3 to do the activities.

Vocabulary, Song, and Spelling

Lesson objectives: identify and talk about things related to space; use syllables to improve spelling

Key vocabulary: *alien, astronaut, galaxy, meteor, moon, orbit, planet, rocket, Solar System, star, universe*

Secondary language: *aliens, infinity, shooting star, whizzing by*

Materials: Tracks 3.6 and 3.7; pictures for Key vocabulary; Phonics Worksheet 3 [TRC printout] (optional)

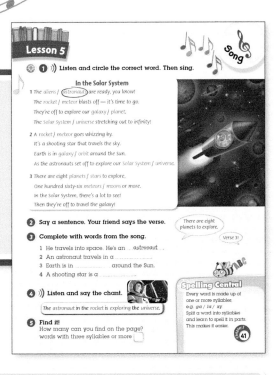

Warmer: Pre-teach vocabulary

Pre-teach the vocabulary using pictures of the space things or draw pictures on the board. Show them twice and have the children repeat. Then play a prediction game by showing the pictures in the same order to elicit what comes next.

1)) 3.6   Listen and circle the correct word. Then sing.

- Have the children look at the picture. Ask *What can you see?* Then give them time to look at the key words.
- Play Track 3.6. The children listen and circle the words.
- Play Track 3.6 again for the children to sing along. Tell them to sing the key words loudly.

Answers

astronauts, rocket, galaxy, universe, meteor, orbit, Solar System, planets, moons

2 Say a sentence. Your friend says the verse.

- Divide the class into pairs. They take turns saying a sentence from the song and calling out the verse number.

3 Complete with words from the song.

- Have the children complete the sentences, referring to the song. Elicit answers.

Answers

1 astronaut **2** rocket **3** orbit **4** meteor

Spelling Central

Split long words into syllables

Say *Ga / la / xy!* clapping your hands for each syllable. Have the children repeat after you. Do the same for other long words, e.g. *interesting, amusement, universe, astronaut.*

4)) 3.7   Listen and say the chant.

- Have the children look at the picture. Ask *What can you see?*
- Play Track 3.7. The children listen and read along. Elicit the long words.
- Play Track 3.7 again, pausing for the children to repeat.

5 Find it!

- Set a time limit for the children to find words with three or more syllables on the page. Elicit answers.
- Elicit any other words with three or more syllables that they know.

Answers

10—aliens, astronaut, meteor, galaxy, universe, infinity, sixty-six, exploring, syllables, easier

Optional activity: Play "Ready, Set, Draw!"

Play the game using *astronaut, galaxy, meteor, moon, planet, rocket, Solar System, universe* (see Games Bank p. 19).

Cooler: Sing loudly, sing quietly ...

))) 3.6

Play the song for the children to sing along. Start loud in each verse, gradually reducing the volume. Have the children sing more quietly to match the volume, so for the last lines they are singing just above a whisper.

Competency Focus

Think! Critical Thinking

The children use critical thinking skills to identify written and spoken forms of new words.

1 Find and circle nine space words. Then write the words in alphabetical order.

The children find the words in the wordsearch, then write them in alphabetical order. Elicit answers.

Answers

astronaut, galaxy, meteor, moon, orbit, planet, rocket, solar system, universe

2 Complete.

The children complete the comic strip using the words supplied. Elicit answers.

Answers

astronauts, rocket, solar system; planet, orbit; meteor

3 Complete the words. Then write the number of syllables.

To practice the **Spelling Central** feature, the children complete the words, writing in the missing letters. They then say the words and write the number of syllables. Elicit answers.

Answers

a planet 2 **b** close 1 **c** Tyrannosaurus 5 **d** unusual 4 **e** galaxy 3 **f** beautiful 3 **g** different 2 **h** dangerous 3

Digital Resources

Student eBook • TIP Display the SB for "heads-up" singing. This will enable you to check all the children are participating and identify any who are struggling.

Teacher Resource Center • For phonics practice, print out Phonics Worksheet 3.

Student's App • Encourage the children to play the games on their smartphone/tablet. Ask them to record their scores to compare in the next lesson. (*The Inks* Apps are free and available on the App Store and Google Play.)

Grammar and Reading

Lesson objective: talk about scientific truths

Key grammar: *When the moon goes in front of the Sun, there is an eclipse. If you look at the Sun, it can damage your eyes.*

Secondary language: *block, damage, safely, solar eclipse*

Materials: Track 3.8; Grammar Worksheet 3B [TRC printout] (optional)

Warmer: Play "Space Ping-Pong"

Divide the class into two teams. Any child can call out a space word as a prompt. The other team has to respond with another space word. If they repeat a word or take longer than five seconds, the other team wins a point. The team with the most points wins.

---

1 **3.8 Listen and read. How can you watch an eclipse of the Sun safely?**

- Ask *What are the children talking about?* (*a solar eclipse*)
- Play Track 3.8. The children listen and read along. Ask *How can you watch an eclipse of the Sun safely?* (*with a pinhole camera*) Ask *How do they make a pinhole camera?* Elicit ideas.
- Play Track 3.8 again. Ask *When is there a solar eclipse?* (*when the moon goes in front of the Sun*) *Is it safe to look at a solar eclipse?* (*No, it's dangerous.*) *When does the solar eclipse finish?* (*when the moon moves past the Sun*)

Grammar Central

When the moon goes in front of the Sun, there is an eclipse. …

Have the children look at the patterns. Elicit the tense of the verbs. (*present simple*) Ask *What are we talking about?* (*a general truth*) Have the children find other sentences with *If* or *When* in the story, and read them out.

For extra practice, try **Grammar Booster** section in the Student Book (p. 47–49)

Answers p. 47

Activity 1: **2** burns **3** When **4** comes **5** turns **6** send **7** can learn **8** If **9** can watch

Activity 2: **2** d **3** f **4** a **5** b **6** e

Activity 3: Children's own answers.

p. 48

Activity 1: moves **3** the fastest **4** the most dangerous **5** safer **6** more interesting **7** can show **8** slower

Activity 2: **2** more **3** faster **4** happen **5** If **6** can

p. 49

Activity 1: **2** stronger **3** faster **4** many **5** more dangerous **6** more **7** wants **8** uses **9** want **10** can look **11** a lot of

Activity 2: Children's own answers.

2 Write the correct letter.

Have the children match the sentence halves. Elicit answers.

Answers

1 d **2** c **3** b **4** a

Optional activity: Play "Stand Up, Sit Down!"

Have the children write a word from Lesson 1 or Lesson 5 on a piece of paper and hold it up. Say *Stand up, please!* and then say *Sit down if you have "rocket"!* Children holding "rocket" sit down. The last person standing wins. Have children take your place and repeat as often as you have time for.

3 Write about what you do in different weather.

Elicit ideas to complete the sentence openings. The children complete the sentences. Have children read a sentence for the class.

Answers

Children's own answers.

Cooler: Unscramble the sentence

Write a sentence on the board, scrambling the order of the words: *If the moon blocks the Sun's light completely, this is a total eclipse.* Have children work in pairs to figure out the sentence. Repeat with *When there's an eclipse, it's dangerous to look at the Sun.*

Competency Focus

Learn

The children develop learning strategies by recognizing and applying language patterns in different contexts.

---

1 Match. Then number the diagram.

Pre-teach *evaporate.* The children match the sentence halves. Elicit answers. Then they number the parts of the diagram to match them to the sentences. Elicit answers.

Answers

1 c **2** a **3** d **4** b

4, 2, 3, 1

2 Circle.

The children complete the sentences by circling the correct verb in each pair. Elicit answers in the form of complete sentences.

Answers

1 become **2** rains **3** goes **4** doesn't rain **5** it's

Digital Resources

Student eBook • Have children use *Highlighter* to identify the *When …* and *If …* sentences in the SB Activity 1 text.

• Have children use *Add personal note* to keep a tally of the teams' scores in the Warmer game.

Teacher Resource Center • For extra grammar practice, print out Grammar Worksheet 3B.

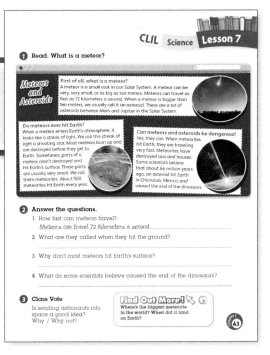

CLIL: Science—Meteors and asteroids

Lesson objective: find out about meteors and asteroids
Materials: CLIL Graphic Organizer 3 [TRC printout] (optional)

① **Read. What is a meteor?**

Meteors and Asteroids

First of all, what is a meteor?
A meteor is a small rock in our Solar System. A meteor can be very, very small, or as big as ten meters. Meteors can travel as fast as 72 kilometers a second. When a meteor is bigger than ten meters, we usually call it an asteroid. There are a lot of asteroids between Mars and Jupiter in the Solar System.

Do meteors ever hit Earth?
When a meteor enters Earth's atmosphere, it looks like a streak of light. We call this streak of light a shooting star. Most meteors burn up and are destroyed before they get to Earth. Sometimes, parts of a meteor aren't destroyed and hit Earth's surface. These parts are usually very small. We call them meteorites. About 500 meteorites hit Earth every year.

Can meteors and asteroids be dangerous?
Yes, they can. When meteorites hit Earth, they are traveling very fast. Meteorites have destroyed cars and houses. Some scientists believe that about 66 million years ago, an asteroid hit Earth in Chicxulub, Mexico, and caused the end of the dinosaurs.

② **Answer the questions.**

1 How fast can meteors travel?
   Meteors can travel 72 kilometers a second.

2 What are they called when they hit the ground?

3 Why don't most meteors hit Earth's surface?

4 What do some scientists believe caused the end of the dinosaurs?

③ **Class Vote**
Is sending astronauts into space a good idea? Why / Why not?

Find Out More!
Where's the biggest meteorite in the world? When did it land on Earth?

43

Play the game with *astronaut, galaxy, meteor, moon, planet, rocket, eclipse, universe, aliens, star* (see Games Bank p. 19).

1 Read. What is a meteor?

- Have the children look at the first picture. Ask *What do you think this is?* Then they look quickly at the text. Ask *What is a meteor?* (*a small rock in our Solar System*)

- The children read the text more carefully. Ask *What's the difference between a meteor and an asteroid?* (*An asteroid is bigger than a meteor.*) *What's a meteorite?* (*a very small meteor that hits Earth's surface*)

2 Answer the questions.

- Read the example. Elicit where this information appears in the text. The children answer the questions about the text.

- Elicit answers.

Answers

1 Meteors can travel 72 kilometers a second.
2 They are called meteorites when they hit the ground.
3 They burn up and are destroyed before they hit Earth's surface.
4 An asteroid that hit Earth in Mexico.

3 Class Vote

- Ask *Is sending astronauts into space a good idea?* Give the children time to think about the question. Divide the board in two and write *Yes* on the left and *No* on the right. Invite children one by one to draw a line on one side of the board. Count the votes.

- Elicit ideas about why sending astronauts to space is a good idea (*learn about space, the Earth, find other forms of life*, etc.) or a bad idea (*too expensive, too dangerous, causes pollution and trash*, etc.).

Find Out More!

Ask the children to research the biggest meteorite in the world. Suggest appropriate resources, e.g. Internet, library books, etc. The children will need to complete this research before doing the follow-up activity in the Activity Book. (It could be set as homework.)

Optional activity: Unscramble the words

Write on the board scrambled versions of planets and adjectives from Chapter 3. Have the children write the words correctly in their notebook. Ask children to write answers on the board for the class to check.

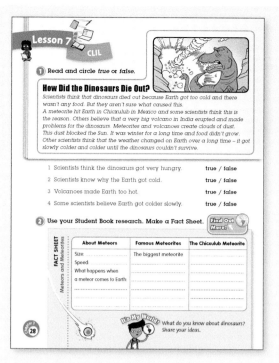

Divide the class into teams. Give them five minutes to come up with five questions about space. Each team takes turns asking another team their questions. A correct answer wins a point. If a team cannot answer, or get the wrong answer, the next team can try to win the point. The team with the most points wins.

Competency Focus

Act

The children carry out research to find out about the biggest meteorite in the world. This helps them expand their learning and relate it to their world, both inside and outside the classroom.

1 Read and circle *true* or *false*.

The children read the text. They circle true or false for each statement. Elicit answers, including the correct versions of the false statements.

Answers

1 true **2** false **3** false **4** true

2 Use your Student Book research. Make a Fact Sheet.

Divide the class into groups of four. Have the children pool the information learned from their research in the Student Book and the Activity Book. They complete the Fact Sheet about meteors and meteorites individually. Have children present information in their Fact Sheet to the class.

Answers

Children's own answers.

It's My World!

Have the children discuss dinosaurs in small groups. Prompt as necessary to encourage them to talk about what they have seen in museums, books they have read, or movies they have watched.

Digital Resources

Student eBook • TIP Help children follow the text as you play the additional audio available for SB Activity 1 or read the text aloud.

• TIP You can use *Add personal note* to log the results of the class vote.

Teacher Resource Center • Print out CLIL Graphic Organizer 3 for the children to use in collating their Find Out More! research.

CLIL eBook • The children can use the CLIL eBook to expand their knowledge of the lesson topic.

Project

Lesson objectives: review language from Chapter 3; make a rocket; find out which rocket goes higher

Materials: colored card, plastic liquid detergent bottles or soda bottles (two or three liters), tape, glue, scissors, colored pencils/markers, paper to decorate; two game pieces and a coin for each pair

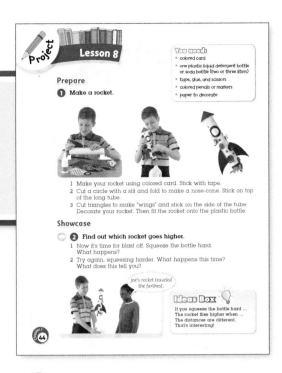

Warmer: Play "Disappearing Text"

Write a sentence on the board, e.g. *I would like to ride on a meteor from the Earth to Venus and back.* Have the children read it aloud. Erase a word and have the children read the whole sentence again. Continue erasing words until children are saying the sentence without any prompts.

Prepare

1 Make a rocket.

- Distribute the materials. Read through the instructions together and ensure the children are clear on what to do.
- They make their rockets individually. Give support as necessary.

Alternative craft activity

An easier project is to have the children make a poster showing a space rocket in as much detail as possible. They could do research on the NASA website. Have the children present their poster to the class, telling them where their rocket will travel, its speed, etc.

Showcase

2 Find out which rocket goes higher.

- Take the children to the playground. Have them follow the instructions. Measure the distances covered by each rocket. Ask *Which rocket flew the highest? Which rocket flew the farthest?*
- Go back to the class. Have children present the results of their experiment to the class using the **Ideas Box** for support.

Optional activity: Play "Tic-Tac-Toe"

Play the game using *far, close, interesting, unusual, dangerous, different, long, high, safe* (see Games Bank p. 19). To win a square, a child has to say the comparative or superlative of the adjective.

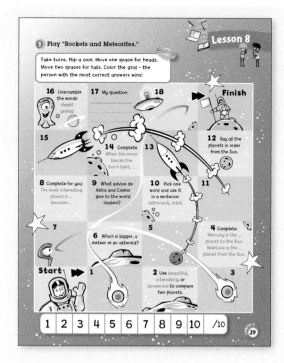

1 Play "Rockets and Meteorites."

See p. 43 for instructions on how to play the game.

Answers

2 … is more beautiful/interesting/dangerous than …
4 closest, farthest **6** an asteroid **8** Children's own answer.
9 *suggested*: don't forget to recycle/grow more trees
10 Children's own answer. **12** Mercury, Venus, Earth, Mars,
Jupiter, Saturn, Uranus, Neptune **14** … it gets dark/it's an
eclipse. **16** planet, galaxy **17** Children's own answer.

Cooler: Play "Sentence Builders"

Divide the class into two teams. Give each team a large
sheet of paper (positioned so the other team cannot see it)
and a pen. Read out a sentence question using key language
from the chapter. The first child writes the first word, the next
child the next word, and so on. When they have finished, the
teams check each other's sentence. Each correct word wins a
point. The team with the most points wins.

Competency Focus

Collaborate and Communicate

By working together, the children consolidate their
understanding of the language learned in a way which
they will find fun and engaging. They also demonstrate
their ability to work with friends and use interpersonal
skills.

Digital Resources

Student eBook • Show the Prepare pictures, stage by
stage, as you talk the class through the activity process.

• Choose vocabulary from Chapters 1–3 to review a
vocabulary topic from previous chapters. Have the
children raise their hands to vote to select a topic. Then
use *Timer* and give the class one minute to recall all the
words in the topic. Repeat with a different topic if you
have time.

Language Review

Lesson objective: review language from Chapter 3
Materials: Tracks 3.9, AB 3.1, AB 3.2 and AB 3.3

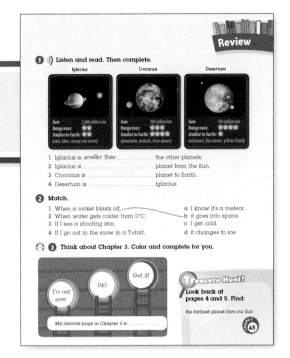

Warmer: True or false?

Say true/false sentences about space, e.g. *Mercury is far from the Sun.* (*F*) *Jupiter is bigger than Saturn.* (*T*) Have the children shout *True!* or *False!* in response. Elicit the correct versions of the false statements.

1))) 3.9 Listen and read. Then complete.

- Elicit the planets pictured. Give the children time to look at the facts.
- Play Track 3.9 twice. The children listen and complete the sentences.
- Elicit answers.

Audioscript

Three Unusual Planets
Iglacius: This planet has clouds and rivers and lakes. It's very cold and it's very snowy on the planet. The planet has one moon. It's smaller than the other planets. It's the farthest planet from the Sun. It has rings of ice.
Croconus: The planet is blue and green. It has rivers, lakes, waterfalls, mountains, and animals. It has three moons and there are a lot of stars in the sky. It's the most similar planet to Earth.
Desertum: Part of this planet has volcanoes. It's very hot and there are no animals or people there. This planet is more different from Earth than Iglacius. It has five moons and yellow clouds. Desertum is the most dangerous planet.

Answers

1 smaller than **2** the farthest **3** the most similar
4 more dangerous than

2 Match.

- Read the example. Have the children match the sentence halves.
- Elicit answers.

Answers

1 b **2** d **3** a **4** c

3 Think about Chapter 3. Color and complete for you.

- Have the children look back at Chapter 3. Elicit their favorite parts. The children then color the circle which represents how they feel about their own progress (self-evaluation).
- Have the children complete the sentence about their favorite page. Elicit responses.

Treasure Hunt!

Have the children look at pp. 4–5 to find the farthest planet from our Sun. They hold up their Student Book and point to the right place on the page.

Cooler: Play "The Telephone Game"

Play the game with *Mars is the most interesting planet in the Solar System.* and *The astronauts explore the galaxy in a very fast rocket.* (see Games Bank p. 19).

Competency Focus

Me: Self-evaluation
The children reflect on the chapter and express their opinions about their own progress.

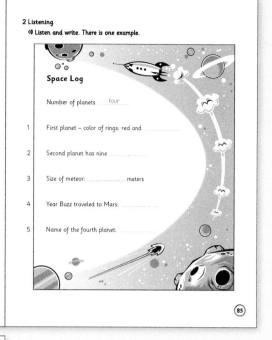

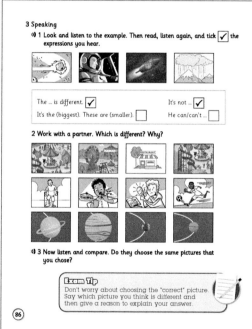

Chapter 3 Exam Booster

1 Reading and Writing

Read the text. Choose the right words and write them on the lines. There is one example.

Earth and Its Moon

The planet Earth is around 4.5 billion years old. It's the fifth _largest_ planet. It's (1) .... away from the Sun than Mercury or Venus but closer (2) .... the other planets.

Earth only has one moon, but other larger planets have (3) .... moons. The Moon goes around Earth and its (4) .... takes 27.3 days. We call the side of the Moon that you can't see from Earth "the dark side of the Moon." It isn't always dark. Like Earth, the Moon spins around, and the Sun shines on every part of it. It's just that we (5) .... see it.

Example	large	larger	(largest)
1	far	farther	farthest
2	than	then	as
3	too	a lot of	much
4	galaxy	rocket	orbit
5	couldn't	can't	didn't

(84)

2 Listening

Listen and write. There is one example.

Space Log

Number of planets .... four

1 First planet – color of rings: red and ....

2 Second planet has nine ....

3 Size of meteor: .... meters

4 Year Buzz traveled to Mars: ....

5 Name of the fourth planet: ....

(85)

3 Speaking

1 Look and listen to the example. Then read, listen again, and tick ✓ the expressions you hear.

The ... is different. ✓	It's not ... ✓
It's the (biggest). These are (smaller). ☐	He can/can't ... ☐

2 Work with a partner. Which is different? Why?

3 Now listen and compare. Do they choose the same pictures that you chose?

Exam Tip
Don't worry about choosing the "correct" picture. Say which picture you think is different and then give a reason to explain your answer.

(86)

---

1 Reading and Writing. Read the text. Choose the right words and write them on the lines.

The children complete the text. Check answers.

Answers

1 farther 2 than 3 a lot of 4 orbit 5 can't

2))) AB 3.1 Listening. Listen and write.

Play Track AB 3.1 twice. Children write the answers.

Answers (Audioscript on p. 222)

1 orange 2 moons 3 eight 4 2012 5 Buzzo

3.1))) AB 3.2 Speaking. Look and listen to the example. Then read, listen again and tick (✔) the expressions you hear.

Play Track AB 3.2 and children tick the correct answer.
(Audioscript on p. 222)

3.2 Speaking. Work with a partner. Which is different? Why?

Children discuss in pairs which picture is different.
Answers (Audioscript on p. 222)

The mountain is not in space.

3.3))) AB 3.3 Speaking. Now listen and compare. Do they choose the same pictures that you choose?

Play Track AB 3.3. Children listen and compare.
Answers (Audioscript on p. 222)

1 the restaurant 2 he can play soccer 3 Saturn is the biggest

Digital Resources

Teacher Resource Center • Print out Test Chapter 3 to use at the end of this lesson. The Test Generator also allows you to create customized tests.

- For the Cambridge English Young Learners Exam preparation activities, there are speaking prompts available for this chapter.

- Print out Festival Worksheet: Christmas to expand the children's knowledge of celebrations throughout the world.

Chapter 4
Going to the Movies
Overview

The children will:

- use critical thinking skills to identify movie types.
- talk about activities they have/haven't done.
- read, understand, and act out a story.
- talk about movie professions.
- ask and answer questions about movies they have/haven't seen.
- find out about how an animated movie is made.
- make a flip-book movie.

Key Vocabulary

Movie genres: action, animation, comedy, fantasy, horror, musical, romance, science fiction
Movie professions: artist, camera operator, composer, designer, director, sound engineer, stylist, writer

Key Grammar

- I've seen (every movie in town).
- We haven't met (Justin Drake).
- Have you seen (*Valley of the Vampires*) yet?
- No, I haven't seen it yet.
  Yes, I've already seen it.

Reading Skills

Story: *The House at the End of the Road*
Genre: scary story

Literacy Development

- predict story content from title and pictures
- interpret and personalize the theme of the story
- find words and pictures that make a story scary

Functional Language

- Hey, how about …ing … ?
- Cool! What about …?
- Yes! This one looks great!

Spelling

Jobs ending in –er, –or, –ist

CLIL: Art—How animated movies are made

The children find out how to make an animated movie.

Competency Focus

The children will:

use critical thinking skills to identify movie types. (Lesson 1)	apply new grammar to previously learned vocabulary. (Lesson 2)	work in threes to act out a dialogue. (Lesson 3)	personalize the story by thinking of their own feelings when reading a scary story. (Lesson 4)	develop cultural understanding by finding out about animation movies. (Lesson 7)
predict the content of a story. (Lesson 3)	talk about whether they have seen a movie. (Lesson 6)	present their flip-book movie to the class. (Lesson 8)	evaluate their own progress in the chapter. (Review)	
identify and talk about professions in the movie industry. (Lesson 5)				

Digital Overview

Teacher Presentation

Student eBook and Digital Activity Book

- Music Video 4.1 (4.2): *We're Making a Movie!*
- Interactive versions of AB activities
- Integrated audio and answer key for all activities

Teacher resources for planning, lesson delivery, and homework

Teacher Resource Center

- Class Planner Chapter 4
- Worksheets to print out (including notes and answers):
  - Grammar Worksheet 4A: I've seen … We haven't met …
  - Grammar Worksheet 4B: Have you seen … yet?
  - Phonics Worksheet 4
  - CLIL Graphic Organizer 4
  - Test Chapter 4
- Test Generator
- Literacy Handbook

Watch the Music Video

Children's resources for consolidation and practice at home

Student eBook

- Music Video 4.1 (4.2): *We're Making a Movie!*

***The Inks* Student's App**

Vocabulary games: Movie genres and movie professions

Going to the Movies

Lesson 1

Vocabulary

Lesson objectives: identify and talk about movie genres
Key vocabulary: *action, animation, comedy, fantasy, horror, musical, romance, science fiction*
Materials: Track 4.1

Warmer: I remember

Ask *What was the last movie you saw? Did you like it? What happened?* Elicit responses.

1))) 4.1   Listen and number. Then say.

- Have the children look at the movies on the website. Ask *Which movies would you like to see?*

- Play Track 4.1 twice. The children listen and point.

- Then they write the number of the movie type by the correct DVD picture. Elicit answers.

- Say the new words for the children to repeat.

Audioscript

Sara: *Dad's taking us to the movies tonight. What movie do you want to see?*
Josh: *What about The Monster Invasion? It's a horror movie about alien monsters. It looks cool!*
Sara: *I am NOT going to a horror movie. I feel scared. How about Mr. Cook's Cats? It's funny. It's a comedy. You'll laugh.*
Josh: *No. We saw a comedy last week. There's a new action movie on—Mountain Escape.*
Sara: *I don't want to see an action movie. Let's go and see Across the Ocean. It's about two people who live on different sides of the world. They fall in love by writing to each other.*
Josh: *No, not romance! Space Explorers sounds good.*
Sara: *But it's science fiction. I don't like movies about the future and other planets.*
Josh: *How about Cool School Musical then? It's about a group*

of kids in New York who start their own dance school. It has a lot of songs and dancing.
Sara: *Um, I don't like musicals. So how about Ride with Dragons?*
Josh: *But you don't like stories about other planets! Ride with Dragons is a fantasy movie about magical animals. They're in another world …*
Dad: *I got tickets for Ellie Elephant's Party.*
Sara: *That's an animated movie, Dad!*
Josh: *Animated movies are for little kids!*
Answers

1, 6, 2, 5; 3, 7, 8, 4

2   Ask and answer.

- Read the example question and elicit the answer. Have the children ask and answer about the movies in Activity 1 in pairs.

- Invite children to ask a question for the whole class to answer without looking in their books.

3   What type of movie do you like? Write a list.

- Have a child read the example list. Say your own list, making it clear that you like number 1 most of all.

- Have the children list their three favorite movie types in their notebook. They then compare their lists in small groups and discuss. Elicit responses, along with examples of movies in each category.

Answers

Children's own answers.

Optional activity: Movies

Brainstorm movies titles and write them on the board. Have the children in pairs take turns saying the name of a movie and its type.

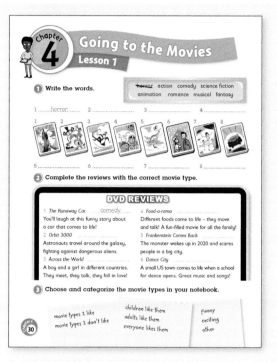

1 Write the words.

The children label the DVDs with the movie type, using the words supplied. Elicit answers.

Answers

1 horror **2** animation **3** comedy **4** science fiction **5** fantasy **6** romance **7** musical **8** action

2 Complete the reviews with the correct movie type.

The children write the movie types. Elicit answers. Ask which movie they would like to see and why.

Answers

1 comedy **2** science fiction **3** romance **4** animation **5** horror **6** musical

3 Choose and categorize the movie types in your notebook.

Elicit an example for each category listed. Ask *Which categories would you choose?* Elicit ideas, prompting children to give a reason for their choice. The children choose a pair of categories and list the words in their notebook, then compare with a friend.

Answers

Children's own answers.

Cooler: Play "The Chain Game"

Divide the class into groups of six. Model the game. Say *I like horror movies.* Have a child say *The teacher likes horror movies and* (e.g.) *I like action movies.* The next child repeats the whole sequence, then adds a new detail. Have the children play the game in groups in this way. If a child makes a mistake or cannot think of a detail to add, the chain starts again.

Competency Focus

Think! Critical Thinking

The children use critical thinking skills to identify movie types by using visual clues and processing the written and spoken forms.

Digital Resources

Student eBook, Digital Activity Book • TIP You can move the answer key pop-up window around the screen to have the activity and the answers side by side.

Grammar

Lesson objective: talk about activities they have/haven't done

Key grammar: *I've seen* (every movie in town). *We haven't met* (Justin Drake).

Secondary language: *actor, movie theater, studio*

Materials: Track 4.2; Grammar Worksheet 4A [TRC printout] (optional)

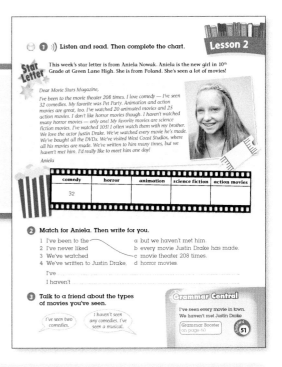

1)) Listen and read. Then complete the chart.

Star Letter This week's star letter is from Aniela Nowak. Aniela is the new girl in 10th Grade at Green Lane High. She is from Poland. She's seen a lot of movies!

Dear Movie Stars Magazine,
I've been to the movie theater 208 times. I love comedy — I've seen 32 comedies. My favorite was Pet Party. Animation and action movies are great, too. I've watched 20 animated movies and 25 action movies. I don't like horror movies though. I haven't watched many horror movies — only one! My favorite movies are science fiction movies. I've watched 105! I often watch them with my brother. We love the actor Justin Drake. We've watched every movie he's made. We've bought all the DVDs. We've visited West Coast Studios, where all his movies are made. We've written to him many times, but we haven't met him. I'd really like to meet him one day!
Aniela

comedy	horror	animation	science fiction	action movies
32				

2 Match for Aniela. Then write for you.

1 I've been to the — a but we haven't met him.
2 I've never liked — b every movie Justin Drake has made.
3 We've watched — c movie theater 208 times.
4 We've written to Justin Drake, d horror movies.

I've _____
I haven't _____

3 Talk to a friend about the types of movies you've seen.

I've seen two comedies.

I haven't seen any comedies. I've seen a musical.

Grammar Central

I've seen every movie in town.
We haven't met Justin Drake

Grammar Booster on page 60

51

Warmer: Play "The Shark Game"

Play the game with *animation* and *fantasy* (see Games Bank p. 19).

---

1)) **4.2 Listen and read. Then complete the chart.**

- Elicit the name of the magazine. (*Movie Stars Magazine*) Ask *Do you read any magazines? What are they about?*

- Play Track 4.2. The children listen and read along. They complete the chart. Elicit answers.

- Play Track 4.2 again. Ask questions, e.g. *Where's Aniela from?* (*Poland*) *How many times has Aniela been to the movie theater?* (*208 times*) *What's her favorite comedy?* (*Pet Party*) *Does she like horror movies?* (*No, she doesn't.*)

Answers

comedy—32, horror—1, animation—20, science fiction—105, action movies—25

2 Match for Aniela. Then write for you.

- Read the example. Have the children match the sentence halves. Elicit answers.

- Then the children complete the sentences about movies they have/haven't seen. Give an example if necessary.

Answers

1 c 2 d 3 b 4 a

Children's own answers.

Grammar Central

I've seen every movie in town. …

Have the children look at the patterns. Point out how the present perfect is formed: *the verb* to be + *the past participle.* (e.g. *I've seen*) Ask *Do we know when she saw the movies?* (*no*) Elicit that we use the present perfect to talk about past experiences at an unspecified time or things that we have not done yet. Elicit children's experiences, e.g. *I've swum in a lake. I haven't traveled by plane.*, etc.

For extra practice, try the **Grammar Booster** section in the Student Book (p. 60)

Answers p.60

Activity 1: **2** haven't seen **3** 've met **4** haven't met **5** 've visited **6** haven't visited **7** 've written **8** haven't written

Activity 2: **2** 've acted **3** 've traveled **4** 've met **5** haven't acted **6** haven't worked

Activity 3: Children's own answers.

3 Talk to a friend about the types of movies you've seen.

- Have two children read the example dialogue.

- Divide the class into pairs to talk about movies they have/haven't seen.

- Have children say their sentences aloud for the class. Have a show of hands for each movie using *Who's seen it? Who hasn't seen it?*

Optional activity: What have you done this week?

Say *This week, I've been to the movie theater.* Have the children work in pairs telling each other what they have done this week. Ask children to report to the class what they have done. Write the activities on the board. Have a class vote on which activity is the most popular.

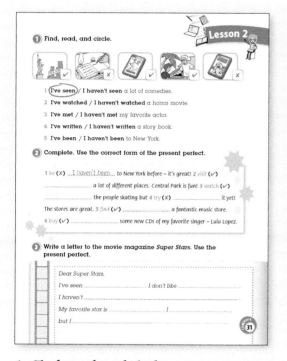

1 Find, read, and circle.

The children look at the pictures and complete the sentences by circling the correct verb form in each pair. Elicit answers.

Answers

1 I've seen **2** I haven't watched **3** I've met
4 I haven't written **5** I've been

2 Complete. Use the correct form of the present perfect.

The children complete the letter with the correct form of the verbs. Elicit answers.

Answers

1 I haven't been **2** I've visited **3** I've watched **4** I haven't tried
5 I've found **6** I've bought

3 Write a letter to the movie magazine *Super Stars*. Use the present perfect.

Read out the prompts in the letter and elicit ideas. The children complete their letter individually. Have children read their letter to the class.

Answers

Children's own answers.

Cooler: Play "Disappearing Words"

Play the game with *horror, action, science fiction, animation, romance, comedy, musical, fantasy*
(see Games Bank p. 19).

Competency Focus

Learn

The children develop learning strategies by recognizing and applying language patterns. They show their understanding of previously acquired vocabulary and use it in a new context.

Digital Resources

Digital Activity Book • Do the AB interactive digital activities as a class or set them for homework.

Teacher Resource Center • For extra grammar practice, print out Grammar Worksheet 4A.

Reading: Story Extract

Lesson objectives: make suggestions; predict story content from title and pictures; read the extract from *The House at the End of the Road* (middle)

Functional language: *Hey, how about …ing … ? Cool! What about …? Yes! This one looks great!*

Secondary language: *neighbors, performance, script, spiderwebs, vampire*

Materials: Tracks 4.3 and 4.4

Warmer: Play "Tic-Tac-Toe"

Play the game using *see, watch, find, like, buy, be, write, visit, meet* (see Games Bank p. 19). To win a square, a child has to ask a *Have you ever …?* question with the past participle of the verb shown.

Functional language

1 🔊 **4.3   Listen and read. Then act out.**

- Have the children look at the picture. Ask *What is Felicity holding?* (a movie)
- Play Track 4.3. The children listen and read along.
- Play Track 4.3 again, pausing for the children to repeat.
- Divide the class into groups of three. They act out the dialogue. Encourage them to substitute different kinds of movies.

Before reading

2   Look at the story. What kind of story do you think this is? Circle the adjectives. 💡

- Have the children read the title of the story and look at the pictures. Ask *What kind of story is it?* Elicit ideas with reasons. (*The extract makes it look like horror.*)
- The children look at the the adjectives and circle the ones which describe the story. Elicit answers.

Answers

scary, old, dark, dirty

3 🔊 **Track 4.4 Listen and read. Answer the questions.**

- Play Track 4.4. The children listen and read along.
- Give time for the children to read the questions and write their answers. Play Track 4.4 again for them to check.
- Elicit answers.

Answers

1 They think there are people because there are candles in the house. **2** Tom and Sadie are going upstairs. **3** Sadie sees spiderwebs on the stairs.

4 Who do you think is in the house?

- Have the children write who they think is in the house. Elicit ideas including reasons but do not confirm. Say they will have to read the story to find out.

Answers

Children's own answers.

1 Unscramble and write. Then act out, changing the underlined word.

Divide the class into pairs to unscramble and write the lines of dialogue, then act it out, changing the underlined words. Have pairs act out for the class.

Answers

Hey, [name]. How about watching a movie?

Cool. Let's watch a scary movie.

2 Read the story in your Student Book. Circle *yes* or *no*.

Read the example and elicit why the answer is no. (*They don't know if there is anyone in the house.*) The children read the Student Book story extract again and circle *yes* or *no* for each sentence. Elicit answers, including the correct versions of the no statements.

Answers

1 no **2** yes **3** yes **4** no **5** no

3 Circle the things you find scary. Then write two more things.

The children circle the things they find scary, and add two more things that they are afraid of. Elicit answers.

Answers

Children's own answers.

Brainstorm things children enjoy doing in their free time, e.g. *watching movies/television, playing computer games/ soccer/tennis, visiting friends*, etc. Write these activities on the board as prompts for the children to make up new dialogues along the lines of the one in Activity 1. Have pairs perform their dialogues for the class.

Competency Focus

Collaborate and Communicate

The children act out an authentic dialogue together, putting into practice the functional language.

Think! Critical Thinking

The children apply reading skills (exploiting pictures and text clues) to understand the story.

Digital Resources

Student eBook • Use *Highlighter* on *scary* and elicit Cheng's question with a different adjective.

Digital Activity Book • To give feedback on AB Activity 3, have a child use *Pen* to circle the things they find scary and then write another item. Elicit who agrees each time with a show of hands. Repeat with children who have different ideas.

The House at the End of the Road

1
There was an old house in Tom and Sadie's neighborhood.
Sadie: I haven't seen lights on in that house before.
Tom: No, it has been empty for years.
Sadie: How about going inside?
Tom: OK. Let's go meet our new neighbors.

2
The back door was unlocked.

3
Tom: Ugh! Bats!

4
Sadie: Hello? Is anyone home?
Tom: Look! There are candles. I think there are people here.

5
Tom: This place looks like something out of a horror movie!
Sadie: We haven't been upstairs yet.
Tom: I think someone's up there. How about going upstairs? Or are you scared?

6
Tom and Sadie climbed the stairs. There were spiderwebs everywhere.
Sadie: They haven't cleaned this place! Look at all these spiderwebs.
Tom: Are you scared yet?
Sadie: No! I like scary movies.

7
Tom: Haven't we been this way already? I don't want to get lost.
Sadie: We haven't looked up here yet.

8
Just then, there was a flash of lightning and a boom of thunder.
Sadie: OK, now I'm scared!
Tom: I was scared already!

9
A figure appeared on the stairs above them. He let out a long, terrifying laugh.
Count Cranium: Mwaaaaa-ha-ha-ha-ha. I am Count Cranium. Welcome to my house.

10
Sadie: Aaaaaaahhhhhh!
Tom: Aaaaaaahhhhhh!

11
Sadie and Tom raced down the stairs.
At the bottom, Sadie tripped over something and fell.
Sadie: Help! It's got my leg! What is it?
Tom: It isn't the vampire, it's just a wire. Where did that come from?

12
Suddenly, the lights went on.
Director: Cut! Wow, fantastic. What a scream! Who is this?
Tom: What's going on? Where's the vampire?
Sadie: Who are these people?
Director: We're making a movie. I'm the director.

13
Director: Has the writer changed the script?
Writer: No, I haven't.
Assistant: What are they doing here?
Tom: I'm sorry, we're exploring.
Sadie: We wanted to meet our new neighbors.

14
Director: I think we've found some new stars. Can you write parts for them?
Writer: Sure!

15
The director liked Sadie and Tom's performance.
Director: How about being in our movie? Luckily we haven't finished it yet.
Sadie and Tom: Yes, please!
Director: And I think you've already met Count Cranium . . .

16
Tom: Hey, you're Mark Major, the famous actor!
Mark: That was an amazing performance! Do you think you can do it again?
Sadie: You haven't seen anything yet!

Lesson objective: read and understand the scary story
The House at the End of the Road in the Reader
Materials: Track 4.5; Reader

Warmer: Review the story

Elicit descriptions of the house in the story extract. Then ask *How do Tom and Sadie feel? Would you feel like that if you were in the house?*

Story Summary

Tom and Sadie visit a spooky house in their neighborhood. The more they explore the house, the more scared they become. Then they discover the house is a movie set for a horror movie and both play a part in the movie.

Value: It's OK to be scared sometimes

)) 4.5 While reading

- Have the children look at the pictures in the Reader. Ask *Is the house scary?*
- Play Track 4.5. The children listen and read along. Ask *Is the house haunted?* (*no*)
- Play Track 4.5 again. Ask questions to check comprehension, e.g. *Why do they go inside the house?* (*to meet their neighbors*) *Do they see their neighbors?* (*no*) *Who do they see upstairs?* (*Count Cranium*) *What are the people doing?* (*They're making a movie*) *What does the director suggest?* (*that Tom and Sadie take part in the movie*)

After reading: Reflect

Ask questions to give the children the opportunity to think about the issues raised by the story, e.g. *Were the children right to go into the house? Is it dangerous to go in strangers' houses? Why were they afraid? Did anything good happen to the children?*

Optional activity: Read with confidence

This activity is fast-paced and lively, and improves the children's speed and confidence in reading. Have the children sit in a circle. Read the first line of the story. Invite children to read a sentence each around the circle. Encourage them to read it loudly, clearly, and with confidence.

Story Time

Showing emotion

The characters in this story experience strong emotions, e.g. fear, surprise, relief, etc. Say some of the lines for the children to repeat and show emotion. For example, *Ugh! Bats!* (Picture 3, in disgust); *I think there are people here.* (Picture 4, whispering in fear); *Mwaaaaa-ha-ha-ha-ha. I am Count Cranium.* (Picture 9, in a scary tone), etc.

Reading Strategy

Sentence Combining

The Sentence Combining strategy helps the children improve their writing skills by combining short sentences into longer, more effective sentences. They need to develop this skill step by step and with structured guidance so that they can apply it in the future when writing longer texts.

For additional explanation and activities, see the Literacy Handbook on the Teacher's Resource Center.

Cooler: That was an amazing performance!

Give an example of an instruction a movie director would give, e.g. *You are very tired. You really want to sleep.*, and have two children act it out at the front of the class. Say *That was an amazing performance!* Repeat with other instructions and different children as the director and actors.

Digital Resources

Reader eBook • To practice the technique described in SB Story Time, use *Highlighter* to identify *Ugh! Bats!* in the text of Picture 3 of the Reader story. Have the children practice saying the phrase in disgust. Repeat with other phrases from the story (see Story Time for more ideas).

Reading Comprehension and Critical Literacy

Lesson objectives: identify scary elements in the story; relate the story to personal experiences

Materials: Track 4.5; Reader

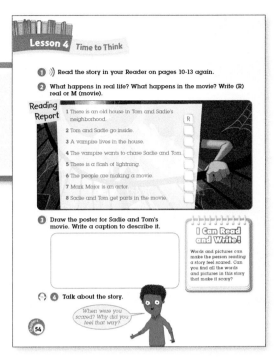

Note: Please ensure that your class has read the Reader story before you do this lesson.

Warmer: Play "Jump the Line"

Play the game with *There was a new house in Tom and Sadie's neighborhood.* (F) *Tom and Sadie went down the stairs.* (F) *There weren't any spiderwebs.* (F) *A friendly monster appeared on the stairs.* (F) *Sadie tripped and fell.* (T) *The lights went out.* (F) *Tom and Sadie became actors in the movie.* (T) (see Games Bank p. 19).

1))) 4.5   Read the story in your Reader.

- Have the children read the story. (Alternatively, play Track 4.5 and have them read along.) Elicit whether they were correct in their predictions in Lesson 3 Activity 4.

- Check comprehension by asking *Do Tom and Sadie know who lives in the house?* (no) *Does the story have a happy or a sad ending?* (happy)

2   What happens in real life? What happens in the movie? Write R (real) or M (movie).

- Have the children read the sentences and decide if they happen in real life or in the movie.

- Elicit answers.

Answers

1 R 2 R 3 M 4 M 5 M 6 R 7 R 8 R

I Can Read and Write!

Have the children look at the story and find scary words (e.g. *empty for years, spiderwebs, scared,* etc.) and pictures (the count, the children screaming, etc.).

3   Draw the poster for Sadie and Tom's movie. Write a caption to describe it.

- Have the chidren talk in pairs about Sadie and Tom's movie.

- Then have them draw the movie poster with the title and draw a caption to describe it. Invite children to present their posters to the class.

Answers

Children's own answers.

4   Talk about the story.

- Ask *How did you feel when you were reading the story?* Elicit responses with reasons, asking the class to agree or disagree. Have the children read Jason's question and think about times when they have been scared. Elicit responses with reasons.

Optional activity: Who said that?

Read out dialogue from the story to elicit who said it.

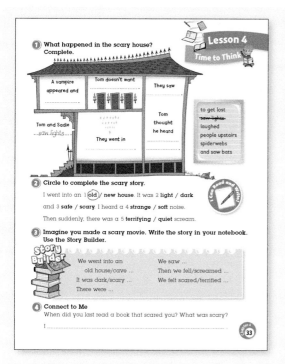

Cooler: Browse the posters

Have the children place their Student Book open on their desks. They walk around looking at the posters designed in Activity 3. Ask them to choose their favorite one. Then have a class vote on the top four posters.

Competency Focus

Me: Critical Literacy

The children use critical literacy skills to reflect on the theme of the story and relate it to their personal experience.

1 What happened in the scary house? Complete.

The children complete the story summary using the words supplied. Elicit answers.

Answers

saw lights; and saw bats; people upstairs; spiderwebs; to get lost; laughed

2 Circle to complete the scary story.

The children practice the **I Can Read and Write!** feature by circling the correct words to complete the story. Elicit answers.

Answers

1 old **2** dark **3** scary **4** strange **5** terrifying

3 Imagine you made a scary movie. Write the story in your notebook. Use the Story Builder.

Use the **Story Builder** prompts to elicit ideas. The children write a story in their notebook, then swap with a friend to check. Have children read out their story for the class.

Answers

Children's own answers.

4 Connect to Me

Elicit ideas on scary books and why they are scary before the children write their own response. Elicit responses.

Answers

Children's own answers.

Digital Resources

Reader eBook • Display the Reader on the board. Show Picture 4. Elicit what happened before and after this. Repeat with pictures 9 and 11.

Student eBook • For SB I Can Read and Write!, children use *Highlighter* to identify scary words and *Pen* to circle scary picture details in the story.

Student eBook, Digital Activity Book • TIP Move the answer key pop-up window around the screen to have the activity and the answers side by side.

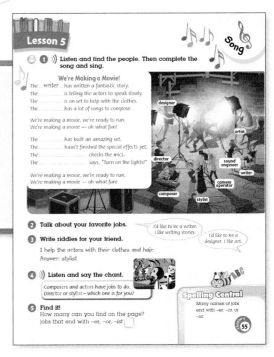

Vocabulary, Song, and Spelling

Lesson objectives: identify and talk about movie professions; practice spelling words ending –*or*, –*er*, – *ist*

Key vocabulary: *artist, camera operator, composer, designer, director, sound engineer, stylist, writer*

Secondary language: *amazing, mics, special effects*

Materials: Tracks 4.6 and 4.7; Phonics Worksheet 4 [TRC printout] (optional)

Warmer: Pre-teach vocabulary

Use the picture in Student Book Activity 1 to pre-teach the vocabulary. Point and say each job twice and have the children repeat. Have them mime each one with you, then mime and repeat, and then mime and say the vocabulary on their own.

1))) 4.6 Listen and find the people. Then complete the song and sing.

- Play Track 4.6. The children listen and find the people.
- Play Track 4.6 again. The children listen and complete the song using the words supplied. Elicit answers.
- Play Track 4.6 again for the children to sing along.

Answers

writer, director, stylist, composer, designer, artist, sound engineer, camera operator

2 Talk about your favorite jobs.

- Read the example with a child. Give the children time to think about which job from Activity 1 they would like to do and why. They discuss in pairs.
- Have a class vote to find out the most popular job.

3 Write riddles for your friend.

- Read the example. Give the children time to write at least two riddles. Give support.

- In pairs, they take turns saying and solving the riddles. Have children read their riddles to the class.

Answers

Children's own answers.

Spelling Central

Jobs ending in –er, –or, –ist

Point out that –*er* and –*or* have the same pronunciation at the end of a word.

4))) 4.7 Listen and say the chant.

- Have the children look at the picture. Ask *What can you see?*
- Play Track 4.7. The children listen and read along. Elicit the –*er*, –*or*, and –*ist* jobs.
- Play Track 4.7 again, pausing for the children to repeat.

5 Find it!

- Set a time limit for the children to find job words ending –*er*, –*or*, and –*ist* on the page. Elicit answers. Point out the pronunciation difference in *engineer*, which ends –*eer*.

Answers

9—designer, sound engineer, writer, composer, director, camera operator, actor, artist, stylist

Optional activity: Visualization

Have the children close their eyes and imagine they are on a movie set. Say *You're working on a great movie. What time of the day is it? What can you smell? Who's there working with you? What are they wearing? What are they doing?* Have them open their eyes and share with a friend what they imagined.

Cooler: Listen and do

Have the children respond with different actions when they hear each job ending, e.g. –*er* clap, –*or* snap their fingers, –*ist* stand up and sit down. Say the movie professions in any order for the children to react. You could add other professions.

Competency Focus

Think! Critical Thinking

The children use critical thinking skills to identify written and spoken forms of new words, and match each word with its visual representation.

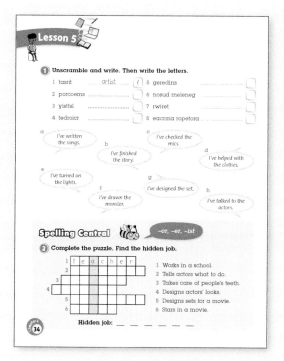

1 Unscramble and write. Then write the letters.

The children unscramble and write the words. Then they write the letter for each speech bubble by the correct job. Elicit answers.

Answers

1 artist f **2** composer a **3** stylist d **4** director h **5** designer g **6** sound engineer c **7** writer b **8** camera operator e

2 Complete the puzzle. Find the hidden job.

To practice the **Spelling Central** feature, the children read the clues and complete the puzzle. Then they find the hidden job. Elicit answers.

Answers

1 teacher **2** director **3** dentist **4** stylist **5** designer **6** actor

Hidden job: artist

Digital Resources

Student eBook • For SB Activity 1, choose the karaoke version of Music Video 4.1 (4.2) and encourage the children to dance and sing along, using the lyrics on screen. Pause for the children to continue dancing and singing.

Teacher Resource Center • For phonics practice, print out Phonics Worksheet 4.

Grammar and Reading

Lesson objectives: ask and answer questions about movies they have/haven't seen

Key grammar: *Have you seen* (Valley of the Vampires) *yet? No, I haven't seen it yet. Yes, I've already seen it.*

Secondary language: *Neither have I.*

Materials: Tracks 4.6 and 4.8; Grammar Worksheet 4B [TRC printout] (optional); a ball (Cooler)

Warmer: Say the next word

))) **4.6**

Play Track 4.6, pausing at random points in the song for the children to tell you how the song continues.

1))) **4.8** **Listen and read. What's the problem for the children?**

- Have the children look at the pictures and ask *In which pictures do the children look worried?* (Pictures 2 and 5) *Why are they worried?* Elicit ideas. Play Track 4.8 and then ask *What's their problem?* (*It's hard to choose which movie to watch.*)

- Play Track 4.8 again. Ask *Who has already seen . . . Harry's Amazing Adventures?* (*Felicity*) *. . . Days in the Sun?* (*Miguel*) *. . . Robo Rat?* (*Felicity and Miguel*)

- Elicit which movie they decide to go and see. (*Cool School Musical 2*)

2 Write movie titles. Read the question and circle the answer.

- Have the children write movie titles before the questions and circle an answer. Do an example with the class, e.g. *Frozen. Have you see it yet?* Elicit answers.

- Have children ask and answer their questions in pairs. They can respond *Me, too!* or *Neither have I!* as appropriate.

Answers

Children's own answers.

Grammar Central

Have you seen *Valley of the Vampires* yet? ...

Have the children look at the patterns. Ask *Which word do we use for the question and the negative?* (*yet*) *Where do we put it?* (*at the end of the sentence*) *Which word do we use for the affirmative?* (*already*) *Where do we put it?* (*between* have *and the verb*) Have children ask questions with *yet* to elicit answers from the class.

For extra practice, try the **Grammar Booster** section in the Student Book (pp. 61–63)

Answers p. 61

Activity 1: **2** yet **3** already **4** yet **5** already **6** yet **7** Have **8** yet **9** Have **10** yet

Activity 2: **2** I haven't been sick all year. **3** I've already washed my hands.

Activity 3: Children's own answers.

p. 62

Activity 1: a **2** b **1** c **4** d **3**

Activity 2: **2** 've built **3** haven't met **4** 've, found **5** Have, made

p. 63

Activity 1: **2** haven't **3** found **4** Have **5** already **6** shouldn't **7** been **8** seen **9** biggest **10** already

Activity 2: Children's own answers.

Optional activity: A chain

Divide the class into small groups. Ask *Have you seen The Hobbit yet?* Have a child in each group answer *Yes, I've already seen it.* or *No, I haven't seen it yet.* Everyone in the group then asks and answers a question about movies in this way.

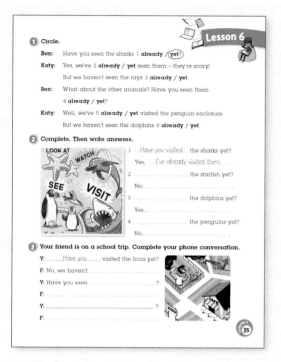

1 Circle.

The children complete the dialogue by circling *already* or *yet.* Elicit answers.

Answers

1 yet **2** already **3** yet **4** yet **5** already **6** yet

2 Complete. Then write answers.

The children complete the questions and answers. Elicit answers.

Answers

1 Have you visited; I've already visited them

2 Have you looked at; I haven't looked at them yet.

3 Have you watched; I've already watched them.

4 Have you seen; I haven't seen them yet.

3 Your friend is on a school trip. Complete your phone conversation.

The children complete the conversation. Divide the class into pairs to practice the conversations. Have pairs say their conversation for the class.

Answers

Children's own answers.

Cooler: Play "Have You ... Yet?"

Divide the class into two teams (A and B), who stand in two rows facing each other. Model the activity. Throw the ball to a child in Team A, and ask a *Have you ... yet?* question, e.g. *Have you read/seen X yet?* The child responds *No, I haven't seen it yet.* or *Yes, I've already seen it.* They then throw the ball to a Team B child and ask another *Have you ... yet?* question. Play continues in this way. Children who make a mistake or who cannot ask/answer are out and sit down. The team with more children standing at the end wins the game.

Competency Focus

Learn

The children develop learning strategies by recognizing and applying language patterns in different contexts.

Digital Resources

Student eBook • Display the SB page. Use *Highlighter* to show the grammar structures in the Story Central story.

Digital Activity Book • Use the AB page to give feedback on activities, using the built-in interactive activity or answer key, as appropriate.

Teacher Resource Center • For extra grammar practice, print out Grammar Worksheet 4B.

CLIL: Art—How animated movies are made

Lesson objective: find out how to make an animated movie
Materials: CLIL Graphic Organizer 4 [TRC printout] (optional)

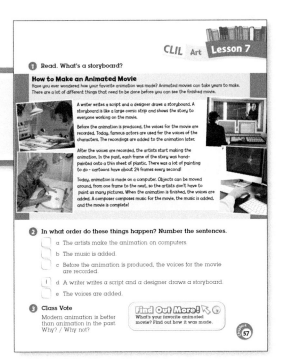

Warmer: Play "Missing Vowels"

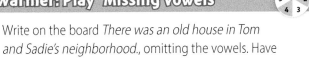

Write on the board *There was an old house in Tom and Sadie's neighborhood.*, omitting the vowels. Have children write in the vowels on the board. Repeat with *Just then, there was a flash of lightning and a boom of thunder.*

1 Read. What's a storyboard?

- Elicit what the children can see in the pictures. Ask *What do you think the people are doing?*
- The children read the text. Ask *What's a storyboard?* (*a large comic strip that shows the story of the movie*) *How long can it take to make an animated movie?* (*years*) *What are the first two things to do?* (*write a script and draw the storyboard*) *Who draws the storyboard?* (*the designer*)

2 In what order do these things happen? Number the sentences.

- Read the example. Have the children number the sentences in the order they happen.
- Elicit answers.

Answers

a 3 b 5 c 2 d 1 e 4

3 Class Vote

- Ask children's opinions about animations. Have them give reasons for preferring modern or old animations before they vote (e.g. *easier and fast to make, better quality, less technology*, etc.).
- Have the class vote. They stand up if they prefer modern animation and they remain seated if they do not. Count the votes.

Find Out More!

Elicit children's favorite animated movies. Ask the children to research how their favorite was made as homework. Suggest appropriate resources, e.g. Internet, library books, etc. The children will need to complete this research before doing the follow-up activity in the Activity Book. (It could be set as homework.)

Optional activity: Animated movie script

Brainstorm different ideas for an animated movie. Ask *Who are the characters? Are they young/old/men/women/children? What do they like? Where do they live? What do they want to do? Why is it difficult? How do they solve the problem? How does the story end?* Write the questions on the board as a guide. Divide the class into groups of four. Have each group discuss the answers to the questions and write a short script for an animated movie. Each group then reads their script to the class.

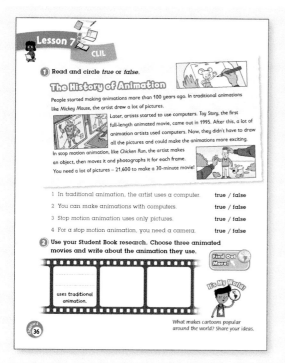

Write a sentence on the board, e.g. *Artists can use computers to draw the pictures for modern animations.* Have the children read it aloud. Erase a word and have the children read the whole sentence again. Continue erasing words until children are saying the sentence without any prompts.

Competency Focus

Act

The children carry out research to find out more about animated movies. This helps them expand their learning and relate it to their world, both inside and outside the classroom.

1 Read and circle *true* or *false*.

The children read the article. They circle true or false for each statement. Elicit answers including the correct versions of the false statements. Ask *What was the first full-length computer-animated movie?* (Toy Story) *How is a stop motion animation different?* (*The artist moves an object and photographs it to make this kind of animation.*)

Answers

1 false **2** true **3** false **4** true

2 Use your Student Book research. Choose three animated movies and write about the animation they use.

Divide the class into groups of four. Have the children pool the information learned from their research in the Student Book and the Activity Book. They write about three animated movies and their type of animation individually. Have children talk about the animated movies to the class.

Answers

Children's own answers.

It's My World!

The children discuss in small groups why cartoons are so popular. Elicit ideas.

Digital Resources

Student eBook • Display the SB page on the board to do Activity 1 point 1, for an alternative "heads-up" introduction to the topic.

Teacher Resource Center • Print out CLIL Graphic Organizer 4 for the children to use in collating their Find Out More! research.

CLIL eBook • The children can use the CLIL eBook to expand their knowledge of the lesson topic.

Project

Lesson objectives: review language from Chapter 4; make and present a flip-book movie

Materials: small sheets of paper, bulldog clips, colored pencils/markers; two game pieces and a coin for each pair

Warmer: Play "Vocabulary Review"

Play the game with *composer, fantasy, romance, designer, sound engineer, comedy, camera operator, musical, stylist, artist* (see Games Bank p. 19).

Prepare

1 Make a flip-book.

- Distribute the materials. Read through the instructions together and ensure the children are clear on what to do.
- Have the children create their character and follow the instructions to create their flip-books. Give support as necessary.

Alternative craft activity

An easier project is for the children to invent an animated character, and draw and write a story about them in a strip cartoon format. They then present their cartoon to the class.

Showcase

2 Show your flip-book movie!

- Divide the class into groups of six. Explain to children that they will now present their flip-book movie to the group, using the **Ideas Box** for support.
- Give the children time to practice, then have them do their presentations.
- Have each group choose one child to present to the class.

Optional activity: Our animation

Divide the class into groups. Each group creates a storyline for an animation, taking turns adding a sentence. Start them off with *It was a dark and stormy night …* Have groups tell the class their animation storyline.

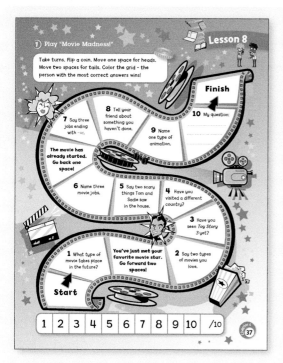

1 Play "Movie Madness!"

See p. 43 for instructions on how to play the game.

Answers

1 Science fiction **2** Children's own answer. **3** Yes, I have. / No, I haven't. **4** Yes, I have. / No, I haven't. **5** spiderwebs, a vampire **6** *any three of:* director, writer, camera operator, artist, sound engineer, designer, actor, composer, stylist, etc. **7** actor, director, doctor **8** Children's own answer: I haven't … yet. **9** *any one of:* traditional animation, computer animation, stop motion animation **10** Children's own answer.

Cooler: Play "Word Steps"

Write *camera* on the board. Have the children use the last letter to start a new word and form steps, e.g. *camera—artist—time*. Play as a class or in groups, starting with a new word from Chapter 4.

Competency Focus

Collaborate and Communicate

By working together, the children consolidate their understanding of the language learned in a way which they will find fun and engaging. They also demonstrate their ability to work with friends and use interpersonal skills.

Digital Resources

Student eBook • Research *flip-book movie examples* on the Internet and store ideas in *Add personal note*, to give the children ideas for their own flip-books.

• Show the Prepare pictures, stage by stage, as you talk the class through the activity process.

• Use *Highlighter* to select the first two sentence openings in the Ideas Box for children to complete about their flip-book. Then highlight the final sentence to elicit who in the class has the best flip-book movie.

Language Review

Lesson objective: review language from Chapter 4
Materials: Tracks 4.9 and AB 4.1

Warmer: Play "The Telephone Game"

Play the game with *A figure appeared on the stairs above Tom and Sadie.* and *Sadie fell at the bottom of the stairs.* (see Games Bank p. 19).

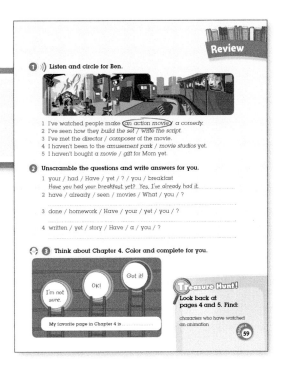

1))) 4.9   Listen and circle for Ben.

- Have the children look at the picture. Ask *What's happening?*
- Give the children time to read the example and sentences. Play Track 4.9 twice. They listen and circle the correct words.
- Elicit answers.

Audioscript

Hi, Mom. We're at the movie studios right now. We're doing the tour.
It's really cool. We're at a movie set now. We've watched the actors make an action movie. And the set designer has built a great set. And there are some amazing special effects.
No, don't worry! A meteor hit the house. No, I'm OK. It's not real! And this is the most amazing thing. I've actually met Peter Jones—he's the director.
No, we haven't been to the amusement park yet. We're going to go there now.
No, I haven't bought you a gift yet. I'm going to stop by the store at the end of the tour.
OK. Bye, Mom. See you later. Yes, I'll stay safe.

Answers

1 an action movie **2** build the set **3** director
4 amusement park **5** gift

2   Unscramble the questions and write answers for you.

- Have the children read the example question and answer.
- They unscramble the questions and write their own answers. Invite pairs of children to read out a question and answer.

Answers

1 Have you had your breakfast yet? **2** What movies have you seen already? **3** Have you done your homework yet?
4 Have you written a story yet? Children's own answers.

3   Think about Chapter 4. Color and complete for you.

- Have the children look back at Chapter 4. Elicit their favorite parts. The children then color the circle which represents how they feel about their own progress (self-evaluation).
- Have the children complete the sentence about their favorite page. Elicit responses.

Treasure Hunt!

Have the children look at pp. 4–5, and find characters who have watched an animation. They hold up their Student Book and point to the right place on the page.

Cooler: He'd be a good director because ...

Ask *What job would your friend be good at on a movie set? Why?* Give the children a minute to think, then elicit ideas.

Competency Focus

Me: Self-evaluation
The children reflect on the chapter and express their opinions about their own progress.

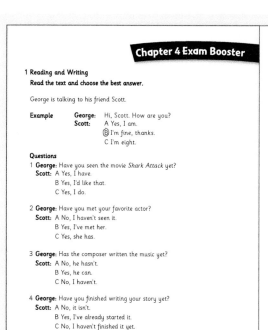

Chapter 4 Exam Booster

1 Reading and Writing
Read the text and choose the best answer.

George is talking to his friend Scott.

Example	George:	Hi, Scott. How are you?
	Scott:	A Yes, I am.
		(B) I'm fine, thanks.
		C I'm eight.

Questions
1 **George:** Have you seen the movie *Shark Attack* yet?
  Scott: A Yes, I have.
    B Yes, I'd like that.
    C Yes, I do.

2 **George:** Have you met your favorite actor?
  Scott: A No, I haven't seen it.
    B Yes, I've met her.
    C Yes, she has.

3 **George:** Has the composer written the music yet?
  Scott: A No, he hasn't.
    B Yes, he can.
    C No, I haven't.

4 **George:** Have you finished writing your story yet?
  Scott: A No, it isn't.
    B Yes, I've already started it.
    C No, I haven't finished it yet.

(87)

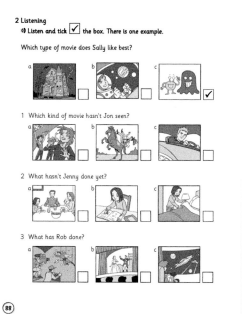

(88)

2 Listening
))) **Listen and tick ✓ the box. There is one example.**

Which type of movie does Sally like best?

a   b   c ✓

1 Which kind of movie hasn't Jon seen?
a   b   c

2 What hasn't Jenny done yet?
a   b   c

3 What has Rob done?
a   b   c

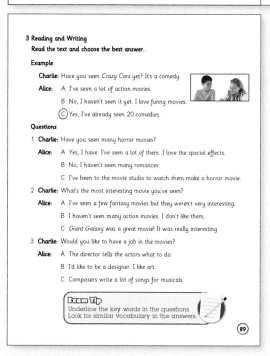

3 Reading and Writing
Read the text and choose the best answer.

Example

Charlie: Have you seen *Crazy Cars* yet? It's a comedy.
Alice: A I've seen a lot of action movies.
    B No, I haven't seen it yet. I love funny movies.
    (C) Yes, I've already seen 20 comedies.

Questions
1 **Charlie:** Have you seen many horror movies?
  Alice: A Yes, I have. I've seen a lot of them. I love the special effects.
    B No, I haven't seen many romances.
    C I've been to the movie studio to watch them make a horror movie.

2 **Charlie:** What's the most interesting movie you've seen?
  Alice: A I've seen a few fantasy movies but they weren't very interesting.
    B I haven't seen many action movies. I don't like them.
    C *Giant Galaxy* was a great movie! It was really interesting.

3 **Charlie:** Would you like to have a job in the movies?
  Alice: A The director tells the actors what to do.
    B I'd like to be a designer. I like art.
    C Composers write a lot of songs for musicals.

Exam Tip
Underline the key words in the questions.
Look for similar vocabulary in the answers.

(89)

3 Reading and Writing. Read the text and choose the best answer.

Children read and choose the correst response.
Answers

1 a **2** c **3** b

1 Reading and Writing. Read the text and choose the best answer.

Children read and choose the correct response.
Answers

1 a **2** b **3** a **4** c

2))) AB 4.1 Listening. Listen and tick (✔) the box. There is one example.

Play Track AB 4.1 twice. They listen and tick the correct box.
Answers (Audioscript on p. 223)

1 a **2** a **3** c

Digital Resources

Teacher Resource Center • Print out Test Chapter 4 to use at the end of this lesson. The Test Generator also allows you to create customized tests.

Student's App • Encourage the children to play the games on their smartphone/tablet. Have a class vote on which of the three games they played is their favorite. (*The Inks* Apps are free and available on the App Store and Google Play.)

Chapter 5

Communication Overview

The children will:

- use critical thinking skills to identify different types of communication.
- talk about past events and what has happened.
- read, understand, and act out a story.
- talk about written communication.
- ask and answer about past events and what has happened.
- find out about Julius Caesar.
- make a code wheel.

Key Vocabulary

Forms of communication: alphabet, cave paintings, hieroglyphics, letter, Morse code, printing press, radio, text message

Written communication and invention verbs: communicate, invent, mail, print, receive, reply, send, write

Key Grammar

- People made (the first cave paintings 30,000 years ago).
- We've discovered (a lot about life then because of cave paintings).
- Have you seen (Miguel)?
- When did he send (the message)?

Reading Skills

Story: *The Secret of Keyhole Island*
Genre: adventure story

Literacy Development

- predict story content from title and pictures
- interpret and personalize the theme of the story
- identify and use imperative instructions

Functional Language

- That's strange! When you …
- Cool! Let's …

Spelling

Double letters

CLIL: History—Julius Caesar

The children find out about Julius Caesar and his cipher.

Competency Focus

The children will:

use critical thinking skills to identify types of communication. (Lesson 1) predict the content of a story. (Lesson 3) identify and talk about written forms of communication. (Lesson 5)	apply new grammar to previously learned vocabulary. (Lesson 2) talk about events in the past. (Lesson 6)	work in pairs to act out a dialogue. (Lesson 3) send a secret message using a code wheel. (Lesson 8)	personalize the story by thinking about other stories which use coded language. (Lesson 4) evaluate their own progress in the chapter. (Review)	develop cultural understanding by finding out about ways of communicating secretly. (Lesson 7)

Digital Overview

Teacher Presentation

Student eBook and Digital Activity Book
- Oral Storytelling Video 5.1: *The Secret of Keyhole Island*
- Interactive versions of AB activities
- Integrated audio and answer key for all activities

Teacher resources for planning, lesson delivery, and homework

Teacher Resource Center
- Class Planner Chapter 5
- Worksheets to print out (including notes and answers):
  - Grammar Worksheet 5A: People made … years ago. We've discovered …
  - Grammar Worksheet 5B: Have you seen …? When did he send …?
  - Oral Storytelling Video Worksheet 5: *The Secret of Keyhole Island*
  - Phonics Worksheet 5
  - CLIL Graphic Organizer 5
  - Festival Worksheet: Valentine's Day
  - Test Chapter 5 and Mid-year Test
- Test Generator

Watch the Oral Storytelling Video

- Literacy Handbook

Student resources for consolidation and practice at home

Student eBook and Reader eBook
- Oral Storytelling Video 5.1: *The Secret of Keyhole Island*

The Inks Student's App
Vocabulary games: Forms of communication and Written communication/invention verbs

Vocabulary

Lesson objective: identify and talk about different types of communication
Key vocabulary: *alphabet, cave paintings, hieroglyphics, letter, Morse code, printing press, radio, text message*
Materials: Track 5.1

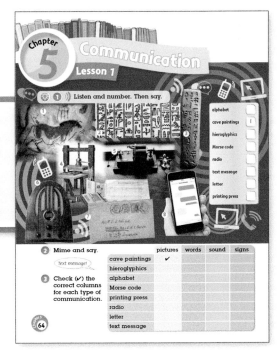

Warmer: Finger writing

Divide the class into pairs, with the child who is going to answer sitting with their back to the board. Write a word on the board. The other child writes the word with their finger on their friend's back. The friend guesses the word. They swap places. Repeat several times. Suggested words: *camera, fantasy, movie, writer, when, small, French, cough.*

1)) 5.1   Listen and number. Then say.

- Ask *How do you communicate with your friends?* Have the children look at the pictures for any ways they use.
- Play Track 5.1 twice. The children listen and point.
- Then they write the number of each picture by the correct label. Elicit answers.
- Say the new words for the children to repeat.

Audioscript

Welcome to the Museum. This is the audio tour of the communication room.

Cave paintings were a form of communication from a long time ago. Cave paintings tell us stories from the past. This brown horse is a cave painting from France.

Hieroglyphics were a type of writing from many years ago. They look like pictures, not letters. These are from Egypt. Can you see a bird and a snake?

Some people say this is the very first alphabet. These are Phoenician letters. The letters are very straight and they were often written from right to left.

The first printing press appeared in 1440 and it was operated by hand. Here, you can see some very old printed books. Because of the printing press, we have the books we read today!

This is a machine from the 1930s. It was used for sending communication in Morse code. Morse code uses long and short sounds to send messages. The code uses circles for short sounds and lines for long sounds.

Look at this big, brown, box. It is a radio from the 1940s. The family sat together and listened to it. The radio is still popular today.

Before cell phones, social networking, and email, people wrote letters by hand. It could often take weeks for letters to arrive from different countries.

After this, communication got easier and easier, with inventions like the modern cell phone, TV, computers, the Internet, and texting. Now, communication is very easy. We can send messages to friends in seconds—even in different countries!

Answers

alphabet 3, cave paintings 1, hieroglyphics 2, Morse code 5, radio 6, text message 8, letter 7, printing press 4

2 Mime and say.

- Mime sending a text message to elicit *Text message*. The first child to guess correctly takes a turn miming a different type of communication. Encourage the children to be inventive.
- Have the children play the miming game in pairs or small groups.

3 Check (✔) the correct columns for each type of communication.

- Have the children check the boxes for the other types of communication. They can do this in pairs. Elicit answers.

Answers

cave painting: pictures; *hieroglyphics:* pictures; *alphabet:* signs; *Morse code:* sound; *printing press:* words; *radio:* sound; *letter:* words; *text message:* words

Optional activity: Do a class presentation

Have the children choose a type of communication and find out more about it. Have them consult library sources in your school or the Internet. Have the children prepare a short class presentation.

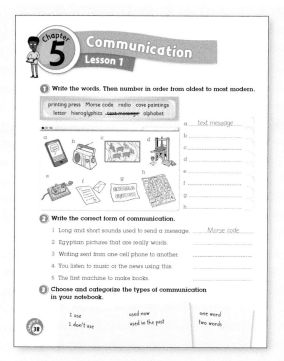

1 Write the words. Then number in order from oldest to most modern.

The children look at the pictures and write the words supplied. Then they number the communication types from oldest to most modern. Elicit answers.

Answers

a text message 8 **b** radio 7 **c** cave paintings 1
d printing press 5 **e** Morse code 6 **f** letter 4
g alphabet 3 **h** hieroglyphics 2

2 Write the correct form of communication.

The children write the correct word/phrase for each definition. Elicit answers.

Answers

1 Morse code **2** hieroglyphics **3** a text message
4 a radio **5** a printing press

3 Choose and categorize the types of communication in your notebook.

Elicit an example for each category listed. Ask *Which categories would you choose?* Elicit ideas, prompting children to give a reason for their choice. The children choose a pair of categories and list the words in their notebook, then compare with a friend.

Answers

Children's own answers.

Cooler: Play "Tic-Tac-Toe"

Play the game using *alphabet, cave painting, hieroglyphics, letter, Morse code, printing press, radio, text message, newspaper* (see Games Bank p. 19). To win a square, a child has to say a sentence using the word.

Competency Focus

Think! Critical Thinking

The children use critical thinking skills to understand the vocabulary by using visual clues and processing the written and spoken forms.

Digital Resources

Student eBook • Play "Kim's Game" with the new vocabulary. Display the SB page and elicit each word. Use *Timer* to give the class one minute to memorize the items, then one minute to recall them. Repeat several times.

Grammar

Lesson objective: talk about past events and what has happened
Key grammar: *People made (the first cave paintings 30,000 years ago).*
We've discovered (a lot about life then because of cave paintings).
Secondary language: *archeologists, Phoenicians, pyramids, tourists*
Materials: Track 5.2; Grammar Worksheet 5A [TRC printout] (optional)

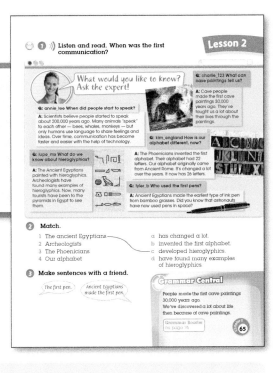

Warmer: Play "Disappearing Words"

Play the game with *alphabet, cave paintings, hieroglyphics, letter, Morse code, printing press, radio, text message* (see Games Bank p. 19).

1))) 5.2 Listen and read. When was the first communication?

- Have the children look at the website page. Pre-teach *archeologists.*

- Play Track 5.2 and ask *When was the first communication?* (*people starting to speak 200,000 years ago*)

- Play Track 5.2 again and ask questions to check comprehension, e.g. *Why are cave paintings important?* (*They teach us about the lives of cave people.*) *What other animals speak to each other?* (*bees, whales, monkeys*) *Who invented the first alphabet?* (*the Phoenicians*)

2 Match.

- Read the example. Have the children match the sentence halves.

- Elicit answers.

Answers

1 c 2 d 3 b 4 a

Grammar Central

People made the first cave paintings 30,000 years ago. ...

Have the children look at the patterns. Point out that we use the simple past when we know <u>when</u> something happened (e.g. *30,000 years ago*) and the present perfect when we do not. Have the children find other sentences with these tenses in the text.

For extra practice, try the **Grammar Booster** section in the Student Book (p. 74)

Answers p. 74

Activity 1: **2** have studied **3** invented **4** 've learned **5** wrote **6** 've developed

Activity 2: **2** sent **3** have **4** 've communicated **5** have discovered

Activity 3: Children's own answers.

3 Make sentences with a friend.

- Have two children read the example dialogue.

- Divide the class into pairs. They take turns choosing a form/tool of communication for their friend to give a piece of information about it. They can refer to the web page if necessary. Alternatively, ask them to do it as a memory test for a more challenging task.

- Have pairs say an example for class agreement.

Optional activity: All about communication

Divide the class into pairs. The children each write two questions based on the text in Activity 1 to test their friend's memory. They take turns asking and answering.

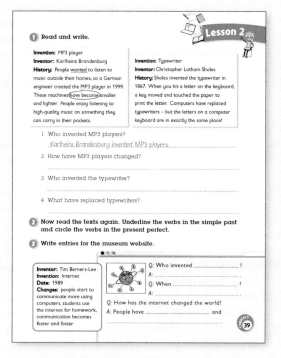

1 Read and write.

The children read about two inventions and write answers to questions. Elicit answers.

Answers

1 Karlheinz Brandenburg invented MP3 players.
2 They've become smaller and lighter.
3 Christopher Latham Sholes invented the typewriter.
4 Computers have replaced typewriters.

2 Now read the texts again. Underline the verbs in the simple past and circle the verbs in the present perfect.

The children read the texts in Activity 1 again and identify the verbs, underlining the verbs in the simple past and circling the verbs in the present perfect. Elicit answers.

Answers

simple past (underlined): wanted, created, invented, hit, moved, touched,

present perfect (circled): have become, have replaced

3 Write entries for the museum website.

The children read the information. Then they complete the questions and write the answers. Elicit questions and answers.

Answers

Q: Who invented the Internet?

A: Tim Berners-Lee invented the Internet.

Q: When did he invent it?

A: He invented it in 1989.

Q: How has the Internet changed the world?

A: People have started to communicate more and students are using the Internet for homework/ communication has become faster and faster.

Cooler: Unscramble the words

Write on the board scrambled versions of *alphabet, cave paintings, hieroglyphics, letter, Morse code, printing press, radio, text message.* Have the children write the words correctly in their notebook. Ask children to write answers on the board for the class to check.

Competency Focus

Learn

The children develop learning strategies by recognizing and applying language patterns. They show their understanding of previously acquired vocabulary and use it in a new context.

Digital Resources

Digital Activity Book • Have children do the AB interactive digital activities or set them for homework.

Teacher Resource Center • For extra grammar practice, print out Grammar Worksheet 5A.

Reading: Story Extract

Lesson objectives: react to a surprising fact/event; predict story content from title and pictures; read the extract from *The Secret of Keyhole Island* (middle)

Functional language: *That's strange! When you … Cool! Let's …*

Secondary language: *map, mirror, pirates*

Materials: Tracks 5.3 and 5.4

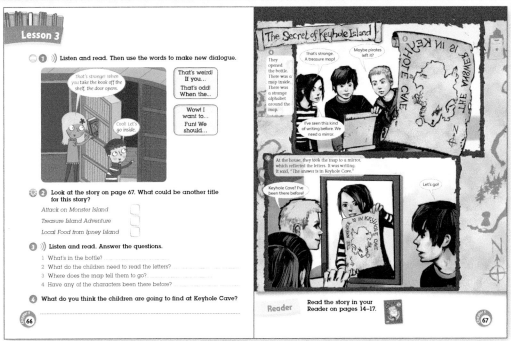

Warmer: Play "The Shark Game"

Play the game with *hieroglyphics* and *printing press* (see Games Bank p. 19).

Functional language

1))) **5.3   Listen and read. Then act out.**

- Have the children look at the picture. Ask *What's the girl doing?* (*She's taking a book off the shelf.*)

- Play Track 5.3. The children listen and read along. Ask *What happens when she takes the book off the shelf?* (*The door opens.*)

- Play Track 5.3 again, pausing for the children to repeat. Have them act out the dialogue in pairs. Encourage children to replace *the door opens* in the dialogue, using e.g. *the TV turns on, the teacher sneezes*, etc.

Before reading

2 Look at the story. What could be another title for this story?

- Elicit the story title. Have the children look at the pictures. Elicit ideas on what the story is about.

- Ask *What could be another title for this story?* The children choose and check one of the three alternative titles. Elicit answers with reasons. (*Treasure Island Adventure*)

3))) **Track 5.4 Listen and read. Answer the questions.**

- Give the children time to read the questions.

- Play Track 5.4. The children listen and read along. Then they answer the questions.

- Play Track 5.4 again for them to check their answers. Elicit answers.

- Ask *Who do you think left the map? What's the message?* (*"The answer is in Keyhole Cave."*)

Answers

1 a map **2** a mirror **3** Keyhole Cave **4** yes (Fred)

4 What do you think the children are going to find at Keyhole Cave?

- Have the children write what they think the characters are going to find. Elicit ideas including reasons but do not confirm. Say they will have to read the story to find out.

Answer

Children's own answers.

1 Complete. Then act out.

Divide the class into pairs to complete and act out the dialogue. Have pairs act out for the class.

Answers

take the book off the shelf

2 Read the story in your Student Book. Complete.

The children read the Student Book story extract again. They complete the sentences using the words supplied. Elicit answers.

Answers

1 Open **2** Take **3** Use **4** Read **5** Go

3 Who put the treasure map in the bottle? Think and write.

Elicit ideas orally. Then the children write down their ideas. Elicit responses.

Answers

Children's own answers.

Cooler: Play "Jump the Line"

Play the game with *There wasn't a message inside the bottle.* (F) *The children needed a bottle to read the message.* (F) *The police left the map inside the bottle.* (F) *There were hieroglyphics around the map.* (F) *The message was "The key is on Keyhole Island."* (F) *One of the children has already been to Keyhole Cave.* (T) *The children are going to Keyhole Cave.* (T) (see Games Bank p. 19).

Competency Focus

Collaborate and Communicate

The children act out an authentic dialogue together, putting into practice the functional language.

Think! Critical Thinking

The children apply reading skills (exploiting pictures and text clues) to understand the story.

Digital Resources

Digital Activity Book • Display the AB page for Activity 3 feedback. Have children use *Pen* to write their answer. Elicit who in the class had the same response. Repeat with a few children who have different ideas.

The Secret of Keyhole Island

1
Fred lived on a small island with his parents. His cousins from the city, Luke and Ella, were coming to stay. Fred was excited to see them, but worried that they would be bored on the island.

2
Luke and Ella arrived by boat. They were excited, too.

Luke: We can explore.

Ella: I brought my spy notebook!

Fred: I can show you a lot of secret places.

3
After lunch, Fred took them to the beach by his house. Ella tripped over something. It looked like it was very old.

Ella: It's an old bottle.

Luke: Look! There's something inside.

4
They opened the bottle. There was a map inside. There was a strange alphabet around the map.

Ella: That's strange. A treasure map!

Fred: Maybe pirates left it?

Ella: I've seen this kind of writing before. We need a mirror.

6
At the house, they took the map to a mirror, which reflected the letters. It was writing. It said, "The answer is in Keyhole Cave."

Fred: Keyhole Cave? I've been there before!

Luke: Let's go!

7
There were a lot of caves in the cliffs.

Fred: There's one which looks like a keyhole.

Luke: I have a light.

8
Inside, there was writing on the wall.

Fred: It looks like pirate code.

Ella: Let's copy it.

Luke: It's a code. For figuring out messages.

9
Further along the beach, they found a boat that had letters painted on it.

Fred: Try using the code.

Ella: It says, "Meet me here at 7:00 p.m."

10
At home, the children made periscopes.

Fred: I've made these before. You can see around corners with them.

11
After dinner, the children went back to the boat. They hid and watched with their periscopes. At 7:00 p.m. a man arrived, then another man. He gave the first man a letter.

12
The children followed the man. He put the letter into the mailbox. There was a piece of paper inside.

Ella: Why did he leave it here?

Luke: That's strange—it's blank.

Fred: Maybe it's invisible ink.

13
At home, the children held the paper over a lightbulb. A message appeared.

FROM THE LIGHTHOUSE DOOR, WALK FOUR STEPS NORTH, THREE STEPS WEST. DIG.

Ella: Let's go! Don't forget a shovel.

Luke: And a compass.

14
The children followed the instructions. They made a hole.

Luke: There's something here!

Ella: Treasure!

15
The treasure chest was filled with candy.

Ella: Was it pirates who left this?

Luke: No, I think someone has helped us all along.

Fred: You're right. I planned all this for you.

Ella: Thanks, Fred!

Luke: We've had a lot of fun.

Lesson objective: read and understand the adventure story *The Secret of Keyhole Island* in the Reader

Materials: Track 5.5; Reader; treasure hunt object (optional); Oral Storytelling Video Worksheet 5 [TRC printout] (optional)

Warmer: Play "Ready, Set, Draw"

Play the game using *bottle, island, message, house, cave, map, mirror* (see Games Bank p. 19).

Story Summary

Fred, a boy who lives on an island, plans a secret treasure hunt for his city cousins, Luke and Ella. His cousins follow clues to discover the treasure—a lot of candy!

Value: Spend time with friends.

)) 5.5 While reading

- Have the children look at the pictures in the Reader. Ask *Is there only one cave?* (*no*)

- Play Track 5.5. The children listen and read along. Ask *What do the children find in the end?* (*a treasure chest full of candy*)

- Play Track 5.5 again. Ask questions to check comprehension, e.g. *Why are Luke and Ella on the island?* (*They're visiting Fred.*) *What do they find inside the cave?* (*a code*) *What does the message on the boat say?* (*Meet me here at 7:00 p.m.*) *Was it really pirates' treasure?* (*no*)

After reading: Reflect

- Ask questions to give the children the opportunity to think about the issues raised by the story, e.g. *Why did Fred plan this adventure? Did his cousins have fun? Have you ever taken part in a treasure hunt?*

Optional activity: A treasure hunt

Choose an object as treasure, e.g. a key. Each group decides on a place to hide the key in the classroom and writes instructions like the ones in Picture 13, e.g. *From the teacher's desk, walk four steps to the window, three steps to Blanca's desk. Pick up the book on the floor.* Have one group leave the classroom and ask another group to hide the key. Then they read out their instructions for the group to follow and find the "treasure." Repeat with different groups.

Story Time

Distinguishing between voices

It is helpful for the children to distinguish between narration and dialogue within a story. Read aloud different phrases to the children—ask them *Dialogue or narration?* This will help them identify better who is talking and what is happening in the story.

Reading Strategy

Page Shrinking

Page Shrinking is a form of summarizing in which the children focus on the main events that take place on each page of the story. By dividing up the story, the children are given support in understanding the plot and identifying the key ideas, so that they can then go on to express them orally or in writing.

For additional explanation and activities, see the Literacy Handbook on the Teacher's Resource Center.

Cooler: Play "Consequences"

Play the game using *What was the pirate's name? What was he like? What was his treasure? Where did he hide it? Where did he put the instructions? Who found them?* (see Games Bank p. 19).

Digital Resources

Reader eBook • Show the Reader story one picture at a time as you play the audio. Pause at the end of each page to elicit a summary of what has happened, and children's ideas on what will happen next.

 • Oral Storytelling Video 5.1 gives the story with a different ending. Watch it together at the end of the lesson, then discuss the differences.

Teacher Resource Center • Print out Oral Storytelling Video Worksheet 5 to help you get the most out of the video.

Reading Comprehension and Critical Literacy

Lesson objectives: learn about imperative instructions; relate the story to personal experiences

Materials: Track 5.5; Reader; Oral Storytelling Video Worksheet 5 [TRC printout] (optional)

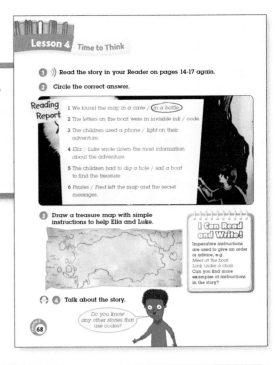

Note: Please ensure that your class has read the Reader story before you do this lesson.

Warmer: Board race

Divide the class into two teams and give each team a board pen. The children on each team take turns running to the board to write a name, place, object, or activity from the story. Teams check each other's answers. Then elicit sentences using some of the key words.

1))) 5.5 Read the story in your Reader.

- Have the children read the story. (Alternatively, play Track 5.5 and have them read along.) Elicit whether they were correct in their predictions in Lesson 3 Activity 4.

- Check comprehension by asking *Were the children good at breaking codes?* (*yes*) *What was the message on the letter?* (*From the lighthouse door, walk four steps north, three steps west. Dig.*) *Who prepared all this?* (*Fred*)

2 Circle the correct answer.

- Have the children complete the sentences by circling the correct answer.

- Elicit answers.

Answers

1 in a bottle 2 code 3 light 4 Ella 5 dig a hole 6 Fred

I Can Read and Write!

Say *Meet at the boat. Look under a chair.* Point out that these are instructions. Have the children read out more instructions from the story. Elicit answers, asking each time if it is an order or advice.

3 Draw a treasure map with simple instructions to help Ella and Luke.

- Have the children make suggestions as to what they would hide for Ella and Luke. Write them on the board.

- The children draw the details on the map in the Student Book. They swap with a friend to check.

Answers

Children's own answers.

4 Talk about the story.

- Have the children read Jason's question. Elicit answers. Ask *Do you use a code to play with your friends? Do you know any stories which use codes? Why did people use a code? Do you know any movies where people use codes?* (e.g. National Treasure)

Optional activity: Unscramble the question

Write these questions in scrambled order on the board: *Where do Luke and Ella live? What did Ella bring? What can you do with a periscope? What did they find inside the treasure chest?* Have children work in groups to unscramble and answer the questions as fast as possible.

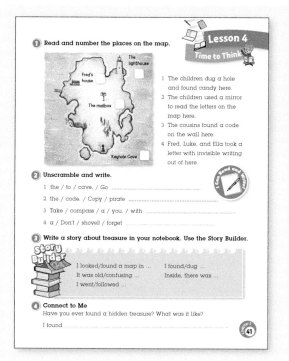

1 Read and number the places on the map.

The children read the sentences and number the places, referring to the Reader if necessary. Elicit answers.

Answers

Fred's house 2, The lighthouse 1, The mailbox 4, Keyhole Cave 3

2 Unscramble and write.

The children practice the **I Can Read and Write!** feature by writing the sentences correctly. Elicit answers.

Answers

1 Go to the cave. **2** Copy the pirate code.
3 Take a compass with you. **4** Don't forget a shovel!

3 Write a story about treasure in your notebook. Use the Story Builder.

Use the **Story Builder** prompts to elicit ideas. The children write a story in their notebook, then swap with a friend to check. Have children read their story for the class.

Answers

Children's own answers.

4 Connect to Me

Elicit ideas on hidden treasure the children have found (e.g. *a jar of cookies in the kitchen, a birthday present,* etc.) before the children write their own response. Elicit responses.

Answers

Children's own answers.

Cooler: Play "Monkey"

Divide the class into two teams (A and B), who stand up facing each other. Have the first child in Team A begin reading the story. When you shout *Monkey!*, the reading switches over to the first child on Team B. Continue in this way, shouting *Monkey!* at random points for the reading to switch.

Competency Focus

Me: Critical Literacy

The children use critical literacy skills to reflect on the theme of the story and relate it to their personal experience.

Digital Resources

Student eBook, Reader eBook • If you haven't already, show Oral Storytelling Video 5.1.

Teacher Resource Center • If you haven't already, print out Oral Storytelling Video Worksheet 5 to do the support activities.

Student eBook • The children can watch Oral Storytelling Video 5.1 at home with their family.

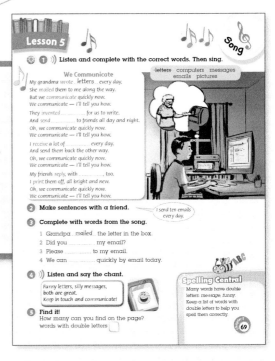

Vocabulary, Song, and Spelling

Lesson objectives: talk about written communication; practice spelling words with double consonants

Key vocabulary: *communicate, invent, mail, print, receive, reply, send, write*

Secondary language: *computers, emails, keep in touch, letters, messages, pictures*

Materials: Tracks 5.6 and 5.7; red and blue pens; Phonics Worksheet 5 [TRC printout] (optional)

Warmer: Pre-teach vocabulary

Pre-teach the key vocabulary by writing the present and simple past pairings on the board (e.g. *write—wrote*). Prompt with the simple past in random order to elicit the present.

1))) **5.6 Listen and complete with the correct words. Then sing.**

- Ask *What do you see in the picture?*
- Play Track 5.6. The children listen and complete the song using the words supplied. Elicit answers.
- Play Track 5.6 again. The children sing along and mime.

Answers

letters, computers, emails, messages, pictures

2 Make sentences with a friend.

- Read the example. Say *I don't write any emails. I send two letters every week.*
- Have the children talk about how they communicate with their friends. Have pairs tell the class their sentences.

3 Complete with words from the song.

- Read the example. The children complete the sentences referring to the song.
- Elicit answers.

Answers

1 mailed **2** receive **3** reply **4** communicate

Spelling Central

Short vowel + double letter

Write on the board *picttures, miror, writing, diferent, comedy, added.* Elicit whether each is correct or not. Have children correct the wrong words on the board.

4))) **5.7 Listen and say the chant.**

- Have the children look at the picture. Ask *What can you see?*
- Play Track 5.7. The children listen and read along. Elicit the words with double letters.
- Play Track 5.7 again, pausing for the children to repeat.

5 Find it!

- Set a time limit for the children to find words with double letters on the page. Elicit answers.
- Elicit any other words with double letters they know.

Answers

16—lesson, correct, communicate, letters, I'll, messages, tell, all, too, off, funny, silly, keep, Spelling, spell, correctly

Optional activity: Words with double letters

Have the children scan the previous pages of their Student Book for words with double letters. Have them say the words and write them on the board.

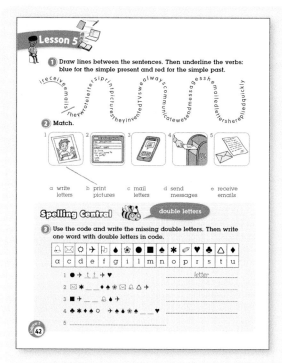

1 Draw lines between the sentences. Then underline the verbs: blue for the simple present and red for the simple past.

The children identify the sentences in the wordsnake by drawing lines. Then they underline the verbs with the correct color—blue for simple present and red for simple past. Elicit answers.

Answers

I receive emails.
They wrote letters.
I print pictures.
They invented TVs.
We always communicate.
We send messages.
She mailed letters.
He replied quickly.

Simple present (blue underline): receive, print, communicate, send

Simple past (red underline): wrote, invented, mailed, replied

2 Match.

The children match the pictures to the phrases. Elicit answers.

Answers

1 b **2** e **3** d **4** c **5** a

3 Use the code and write the missing double letters. Then write one word with double letters in code.

To practice the **Spelling Central** feature, the children decode the words, writing the missing double letters and the complete word. Elicit answers. Then they write their own coded word with double letters. They swap with a friend to decode each other's word.

Answers

1 letter **2** communicate **3** message **4** sound engineer
5 Children's own answer.

Cooler: Sing a line

))) 5.6

Play Track 5.6 for the children to sing along. Then divide the class into two groups. Have a child in each group sing a line of the song—child 1 sings *My grandma wrote letters every day*; child 2 sings *She mailed them to me along the way*, and so on. Continue the song around the circle, until it is finished.

Competency Focus

Think! Critical Thinking

The children use critical thinking skills to identify written and spoken forms of new words, and complete the activity.

Digital Resources

Student eBook • TIP Children use *Highlighter* to identify the words which illustrate the spelling feature on the page.

• TIP Use *Timer* to set a time limit for SB Activity 5.

Student's App • Encourage the children to play the games on their smartphone/tablet. They could do this with a friend as a fun way to review the chapter vocabulary together. (*The Inks* Apps are free and available on the App Store and Google Play.)

Teacher Resource Center • For phonics practice, print out Phonics Worksheet 5.

Grammar and Reading

Lesson objectives: ask and answer about past events and what has happened

Key grammar: *Have you seen (Miguel)? When did he send (the message)?*

Secondary language: *message, reply, text language*

Materials: Track 5.8; Grammar Worksheet 5B [TRC printout] (optional)

Warmer: Verb listen and do

Ask the class to stand up. Say sentences featuring the simple past tense (e.g. *made, saw, sent*) or the present perfect (e.g. *have made, have seen, have sent*) in random order. Have the children wave both arms in the air for the simple past and jump up and down for the present perfect.

1))) 5.8 Listen and read. What's the message for Felicity?

- Have the children look at the pictures. Ask *What are they looking at?* (phone, computer)

- Play Track 5.8. The children listen and read along. Ask *What is the message for Felicity?* (Busy at work. See you later. Miguel)

- Play Track 5.8 again and ask further questions, e.g. *What's the problem?* (Miguel sent a message they can't understand.) *What has Miguel invented?* (a machine for sending messages in text language) *Is it useful?* (No, because it does what a cell phone can do.) *Would you like to have this machine? Why?*

Grammar Central

Have you seen Miguel? …

Have the children look at the patterns. Elicit the tense in each question. (*present perfect* and *simple past*) Point out the word order in each question. Have children work in pairs, taking turns asking and answering questions using the present perfect and the simple past. Make sure they specify the time in the simple past questions, e.g. *What did you eat yesterday/last night/on Tuesday?*

For extra practice, try the **Grammar Booster** section in the Student Book (pp. 75–77)

Answers p.75

Activity 1: **2** did, hear **3** Have, replied **4** did, meet **5** Has, been **6** did, play

Activity 2: **2** Have you visited your grandparents? **3** When did you visit them? **4** Did you have lunch with them? **5** Have you e-mailed your cousins?

p. 76

Activity 1: **2** did **3** ago **4** loved **5** I've **6** haven't

Activity 2: **2** has **3** tried **4** loved **5** has tried **6** hasn't been

p. 77

Activity 1: **2** made **3** made **4** worked **5** found **6** much **7** did you use **8** played **9** had **10** try

Activity 2: Children's own answers.

2 Complete the sentences with the correct form of verbs from the box.

- The children complete the sentences using the correct form of the verbs supplied. Elicit answers.

Answers

1 seen **2** speak to **3** send **4** invented

Optional activity: A coded text message

Write more text message abbreviations on the board: *2mrw* (*tomorrow*), *asap* (*as soon as possible*), *BBIAM* (*be back in a minute*), *bday* (*birthday*), *2nite* (*tonight*), etc. Have the children break the coded messages in pairs or small groups. Then they write their own abbreviated text message and exchange in pairs to decode.

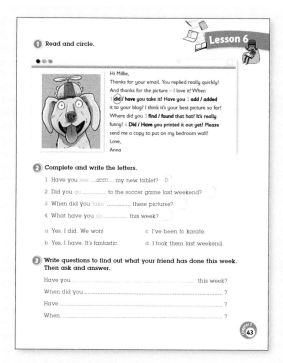

1 Read and circle.

The children circle the correct words to complete Anna's email. Elicit answers.

Answers

1 did **2** added **3** find **4** Have

2 Complete and write the letters.

The children complete the questions, then write the letter of the correct answer by each one. Elicit answers.

Answers

1 seen b **2** go a **3** take d **4** done c

3 Write questions to find out what your friend has done this week. Then ask and answer.

The children complete the questions. Then they take turns asking and answering in pairs.

Answers

Children's own answers.

Cooler: Play "The Telephone Game"

Play the game using *Has Felicity replied to Miguel's message yet?* and *The children didn't understand Miguel's message because it was in code.* (see Games Bank p. 19).

Competency Focus

Learn

The children develop learning strategies by recognizing and applying language patterns in different contexts.

Digital Resources

Student eBook • Use *Highlighter* to identify questions in SB Activity 1. Elicit the tense used.

Teacher Resource Center • For extra grammar practice, print out Grammar Worksheet 5B.

CLIL: History—Julius Caesar

Lesson objectives: find out about secret codes and how to make them
Materials: CLIL Graphic Organizer 5 [TRC printout] (optional); cotton swabs, lemon juice (optional)

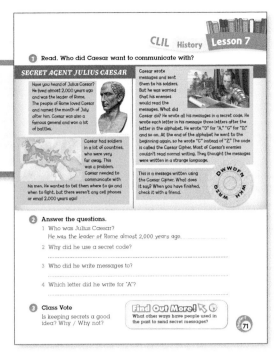

Warmer: Speaking Z

Write on the board *Hzi, chzildrzen. Hzow zare yzou?* Divide the class into pairs and tell them this is a secret message. Ask them to try and find out what the message is. Give them a few minutes and elicit the message. (*Hi, children. How are you?*) Explain that you were writing your own code language—*Z*! Prompt as necessary to help the children figure out that you write *z* before each vowel sound, so *Hi* becomes *Hzi*. Have pairs write other messages in *Z* for the class.

1 Read. Who did Caesar want to communicate with?

- Elicit the countries the children can recognize on the map (e.g. *Spain, Italy, Greece, Turkey, England, France,* etc.).

- Have the children read the first paragraph of the text. Ask *Who was Julius Caesar?* (*the leader of Rome / a famous Roman general*)

- The children read the rest of the text. Ask *Who did Caesar want to communicate with?* (*his men*) *Why was he worried?* (*because his enemies could read his messages*) *How does the code work?* (*He wrote each letter three letters after the one in the alphabet.*)

- Have them work in pairs to decode the message. (*Attack the town.*)

2 Answer the questions.

Read the example. The children answer the questions on the text, then compare answers in pairs. Elicit answers.

Answers

1 He was the leader of Rome almost 2,000 years ago.
2 Because he didn't want his enemies to read his messages.
3 He wrote messages to his soldiers.
4 He wrote "D" for "A."

3 Class Vote

- Have the children discuss the question in pairs. Then ask them to write *good* or *bad* on a piece of paper. They hold up their answers for you to count the votes.

- Elicit ideas on why secrets might sometimes be a good idea (*to protect people, to organize a surprise party*) and why it is a bad idea (*better to get advice/help, hurt people, people will get angry/upset when they find out, lose friends*).

Find Out More!

Ask the children to research other ways of sending secret messages, e.g. invisible ink, messages sent with pigeons, etc. Suggest appropriate resources, e.g. Internet, library books, etc. The children will need to complete this research before doing the follow-up activity in the Activity Book. (It could be set as homework.)

Optional activity: Write an invisible message

Give each child a sheet of paper, a cotton swab, and some lemon juice in an open container. Have the children dip the cotton swab in the juice and write a message on the paper. Allow it to dry, and have them hold it to the sunlight or a heat source.

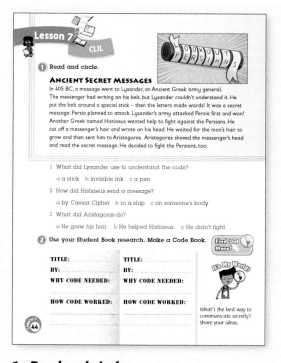

Cooler: Make up a code

Divide the class into pairs. Elicit ideas as a class for making up codes (e.g. using the letter which comes before in the alphabet, using numbers for letters, etc.). Each pair then decides on an idea for their own code. Elicit ideas. Have a class vote on which would be best code for keeping a message secret.

Competency Focus

Act

The children carry out research to find out more about secret codes. This helps them expand their learning and relate it to their world, both inside and outside the classroom.

1 Read and circle.

The children read the text and answer the questions by circling the correct option from three each time. Elicit answers, asking children to identify the part of the text that provides the answer.

Answers

1 a 2 c 3 b

2 Use your Student Book research. Make a Code Book.

Divide the class into groups of four. Have the children pool the information learned from their research in the Student Book and the Activity Book. They complete the information in the Code Book individually. Have children talk about the codes to the class.

Answers

Children's own answers.

It's My World!

The children discuss in small groups the best way to communicate secretly. Elicit ideas.

Digital Resources

Student eBook • To give feedback on SB Activity 2, have children use *Highlighter* to identify the section of the text which gives them the answer to each question.

• TIP Remember—you can use *Add personal note* to log the results of the class vote.

Teacher Resource Center • Print out CLIL Graphic Organizer 5 for the children to use in collating their Find Out More! research.

CLIL eBook • The children can use the CLIL eBook to expand their knowledge of the lesson topic.

Project

Lesson objectives: review language from Chapter 5; make a code wheel and use it to write a secret message

Materials: rulers, 12 cm. and 15 cm. colored construction paper circles (one per child), scissors, split pins, colored pens/pencils; small pieces of colored paper (optional); two game pieces and a coin for each pair

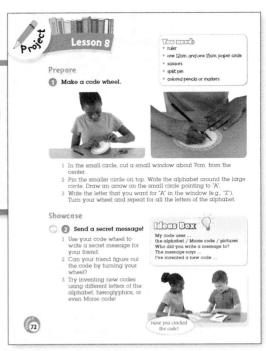

Warmer: Play "Vocabulary Review"

Play the game with *communication, hieroglyphics, Morse code, printing press, radio, text message, cave paintings, reply, receive* (see Games Bank p. 19).

Prepare

1 Make a code wheel.

- Distribute the materials. Read through the instructions together and ensure the children are clear on what to do.

- Have the children make their code wheels individually. Give support as necessary.

Alternative craft activity

An easier project is to have the children write the normal alphabet horizontally in their notebook, and beneath it write the alphabet starting with the letter they want for *A*, e.g. *Z* or *D*. They then use this to write a coded message.

Showcase

2 Send a secret message!

- Have children write coded messages using their code wheel.

- Then they exchange secret messages and code wheels with a friend. Give them a time limit to break the code and decipher the message. They should talk to each other using the **Ideas Box** for support. Give support as necessary.

- Repeat with different pairs.

Optional activity: Happy messages

Give the children small pieces of colored paper or have them cut out a piece from their notebook. Tell them to write a "happy" message to their class/the people in their town/ the whole world. Elicit examples, e.g. *Life is smiling at you! / Sing a song every day.*, etc. Have them mingle and say their messages to each other. Then display the messages on a cork board or stick them around the classroom.

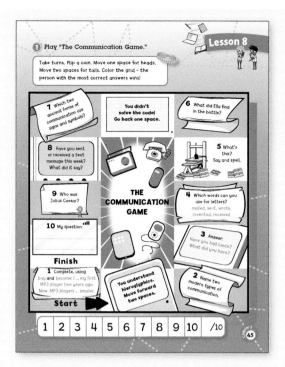

1 Play "The Communication Game."

See p. 43 for instructions on how to play the game.

Answers

1 bought, have become **2** *any two of:* radio, text message, email **3** Yes, I have. I had … / No, I haven't. **4** mailed, sent, wrote, received **5** printing press **6** a map **7** hieroglyphics, cave paintings **8** Yes, I have. It said … / No, I haven't. **9** A Roman leader who invented a secret code. **10** Children's own answer.

Cooler: Understand silent speech

Write key vocabulary from Chapter 5 on the board. Tell the children to listen carefully. When you have their full attention, mouth a word silently for the children to identify just by watching the movement of your mouth. The first child to guess correctly takes your place.

Language Review

Lesson objective: review language from Chapter 5
Materials: Tracks 5.6, 5.9, AB 5.1 and AB 5.2

Warmer: Who said it?

Read out two phrases spoken by people in the chapter to elicit who said it (from the story, dialogues in Lessons 3 and 6, etc.). Then have the children continue the task in pairs, taking turns prompting and responding.

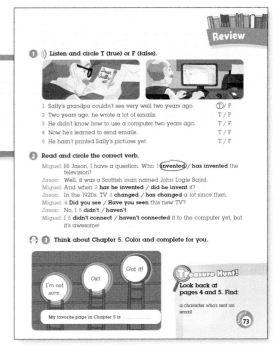

1)))) **5.9**   **Listen and circle T (true) or F (false).**

- Give the children time to read the example and the sentences. Play Track 5.9 twice. They listen and circle T (true) or F (false) for each sentence.

- Elicit answers, including the correct version of the false sentences.

Audioscript

Rick: *Sally, you've got mail.*
Sally: *Great, it's from my grandpa—he's amazing! Two years ago, he couldn't see very well. He wrote letters and mailed them to the wrong address because he didn't write very well.*
Rick: *What happened then?*
Sally: *Then he went to the hospital for an operation. The doctors helped him. When they took the bandages off his eyes, it was amazing—he could see again!*
Rick: *Fantastic! What did he do then?*
Sally: *Well, he's changed a lot in the past two years. He bought a computer and he's learned to use it. This week, he's sent me three emails already! And I've sent him some pictures of me ... but he hasn't printed them yet.*
Rick: *Does he have a cell phone, too?*
Sally: *Yes ... Look, he sent me a text message.*
Rick: *Have you replied yet?*
Sally: *Not yet.*
Rick: *I don't understand the text message.*
Sally: *That's because it's in code. I told you my grandpa was amazing!*

Answers

1 T 2 F 3 T 4 T 5 T

2   **Read and circle the correct verb.**

- Read the example. Have the children circle the correct verbs to complete the dialogue.

- Invite pairs of children to read out parts of the dialogue.

Answers

1 invented **2** did he invent **3** has changed **4** Have you seen **5** haven't **6** haven't connected

3   **Think about Chapter 5. Color and complete for you.** 🎧

- Have the children look back at Chapter 5. Elicit their favorite parts. The children then color the circle which represents how they feel about their own progress (self-evaluation).

- Have the children complete the sentence about their favorite page. Elicit responses.

Treasure Hunt!

Have the children look at pp. 4–5, and find a character who has sent an email. Have the children hold up their Student Book and point to the right place on the page.

Cooler: Sing loudly, sing quietly ...

)))) **5.6**

Play the song for the children to sing along. Start loud in each verse, gradually reducing the volume. Have the children sing more quietly to match the volume, .

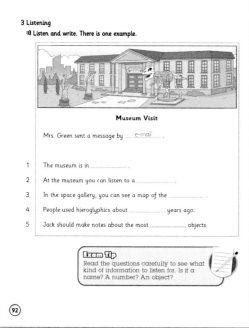

1 Reading and Writing. Look and read. Choose the correct words and write them on the lines. There is one example.

The children complete the text.

Answers

1 ago **2** used **3** have invented **4** made **5** see

2))) AB 5.1 Listening. Listen and write. There is one example.

Play Track AB 5.1 twice. Children listen and write an answer for each prompt.

Answers (Audioscript on pp. 223)

1 Lucy **2** October 25th **3** Kingsley **4** email **5** sneakers

3))) AB 5.2 Listening. Listen and write. There is one example.

Play Track AB 5.2 twice. They listen and write an answer for each sentence.

Answers (Audioscript on p. 223)

1 Lakestone **2** morse code machine **3** planets **4** 5,000 years ago **5** unusual

Competency Focus

> Me: Self-evaluation
>
> The children reflect on the chapter and express their opinions about their own progress.

Digital Resources

Teacher Resource Center • Print out Test Chapter 5 and Mid-year Test to use at the end of this lesson. The Test Generator also allows you to create customized tests.

• Print out Festival Worksheet: Valentine's Day to expand the children's knowledge of celebrations throughout the world.

Chapter 6
Fun and Fantasy
Overview

The children will:

- use critical thinking skills to identify costumes and props.
- ask and answer about possessions.
- read, understand, and act out a story.
- learn verbs to retell a story.
- talk about two or more actions that happen at the same time in the past.
- find out about real-world magic.
- make an optical illusion.

Reading Skills

Story: *Aladdin*
Genre: Middle Eastern folk tale

Key Vocabulary

Dressing up props: cloak, hat, jewels, lamp, mirror, ring, sword, treasure chest
Story verbs: appeared, disappeared, found, hid, put (it) on, rubbed, stole

Literacy Development

- predict story content from title and pictures
- interpret and personalize the theme of the story
- find words and details about a character's personality

Key Grammar

- Whose (cloak) is this?
- (This cloak) is mine/yours/hers/his/theirs/ours.
- When I opened (my eyes), I saw (my dog).
- When I rubbed (his nose), he disappeared.

Functional Language

- Whose … is this?
- It's … 's.
- Are you sure it's hers?
- Yes, it has …

Spelling

Letters *j* and *g* for the *j* sound

CLIL: Science—Real-world magic

The children find out about natural phenomena which seem magic.

Competency Focus

The children will:

use critical thinking skills to identify costumes and props. (Lesson 1)	apply new grammar to previously learned vocabulary. (Lesson 2)	work in pairs to act out a dialogue. (Lesson 3)	personalize the story by thinking of other stories based on magic wishes. (Lesson 4)	develop a wider understanding of nature. (Lesson 7)
predict the content of a story. (Lesson 3)	talk about simultaneous events in the past. (Lesson 6)	present an optical illusion to the class. (Lesson 8)	evaluate their own progress in the chapter. (Review)	
identify verbs to retell a story. (Lesson 5)				

Digital Overview

Teacher Presentation

Student eBook and Digital Activity Book

- Music Video 6.1 (6.2): *The Magic Ring*
- Interactive versions of AB activities
- Integrated audio and answer key for all activities

Teacher resources for planning, lesson delivery, and homework

Teacher Resource Center

- Class Planner Chapter 6
- Worksheets to print out (including notes and answers):
  - Grammar Worksheet 6A: Whose … is this? This … is mine, yours, …
  - Grammar Worksheet 6B: When I opened …, I saw …
  - Phonics Worksheet 6
  - CLIL Graphic Organizer 6
  - Test Chapter 6
- Test Generator
- Speaking Assessment: Cambridge English Young Learners Exams
- Literacy Handbook

Watch the Music Video

Children's resources for consolidation and practice at home

Student eBook

- Music Video 6.1 (6.2): *The Magic Ring*

Student's App

Vocabulary games: Dressing up props and story verbs

Vocabulary

Lesson objective: identify and talk about costumes and props
Key vocabulary: *cloak, hat, jewels, lamp, mirror, ring, sword, treasure chest*
Materials: Track 6.1; a ball (Warmer); cards for "Board Pelmanism" (optional)

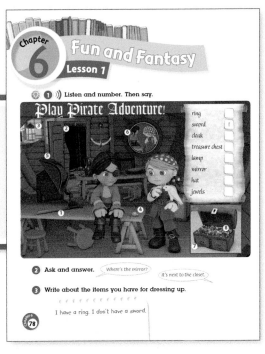

Warmer: Play "Don't Say 3!"

Have the children sit in a circle. They pass a ball around counting from 1. When they reach 3 (or a multiple of 3), instead of saying the number, the child has to say an item of clothing, e.g. *1, 2, skirt, 4, 5, coat, 7, 8, jacket.*, etc. If they make a mistake, they leave the circle. The last person sitting wins.

1))) 6.1 Listen and number. Then say.

- Ask *What is the game about?* Elicit ideas. (They may need L1.) Ask *Where are the pirates?* (on their ship)
- Play Track 6.1 twice. The children listen and point.
- Then they write the number of each object by the correct word. Elicit answers.
- Say the new words for the children to repeat.

Audioscript

Girl: OK, Let's play All Aboard—Pirate Adventure. There are two pirates. What do they need?
Boy: Let's see … my pirate needs this sword. It's very long. It's on the table.
Girl: I want my pirate to have the cloak! It's long and black. It's in the closet. Hm, what else …
Boy: Don't forget the lamp! It's on the shelf.
Girl: Oh, yes, it's gold. My pirate needs that.
Boy: And I'll choose the ring.
Girl: The one on the table? That's a beautiful ring. It's so shiny and green!

Boy: OK. What is your pirate going to wear on his head?
Girl: The hat on the chair! Look, it's red and black—a real pirate hat.
Boy: Perfect. Ready to play the adventure?
Girl: Yes. Look at the pirates in the mirror. It's next to the closet. They look great.
Boy: OK. It's time for the pirates to look for the treasure chest!
Girl: Oh, yes, I hope they find it. It has all the jewels inside.
Boy: Let's go!

Answers

ring 4, sword 1, cloak 2, treasure chest 7, lamp 3, mirror 6, hat 5, jewels 8

2 Ask and answer.

- Do the example with the class. If necessary, review *next to, on, behind.*
- Divide the class into pairs. They take turns asking and answering about the position of the objects in the picture. Elicit answers.

3 Write about the items you have for dressing up.

- Say *You're going to a costume party. What items do you have in Activity 1 that you can use for the party?* Ask a child to read the example, then elicit further ideas.
- The children write about what items they have and don't have for dressing up in their notebook. Elicit sentences. Have a class vote to see which object most people have.

Answers

Children's own answers.

Optional activity: Play "Board Pelmanism"

Prepare cards using key vocabulary from the lesson (sw/ord, cloa/k, h/at, ri/ng, j/ewels, la/mp, mirr/or, treasure/chest). Put the cards face down on the board. Have children turn over the cards to try and make a pair.

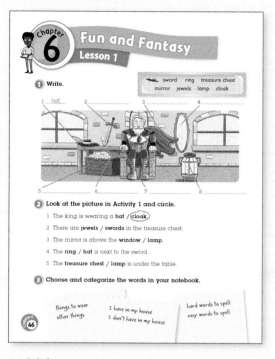

1 Write.

The children label the items in the picture using the words supplied. Elicit answers.

Answers

1 hat **2** sword **3** cloak **4** mirror **5** treasure chest **6** jewels **7** ring **8** lamp

2 Look at the picture in Activity 1 and circle.

The children look at the picture again and choose the correct words to complete the sentences. Elicit answers.

Answers

1 cloak **2** jewels **3** lamp **4** hat **5** treasure chest

3 Choose and categorize the words in your notebook.

Elicit an example for each category listed. Ask *Which categories would you choose?* Elicit ideas, prompting children to give a reason for their choice. The children choose a pair of categories and list the words in their notebook, then compare with a friend.

Answers

Children's own answers.

Cooler: Find the words

Write a wordsnake on the board.

writewearcomecommunicategosendplayreplyprintreceivemail

Have children come to the front, circle a verb, and give its past tense. Ask for class agreement.

Competency Focus

Think! Critical Thinking

The children use critical thinking skills to understand the vocabulary by using visual clues and processing the written and spoken forms.

Digital Resources

Digital Activity Book • Use the AB page to give feedback on activities, using the built-in interactive activities or answer keys.

Grammar

Lesson objective: ask and answer about possessions
Key grammar: *Whose (cloak) is this? (This cloak) is mine/yours/hers/his/theirs/ours.*
Secondary language: *costume, magic lamp, money, pants, party dress*
Materials: Track 6.2; Grammar Worksheet 6A [TRC printout] (optional)

Warmer: Play "The Shark Game"

Play the game with *treasure* and *jewels*
(see Games Bank p. 19).

---

1))) 6.2 Listen and read. What are the children looking for?

- Have the children look at the pictures. Ask *Where are they?* (*in a store*) *What can you do in this store?* (*rent costumes*)

- Play Track 6.2. The children listen and read along. Ask *What are the children looking for?* (*a Cinderella costume, a queen costume, an Aladdin costume, and a pirate costume*)

- Play Track 6.2 again. Ask further questions, e.g. *Whose glass shoes are they?* (*Cinderella's*) *Whose cloak is it?* (*the queen's*) *Whose sword is it?* (*the pirate's*) *Whose magic lamp is it?* (*Aladdin's*) Have the children vote on the best costume.

Grammar Central

Whose cloak is this? ...

Have the children look at the patterns. Point out the difference between *This is her cloak.* and *This cloak is hers.* (*We don't use a noun after hers.*) Take one of your pens, and ask *Whose is this?* Elicit *It's yours.* Ask about other children's objects to elicit all the possessive pronouns.

For extra practice, try the **Grammar Booster** section in the Student Book (p.88)

Answers p. 88

Activity 1: **2** hers **3** yours **4** his **5** your **6** their **7** Whose **8** mine **9** Whose **10** hers

Activity 2: **2** **3** mine **4** yours **5** Whose **6** hers **7** theirs **8** mine

2 Write about the people.

- Read the example sentence. Ask *What else is hers?* (*the glass shoes*)

- Have the children choose one item for each person and write a sentence about it. Elicit sentences and check with the class.

Answers

1 The dress is hers. **2** The pants are / magic lamp is his.
3 The hat/sword/treasure chest is his. **4** The money is hers.

3 Ask and answer about things in the classroom.

- Have two children read the example dialogue.
- Divide the class into pairs. They take turns asking and answering questions about things in the classroom. Give support as necessary.
- Invite pairs to ask and answer a question for the class.

Optional activity: Play "The Yes/No Game"

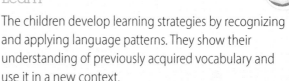

Have a child stand up. Hold up children's objects and ask *Is this Lucy's eraser? Is this Tomas' backpack?* Have the child answer truthfully without using *yes* or *no*, but *It isn't. It's Bert's.*, or *It's mine.* If the child answers *yes* or *no*, they are out, and another child takes their place. If within a minute the child has not said *yes* or *no*, they win.

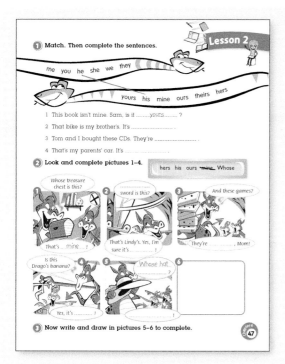

1 Match. Then complete the sentences.

The children match the pronouns. Elicit answers. Then they complete the sentences using the correct possessive forms. Elicit answers.

Answers

me—mine, you—yours, he—his, she—hers, we—ours, they—theirs

1 yours **2** his **3** ours **4** theirs

2 Look and complete pictures 1–4.

The children complete the speech bubbles using the words supplied. Elicit answers.

Answers

1 mine **2** Whose, hers **3** ours **4** his

3 Now write and draw in pictures 5–6 to complete.

The children write speech bubbles for picture 5 and write and draw an ending for the story in picture 6. Invite children to read their ending to the class.

Answers

5 Whose hat is this? It's yours.
6 Children's own answer.

Cooler: Make a wordsearch

Show how to make a wordsearch by drawing a 10 by 10 grid on the board. There should be space for one letter in each square. Insert a few possessive pronouns, some horizontally and some vertically, with some intersecting. Have the children draw their grids in their notebook, and write in seven possessive pronouns, then fill in the empty spaces with random letters. Then they swap and do a friend's wordsearch. Monitor and check spelling.

Competency Focus

Learn

The children develop learning strategies by recognizing and applying language patterns. They show their understanding of previously acquired vocabulary and use it in a new context.

Digital Resources

Student eBook • Use *Highlighter* to focus on key grammar structures in SB Activity 1.

Teacher Resource Center • For extra grammar practice, print out Grammar Worksheet 6A.

Reading: Story Extract

Lesson objectives: check who something belongs to; predict story content from title and pictures; read the extract from *Aladdin* (middle)
Functional language: *Whose … is this? It's … 's. Are you sure it's hers? Yes, it has …*
Secondary language: *command, feast, genie, rub, sneaky, wish*
Materials: Tracks 6.3 and 6.4

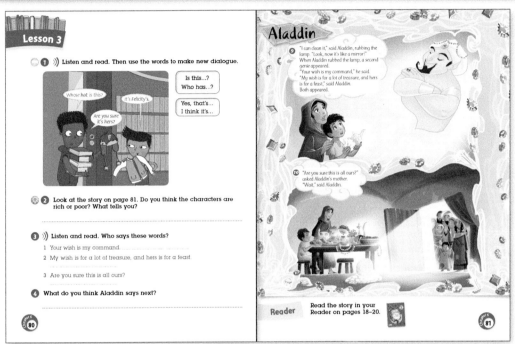

Warmer: Play "Tic-Tac-Toe"

Play the game with *ring / hers, sword / ours, cloak / his, treasure chest / theirs, lamp / mine, mirror / hers, hat / his, jewels / yours, shoes / mine* (see Games Bank p. 19). To win a square, two children have to ask and answer a question using *Whose* and the word pairs, e.g. *Whose ring is it? It's hers.*

Functional language

1))) 6.3 Listen and read. Then act out.

- Ask *What's Jason holding?* (*books and a hat*)
- Play Track 6.3. The children listen and read along. Ask *Whose hat is it?* (*Felicity's*) *Why is Cheng sure?* (*There's an F for Felicity on it.*)
- Play Track 6.3 again, pausing for the children to repeat. Then they act out in pairs. Encourage them to sustitute different items and people.

Note: The **Reading Strategy** activity for this chapter is best done *before* you read the extract. See p. 143 and the Literacy Handbook for details.

Before reading

2 Look at the characters. Do you think they are rich or poor? What tells you?

- The children look at the story title and the pictures. Elicit what characters they see. (*a woman and a boy, a genie*) They write whether the woman and her son are rich or poor, giving reasons. Elicit answers. (*I think they are rich because there's a lot of food on the table / poor because they look hungry and have old clothes.*)
- Elicit ideas on what the story is about.

3))) 6.4 Listen and read. Who says these words?

- Play Track 6.4 and have the children listen and read along.
- Give the children time to read the words and write who says them—Aladdin, his mother, or the genie.

- Play Track 6.4 again for the children to check their answers. Elicit answers.

Answers

1 genie **2** Aladdin **3** Aladdin's mother

4 What do you think Aladdin says next?

- Have the children write what they think Aladdin says next. Elicit ideas including reasons but do not confirm. Say they will have to read the story to find out.

Answers

Children's own answers.

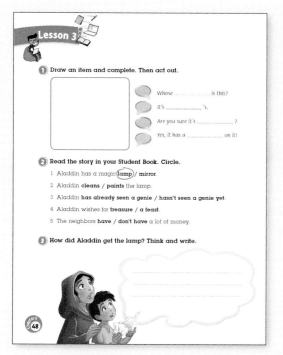

1 Draw an item and complete. Then act out.

The children draw an item and complete the dialogue, then act it out. Have pairs act out for the class.

Answers

Children's own answers.

2 Read the story in your Student Book. Circle.

The children read the Student Book story extract again. They answer the questions by circling the correct option in each pair. Elicit answers.

Answers

1 lamp **2** cleans **3** has already seen a genie **4** treasure **5** don't have

3 How did Aladdin get the lamp? Think and write.

Elicit ideas orally. The children write their answers then compare them in small groups. Do they agree? Elicit responses.

Answers

Children's own answers.

Cooler: It has an "M" on it!

In pairs, the children act out the dialogue from Activity 1 again, replacing *Felicity* and *F* with the name of a child from the class, e.g. *It's Marco's. Are you sure it's his? Yes, it has an "M" on it!*

Competency Focus

Collaborate and Communicate

The children act out an authentic dialogue together, putting into practice the functional language.

Think! Critical Thinking

The children apply reading skills (exploiting pictures and text clues) to understand the story.

Digital Resources

Student eBook • Look at the picture numbers in the story extract. Explain it comes from near the end and elicit ideas on what happened before.

Aladdin

1

Once upon a time, a poor boy named Aladdin lived with his mother.

A bad magician met Aladdin in the market. He needed a boy to steal treasure from a magic cave.

2

"I'm your uncle!" said the magician.

Aladdin was surprised. The sneaky magician gave Aladdin beautiful gifts.

"Take this ring, it's yours. Your mother needs money. I can take care of you both."

3

Aladdin took the magician to meet his mother.

Aladdin's mother was surprised. "I haven't met this man before, but you should do what your uncle says," she told her son. "We need his help."

"Well," said the magician, "there is something you can do to help me."

4

He took Aladdin into the desert. They walked and walked over the sand. Finally, they stopped at a door in the ground. The magician opened it with magic words.

"Find the lamp," said the magician. "It's mine. Bring it to me."

5

Aladdin climbed down into the cave. Treasure sparkled in chests all around. He took a lot of jewels, and put them in his pockets. He shouted, "I've found the lamp!" He reached up and took the lamp.

6

"It's mine. Give it to me," said the magician. But Aladdin saw a dangerous look in his eye.

"Help me climb out," Aladdin said.

"Give me the lamp first," the magician shouted.

"Are you sure it's yours?" asked Aladdin.

The magician was very angry with Aladdin. He called up a desert wind so strong it blew the magician away and he disappeared forever.

Suddenly, the door closed.

7

Aladdin cried. He didn't know what to do. Wiping his eyes, he put on the ring from the magician. When he put it on, a genie appeared.

Aladdin couldn't believe his eyes.

"Make a wish," said the genie.

"I wish to be home!"

8

FLASH! Aladdin was home.

When Aladdin's mother saw him, she was very happy. He showed her the jewels and the lamp.

"We can sell the lamp to buy food."

9

"I can clean it." said Aladdin, rubbing the lamp. "Look, now it's like a mirror!"

When Aladdin rubbed the lamp, a second genie appeared.

"Your wish is my command," he said.

"My wish is for a lot of treasure, and hers is for a feast," said Aladdin. Both appeared.

10

"Are you sure this is all ours?" asked Aladdin's mother.

"Wait," said Aladdin.

12

"As long as the lamp is ours, we can all eat," said Aladdin.

Lesson objective: read and understand the Middle Eastern folk tale *Aladdin* in the Reader
Materials: Track 6.5; Reader

Warmer: Aladdin's lamp

Draw a magic lamp on the board. Ask two children to demonstrate. One (Aladdin) rubs the lamp. The other (the genie) says *Your wish is my command.*, and Aladdin responds, e.g. *I'd like an ice cream.* Repeat with other children.

Story Summary

An evil magician, claiming to be Aladdin's uncle, tricks him into stealing treasure. The magician escapes, leaving Aladdin trapped in a cave. A genie helps Aladdin return home. Aladdin and his mom ask a second genie to give them treasure and a feast. They share the feast with all of their neighbors.

Value: Don't trust strangers

))) 6.5 While reading

- Have the children look at the pictures in the Reader. Elicit where Aladdin is in different pictures.

- Play Track 6.5. The children listen and read along. Ask *Does Aladdin's life change?* (*Yes—at the beginning he's poor and at the end he's rich.*)

- Play Track 6.5 again. Ask questions to check comprehension, e.g. *What lie did the magician tell Aladdin?* (that he was his uncle) *What did he give Aladdin?* (a ring) *Where did he take Aladdin?* (to a cave in the desert) *What did he do?* (He left Aladdin in the cave.) *What did Aladdin do?* (He put on the ring and the genie took him home.)

After reading: Reflect

- Ask questions to give the children the opportunity to think about the issues raised by the story, e.g. *Was it a good idea for Aladdin to go with the magician? Aladdin shared his treasure with his neighbors: was he generous or silly? Would you do the same thing?*

Optional activity: A wish for the world

The children draw a magic lamp on one side of a piece of paper and on the other write a wish that will help everyone in the world. Elicit responses.

Story Time

Practice telling the story first

Practice telling the story before you do so in the classroom. When there is little or no dialogue, you can ask a lot of questions without interrupting the story: ask questions about the pictures, the feelings of the characters, what happens next, etc. The children will feel more involved with the story.

Reading Strategy

Possible Sentences

Possible Sentences is a strategy that encourages readers to anticipate what will happen in the story. The children use key words taken from the story to try and guess what the plot is. With this strategy, the children expand their vocabulary and develop their critical thinking skills.

For additional explanation and activities, see the Literacy Handbook on the Teacher's Resource Center.

Cooler: Play "Who said it?"

In pairs, have the children take turns reading a line of dialogue from the story and identifying the character speaking.

Digital Resources

Reader eBook • Run through the story as a class. Focus on the characters in key scenes and elicit how they are feeling, e.g. the magician in Picture 6, Aladdin's mother in Picture 8, Aladdin in Picture 12.

Reading Comprehension and Critical Literacy

Lesson objectives: identify words with negative connotations; relate the story to personal experiences

Materials: Track 6.5; Reader

Lesson 4 Time to Think

1.))) Read the story in your Reader on pages 18–20 again.

2. Number the events from the story in order.

Reading Report

a Aladdin wished to be home. ☐

b At home, Aladdin rubbed the lamp. ☐

c A second genie appeared and gave Aladdin treasure and food. ☐

d A magician asked Aladdin to help him find a lamp. ☐

e Aladdin was trapped in a cave with the lamp. ☐

f When Aladdin rubbed his ring, a genie appeared. ☐

g Aladdin and his mother shared food with their neighbors. ☐

3. Write another wish for Aladdin and his mother to help their neighborhood.

I Can Read and Write!
How do we know that the magician is bad? Find words and details that tell us this.

4. Talk about the story.
Do you know any other stories about people who have wishes?

82

Note: Please ensure that your class has read the Reader story before you do this lesson.

Warmer: Play "Ready, Set, Draw!"

Play the game using *cloak, hat, jewels, lamp, mirror, ring, sword, treasure chest* (see Games Bank p. 19).

---

1))) 6.5 Read the story in your Reader.

- Have the children read the story. (Alternatively, play Track 6.5 and have them read along.) Elicit whether they were correct in their predictions in Lesson 3 Activity 4.

- Check comprehension by asking *Did Aladdin do the right thing in going with his "uncle?" What was Aladdin's wish when he got home?* (for a lot of treasure) *Was it a good one? Is everyone happy at the end? Why?*

2 Number the events from the story in order.

- Have the children do the activity in pairs. Have children read their answers for the class to agree.

Answers

a 4 b 5 c 6 d 1 e 2 f 3 g 7

I Can Read and Write!

Say *Sneaky—good or bad?* (bad) Have the children look at the story and find other words and details about the magician that indicate he is bad. Elicit answers.

3 Write another wish for Aladdin and his mother to help their neighborhood.

- Have the children read out Aladdin's wishes. (*I wish to be home. My wish is for a lot of treasure.*) Have the children write another wish for Aladdin and his mother. They can decide in pairs.

- Elicit ideas.

Answers

Children's own answers.

4 Talk about the story.

- Have the children read Jason's question, and think about other stories with magic wishes. Elicit answers.

- Ask *Would you ask the genie for a wish for you, for your family, for your neighborhood, or for the planet?* Give the children time to think. Have children say their wishes and discuss them with the class.

Optional activity: Play "Sit Down If …"

Have the class stand and hold up a picture they drew for the Warmer. Say *Sit down if you have a cloak!* Children holding a cloak sit down. Continue until all the children are sitting down. Repeat, with different children prompting in your place.

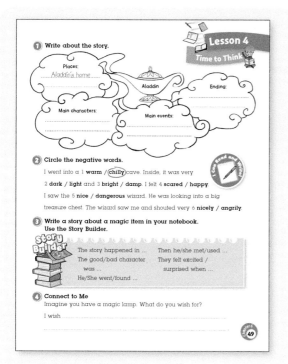

1 Write about the story.

The children complete the activity in pairs, referring to the Reader if necessary. Elicit answers.

Answers (suggested)

Places: Aladdin's home, a cave in the desert, the market

Main characters: Aladdin, Aladdin's mom, genies, magician, neighbors

Main events: Aladdin meets the magician. Aladdin finds the lamp in the cave. The genies give Aladdin his wishes.

Ending: Aladdin is rich. He shares the food and treasure. They have a feast.

2 Circle the negative words.

The children practice the **I Can Read and Write!** feature by circling the negative words to complete the story. Elicit answers.

Answers

1 chilly **2** dark **3** damp **4** scared **5** dangerous **6** angrily

3 Write a story about a magic item in your notebook. Use the Story Builder.

Use the **Story Builder** prompts to elicit ideas. The children write a story in their notebook, then swap with a friend to check. Have children read their story for the class.

Answers

Children's own answers.

4 Connect to Me

Elicit ideas on what the children would wish for if they had a magic lamp (e.g. *a new bike, a vacation,* etc.) before they write their own response. Elicit responses.

Answers

Children's own answers.

Cooler: Continue the story

 6.5

Tell the children to listen carefully because you are going to stop the CD so they can continue the story. Play the CD, pausing every so often to elicit what happens next.

Competency Focus

Me: Critical Literacy

The children use critical literacy skills to reflect on the theme of the story and relate it to their personal experience.

Digital Resources

Student eBook • For SB I Can Read and Write!, have children use *Highlighter* to identify the words and details in the story that show the magician is bad.

Digital Activity Book • TIP For AB Activity 3, use *Highlighter* to focus on the Story Builder sentence openings, one by one, and elicit a range of endings.

Student eBook, Digital Activity Book • TIP You can move the answer key pop-up window to show the answers by the activity.

Vocabulary, Song, and Spelling

Lesson objectives: practice storytelling; practice spelling words with *j* and *g*
Key vocabulary: *appeared, disappeared, found, hid, put (it) on, rubbed, stole*
Secondary language: *bazaar, in a flash*
Materials: Tracks 6.6 and 6.7; Phonics Worksheet 6 [TRC printout] (optional)

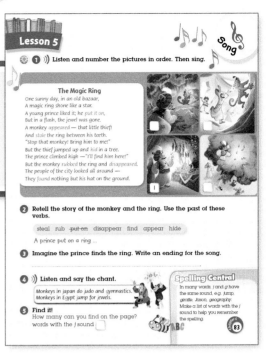

Warmer: Pre-teach vocabulary

Pre-teach the vocabulary using mimes. Have the children mime each one with you, then mime and repeat. Then mime to elicit the words.

1))) 6.6 Listen and number the pictures in order. Then sing.

- Have the children look at the pictures and say what is going on. (They may need L1.)
- Play Track 6.6. They listen and number the pictures in the order they are mentioned. Elicit answers.
- Play Track 6.6 again, and have the children sing along. Half the class can mime being the prince and the other half the monkey.

Answers

3, 2, 1, 4

2 Retell the story of the monkey and the ring. Use the past of these verbs.

- Elicit the past tense of the verbs.
- Retell the story as a class with as many children as possible saying something about it.
- Have the children retell the story in pairs, using the verbs and without referring to the song if possible. Monitor and check pronunciation.

3 Imagine the prince finds the ring. Write an ending for the song.

- Elicit ideas. The children write a new ending in pairs, if possible making their endings rhyme.
- Invite children to read their endings to the class.

Answers

Children's own answers.

Spelling Central

Letters *j* and *g* for the *j* sound

Say the *j*/*g* words for the children to repeat. Have them say other words with *j* and *g* and write them on the board, e.g. *Jupiter, jeans, orange, gym*.

4))) 6.7 Listen and say the chant.

- Ask *What can you see?*
- Play Track 6.7. The children listen and read along. Elicit the words with *j* and *g*.
- Play Track 6.7 again, pausing for the children to repeat.

5 Find it!

- Set a time limit for the children to find words with the *j* sound on the page. Elicit answers.
- Elicit any other words with the *j* sound they know.

Answers

13—magic, jewel, jumped, imagine, Japan, judo, gymnastics, Egypt, jump, jewels, giraffe, Jason, geography

Optional activity: Guess the word

Divide the class into three groups. Have a child from each group sit in a chair with their backs to the board, facing their group. Write a story verb on the board (e.g. *appear, disappear, find, hide, put on, rub, steal*) so that the children cannot see it but their groups can. The groups have to mime the action so that their teammate guesses the word first. The first child to guess the word gets a point for their team.

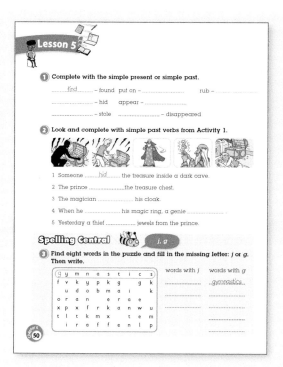

1 Complete with the simple present or simple past.

The children write the missing verbs. Elicit answers.

Answers

find—found, hide—hid, steal—stole, put on—put on, appear—appeared, disappear—disappeared, rub—rubbed

2 Look and complete with simple past verbs from Activity 1.

The children complete the sentences with the verbs from Activity 1. Elicit answers.

Answers

1 hid **2** found **3** put on **4** rubbed, appeared **5** stole

3 Find eight words in the puzzle and fill in the missing letter: *j* or *g*. Then write.

To practice the **Spelling Central** feature, the children find the words in the wordsearch, writing in *j* or *g* each time to complete them. Then they write the words in the correct category. Elicit answers.

Answers

Words with j: judo, jewel, jump

Words with g: gymnastics, garage, giant, orange, giraffe

Cooler: Sing and do

 6.6

Agree on actions for the different verbs in the song. Play Track 6.6 twice for the children to sing along and do the actions.

Competency Focus

Think! Critical Thinking

The children use critical thinking skills to identify written and spoken forms of new words, and match each word with its visual representation.

Digital Resources

Student eBook • Choose the karaoke version of Music Video 6.1 (6.2) and encourage the children to dance and sing along, using the lyrics on screen. Pause the video for the children to continue dancing and singing.

Teacher Resource Center • For phonics practice, print out Phonics Worksheet 6.

Student eBook • Remind the children they can access Music Video 6.1 (6.2) at home to practice the song and dance moves.

Grammar and Reading

Lesson objective: talk about simultaneous events in the past

Key grammar: *When I opened (my eyes), I saw (my dog). When I (rubbed his nose), he disappeared.*

Secondary language: *author, latest, rub*

Materials: Track 6.8; Grammar Worksheet 6B [TRC printout] (optional)

Warmer: Play "Verb Ping-Pong"

Divide the class into two teams. You "serve" the first verb in the present tense, e.g. *open.* The first team gives the simple past form, e.g. *opened.* The teams continue taking turns with different verbs. Each correct answer gets a point. The team with the most points wins.

1))) 6.8 Listen and read. Has Cheng read *My Dog's Magic?*

- Have the children look at the pictures. Point to Bob Black and ask *Who do you think this is?* Elicit ideas. Pre-teach *author* and *latest.*

- Play Track 6.8. The children listen and read along. Ask *Has Cheng read* My Dog's Magic*? (Yes, he has.)*

- Play Track 6.8 again and ask *What's happening at Story Central? (An author is giving a talk.) What's going to come out in November? (a movie of* My Dog's Magic*) What did Bob Black give Miguel? (a copy of* My Dog's More Magic*)*

2 Imagine and write about your dog.

- Ask *Do you have a dog?* Elicit answers. Tell children who do not have a dog to imagine one.

- Do an example with the class, e.g. *When I rubbed his nose, he started to fly.* Have the children complete the sentences. Encourage them to be as inventive as possible! Then they compare answers in pairs.

- Invite children to read a sentence for the class.

Answers

Children's own answers.

Grammar Central

When I opened my eyes, I saw my dog. …

Have the children look at the patterns. Elicit the tense of the verbs. (*simple past*) Ask the children which action happened first and which second. (*the* when *action happened first*)

For extra practice, try the **Grammar Booster** section in the Student Book (pp. 89–91)

Answers p. 89

Activity 1: **2** saw **3** arrived **4** sat **5** When **6** cried **7** went **8** started

Activity 2: **2** When, covered **3** rubbed, appeared **4** When, changed **5** spoke, understood

Activity 3: Children's own answers.

p. 90

Activity 1: **2** appeared **3** mine **4** yours **5** When **6** sat **7** saw

Activity 2: **2** When he went into the water, he saw a giant crab. **3** The giant said the rock was his. **4** Whose guitar was it?

p. 92

Activity 1: **2** his **3** hers **4** looked **5** found **6** seen **7** mine **8** When **9** put **10** jumped **11** couldn't

Activity 2: Children's own answers.

Optional activity: Play "My Dog's Magic"

Divide the class into two teams. Prompt with *"When I …"* sentence openings from the story (in random order) for the teams to complete. A correct answer wins one point. The team with the most points wins.

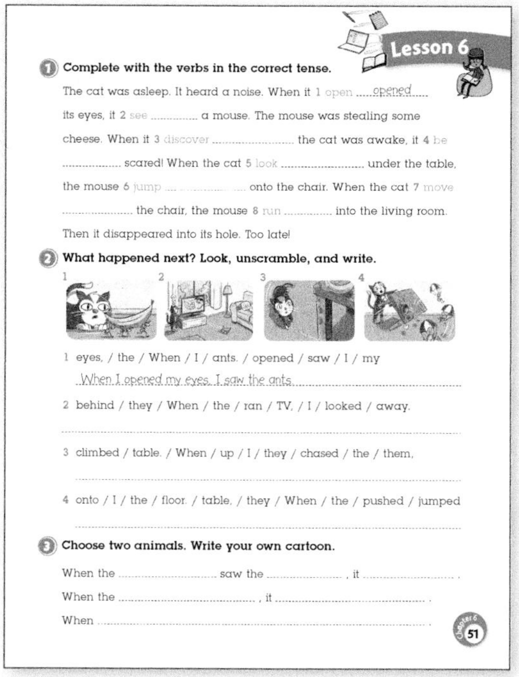

Elicit ideas for situations, e.g. … *I went to Mars / I met a pirate*. Write them on the board with *When* (e.g. *When I went to Mars, …*). Give the children two minutes to discuss possible conclusions to the sentences. Encourage them to be inventive. Elicit responses.

Competency Focus

Learn

The children develop learning strategies by recognizing and applying language patterns in different contexts.

(Student Book page reproduction)

1 Complete with the verbs in the correct tense.

The cat was asleep. It heard a noise. When it 1 open ____opened____ its eyes, it 2 see _____ a mouse. The mouse was stealing some cheese. When it 3 discover _____ the cat was awake, it 4 be _____ scared! When the cat 5 look _____ under the table, the mouse 6 jump _____ onto the chair. When the cat 7 move _____ the chair, the mouse 8 run _____ into the living room. Then it disappeared into its hole. Too late!

2 What happened next? Look, unscramble, and write.

1 eyes, / the / When / I / ants. / opened / saw / I / my
When I opened my eyes, I saw the ants.

2 behind / they / When / the / ran / TV, / I / looked / away.

3 climbed / table. / When / up / I / they / chased / the / them.

4 onto / I / the / floor. / table, / they / When / the / pushed / jumped

3 Choose two animals. Write your own cartoon.

When the _____ saw the _____ , it _____ .
When the _____ , it _____ .
When _____ .

51

---

1 Complete with the verbs in the correct tense.

The children complete the story with the correct form of the verbs supplied, then compare in pairs. Elicit answers.

Answers

1 opened 2 saw 3 discovered 4 was 5 looked 6 jumped 7 moved 8 ran

2 What happened next? Look, unscramble, and write.

The children unscramble and write the sentences. Elicit answers.

Answers

1 When I opened my eyes, I saw the ants.
2 When I looked behind the TV, they ran away.
3 When I chased them, they climbed up the table.
4 When I pushed the table, they jumped onto the floor.

3 Choose two animals. Write your own cartoon.

Elicit ideas. The children write a short story for a cartoon. Invite children to read their story to the class.

Answers

Children's own answers.

Digital Resources

Student eBook • Use *Timer* to give the class one minute to look at SB Activity 1. Elicit what happens in that picture. Repeat with a different picture.

Teacher Resource Center • For extra grammar practice, print out Grammar Worksheet 6B.

CLIL: Science—Real-world magic

Lesson objective: find out about real-world phenomena which seem magic
Materials: CLIL Graphic Organizer 6 [TRC printout] (optional)

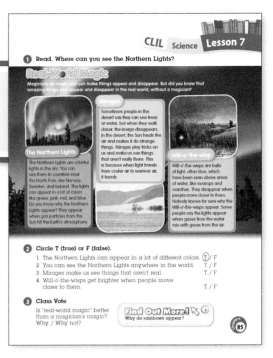

Warmer: Play "Vocabulary Review"

Play the game with *sword, cloak, treasure chest, jewels, appear, disappear, steal* (see Games Bank p. 19).

1 Read. Where can you see the Northern Lights?

- The children look at the pictures. Ask *What's the article about?* Elicit ideas.

- The children read the first text. Ask *Where can you see the Northern Lights?* (*near the North Pole, e.g. in Norway, Sweden, Iceland*)

- The children read the rest of the text. Ask *Where can you see a mirage?* (*in the desert*) *What is the will-o'-the-wisp?* (*balls of light which people see in swamps or marshes*) *What do all three phenomena have in common?* (*They're light effects.*)

2 Circle T (true) or F (false).

- Have the children circle T (true) or F (false) for each sentence.

- Elicit answers, including the correct version of the false sentences.

Answers

1 T 2 F 3 T 4 F

3 Class Vote

- Elicit other real-world magic (e.g. *lightning, rainbows, shooting stars, tornadoes,* etc.) and tricks a magician does (e.g. *card tricks, making coins disappear, moving things without touching them,* etc.).

- Have the children think about the question and then vote. They put their hands on the desk if they think real-world magic is better. They put their hands under the desk if they think a magician's magic is better. Count the votes.

- Elicit why the children think as they do: real-world magic better (*real, can be very big and impressive*); magician's magic better (*smart, can be funny*).

Find Out More!

Ask the children to research why rainbows appear. Suggest appropriate resources, e.g. Internet, library books, etc. The children will need to complete this research before doing the follow-up activity in the Activity Book. (It could be set as homework.)

Optional activity: When I …

Start by saying *When I got home, …* Have a child complete the sentence, e.g. *I ate dinner.* The next child continues, saying another sentence starting with *When,* e.g. *When I ate dinner, …* Continue in this way around the class or play in small groups.

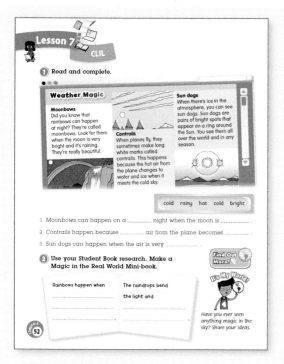

Divide the class into small groups. Say *When I got home, I had dinner. What did you do?* Have the first child in each group answer, then turn to the next child on the right and ask the question.

Competency Focus

Act

The children carry out research to find out more about rainbows. This helps them expand their learning and relate it to their world, both inside and outside the classroom.

1 Read and complete.

The children read the texts and then complete sentences using the words supplied. Elicit answers.

Answers

1 rainy, bright **2** hot, cold **3** cold

2 Use your Student Book research. Make a Magic in the Real World Mini-book.

Divide the class into groups of four. Have the children pool the information learned from their research in the Student Book and the Activity Book. They write about rainbows to make their mini-book individually. Have the children read their sentences to the class.

Answers

Children's own answers.

It's My World!

The children discuss in small groups anything magic they have seen in the sky. Elicit ideas, e.g. *an eclipse, a shooting star, lightning,* etc. Ask *Do you know how/why this phenomenon happens?*

Digital Resources

Student eBook, Digital Activity Book, Reader eBook, CLIL eBook • Remember—do not be afraid to turn off the screen! Work the materials into your teaching in the way that suits you best.

Teacher Resource Center • Print out CLIL Graphic Organizer 6 for the children to collate their Find Out More! research.

CLIL eBook • The children can use the CLIL eBook to expand their knowledge of the lesson topic.

Project

Lesson objectives: review language from Chapter 6; make and present an optical illusion

Materials: posterboard, paper, colored pencils/markers, scissors, glue, hole punch, rubber bands; two game pieces and a coin for each pair

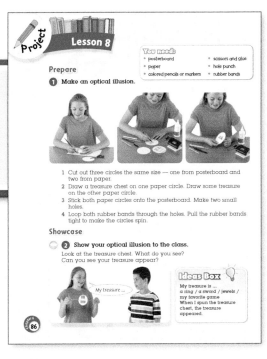

Warmer: Play "Disappearing Text"

Write a few sentences on the board, e.g. *The magician said the magic lamp was his. "It's not yours," said the dragon. "It's mine."* Have the children read it aloud. Erase a word and have the children read the whole sentence again. Continue erasing words until children are saying the text without any prompts.

Prepare

1 Make an optical illusion.

- Distribute the materials. Read through the instructions together and ensure the children are clear on what to do.

- Have the children follow the instructions to make an optical illusion. Give support as necessary.

Alternative craft activity

An easier project is for the children to hold their hands in front of them at eye level, with their index fingers pointing towards each other. They leave a little space between their fingers, and stare at a wall or an object in the distance. They should see a finger with two ends floating in between their two index fingers. If they have problems seeing it, have them try moving their fingers towards their eyes, but keeping them at eye level.

Showcase

2 Show your optical illusion to the class.

- Divide the class into small groups. Explain to the children that they will now present their optical illusion to the group, using the **Ideas Box** for support.

- Listen in to the presentations. Have each group choose a child to present to the class.

Optional activity: Play "The When Game"

Brainstorm verbs the children know and write about 20 on the board, e.g. *steal, hide, go out, find, rub, appear, put on, leave,* etc. Divide the class into two teams. Have a child from Team A begin a sentence (e.g. *When I walked out, I …*) for a child from Team B to complete. If the child completes the sentence correctly, both teams get a point. If they do not, only Team A gets a point. Have the teams take turns providing beginnings and endings.

1 Play "Magic Worlds!"

See p. 43 for instructions on how to play the game.

Answers

1 cloak **2** disappeared **3** . . . is mine! **4** When Aladdin rubbed the lamp, a genie appeared. **5** hers **6** Children's own answer. **7** *any words starting with j*, e.g. jump, judo **8** *any two of:* Northern lights, mirage, contrails, moonbows, sundogs **9** a mirror **10** Children's own answer.

Cooler: Play "Sentence Builders"

Divide the class into two teams. Give each team a large sheet of paper (positioned so the other team cannot see it) and a pen. Read out a sentence question using key language from the chapter. The first child writes the first word, the next child the next word, and so on. When they have finished, the teams check each other's sentence. Each correct word wins a point. The team with the most points wins.

Competency Focus

Collaborate and Communicate

By working together, the children consolidate their understanding of the language learned in a way which they will find fun and engaging. They also demonstrate their ability to work with friends and use interpersonal skills.

Digital Resources

Student eBook • Show the Prepare pictures, stage by stage, as you talk the class through the activity process.

Language Review

Lesson objective: review language from Chapter 6
Materials: Tracks 6.6, 6.9, AB 6.1, AB 6.2 and AB 6.3

Warmer: Play "Board Race"

Divide the class into two or more teams. Have a child from each team stand up and give them a board marker. Define a word from Lesson 1 or a verb from Lesson 2. The children race to write it first on the board. The first to write it correctly wins a point. Repeat with different words and children.

1))) **6.9 Listen and write K (Katy), J (Joe), or T (Toby).**

- Have the children look at the picture and name the objects they can see.
- Play Track 6.9. The children listen and label the objects with the initial of the person they belong to (K, J, or T). Elicit answers.

Audioscript

Katy: *Look! Here's our dress-up box. Let's put on some costumes and play.*
Joe: *OK. Look at this cloak. Is that yours, Toby?*
Toby: *No, it's not mine. That's for the princess costume, so it's Katy's.*
Joe: *How about this hat?*
Toby: *That's the spy's hat, so it's mine.*
Joe: *Well, what about these boots?*
Katy: *They're for the pirate, Joe—so they're yours.*
Toby: *Hey, look at this sword! Whose is that?*
Joe: *That's mine, too. The pirate likes to fight.*
Toby: *What about the magic ring?*
Joe: *Give that to Katy—it's hers for the princess.*
Katy: *Thanks, Toby. What's left now?*
Joe: *Just these glasses.*
Katy: *Give them to Toby—they're for the spy.*
Joe: *OK. Let's put our costumes on and have some fun!*

Answers

boots J, hat T, ring K, glasses T, cloak K, sword J

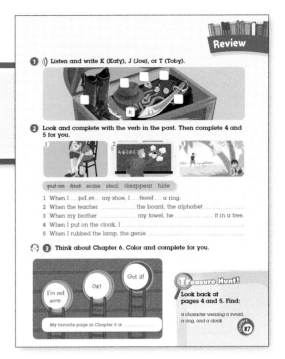

2 Look and complete with the verb in the past. Then complete 4 and 5 for you.

- Have the children complete the sentences.

Answers

1 put on, found **2** erased, disappeared **3** stole, hid
4–5 Children's own answers.

3 Think about Chapter 6. Color and complete for you.

- Children color the circle which represents how they feel about their own progress (self-evaluation).

Treasure Hunt!

Have the children look at pp. 4–5, and find a character wearing a sword, a ring, and a cloak.

Cooler: Sing a line

))) **6.6**

Play Track 6.6 for the children to sing along. Then divide the class into two groups. Have a child in each group sing a line of the song. Continue the song between the groups.

Competency Focus

Me: Self-evaluation
The children reflect on the chapter and express their opinions about their own progress.

Chapter 6 Exam Booster

1 Reading and Writing
Look at the picture and read the story. Write some words to complete the sentences about the story. You can use 1, 2, or 3 words.

The Princess and the Dragon

A beautiful princess lived in a palace with her father, the King. She wanted to find the King's lost treasure. So she put on her father's cloak and hat and took his sword. She went out into the forest.
It was dark and she couldn't see well. She fell over something. What was it? She looked carefully and saw an old lamp. When she rubbed it, a yellow light appeared. Now she could see the path through the forest.
The princess arrived at the mountain. She went into the dark cave, holding her magic lamp. She saw a treasure chest full of jewels. She heard a noise. She turned around and saw the dragon.
"That treasure is mine," said the dragon. "No, it isn't. It belongs to the King – it's his!" She picked up the treasure chest. Then she rubbed the lamp – and disappeared!
The dragon was very surprised and unhappy because he lost the treasure.

Example

The princess decided to find her ....father's........ treasure.

Questions

1 When she went into the forest, she wore a cloak and ....

2 She found .... in the forest.

3 The treasure chest was in ....

4 The dragon thought that .... were his.

5 The dragon wasn't .... when the princess took the treasure. (93)

(94)

2 Listening
))) Listen and draw lines. There is one example.

Sue   Jenny   Tim   Kate

Mike   Daisy   Pete

3 Speaking
)) 1 Listen to the beginning of the story and complete the sentences.

Treasure Tale

(1) ....Today....... , Paul played soccer.

Afterward, he felt very (2) ....

He has already finished reading

his (3) ....

Now he is (4) ....

2 Work with a partner. Look at the pictures and tell the story.

Where is Paul?   What can he see?   What happened?

What is he doing?   What is he wearing?

)) 3 Now listen and compare. Find one detail that is different to the story that you told.

Exam Tip
Read the name of the character and the name of the story. Listen for these names when the examiner describes the first picture.

(95)

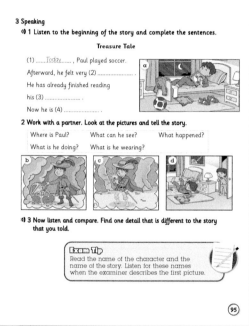

1 Reading and Writing. Look at the picture and read the story. Write some words to complete the sentences about the story. You can use 1, 2, or 3 words.

The children read the text and complete the sentences.
Answers

1 a hat **2** an old lamp **3** a dark cave **4** the jewels **5** happy

2))) AB 6.1 Listening. Listen and draw lines.

Play Track AB 6.1 twice. Children listen and match.
(Audioscript on p. 223)

3.1))) AB 6.2 Speaking. Listen to the beginning of the story and complete the sentences.

Play Track AB 6.2 twice. Children write the missing words.
Answers (Audioscript on p. 223)

2 tired **3** book **4** sleeping

3.2 Speaking. Work with a partner. Look at the pictures and tell the story.

Children discuss what is happening.

3.3))) AB 6.3 Speaking. Now listen and compare. Find one detail that is different to the story that you told.

Play Track AB 6.3 again. The children listen and find differences in the two stories.
(Audioscript on p. 223)

Digital Resources

Teacher Resource Center • Print out Test Chapter 6 to use at the end of this lesson. The Test Generator also allows you to create customized tests.

• For the Cambridge English Young Learners Exam preparation activities, there are speaking prompts available for this chapter.

Student's App • Encourage the children to play the games on their smartphone/tablet. Ask them to record their scores to compare in the next lesson. (*The Inks* Apps are free and available on the App Store and Google Play.)

Chapter 7

Clues and Crimes
Overview

The children will:

- use critical thinking skills to identify clothes and accessories.
- talk about what was happening at a specific time in the past.
- read, understand, and act out a story.
- talk about clues in a crime.
- talk about what was happening when something occurred.
- find out about catching thieves.
- make a thumbprint database.

Key Vocabulary

Clothes and accessories: belt, button, earring, gloves, handbag, necklace, scarf, tie
Clues and crimes: clue, crime, detective, fingerprints, footprints, thief, witness

Key Grammar

- What were you doing (at 2 o'clock yesterday)?
- I was working (in my classroom).
- Was he wearing (a tie)?
- No, he wasn't wearing (a tie).
- I was talking (on the phone) when he took (it).

Reading Skills

Story: *Whodunit?*
Genre: modern detective story

Literacy Development

- predict story content from title and pictures
- interpret and personalize the theme of the story
- learn about narratives in the first person (*I*)

Functional Language

- Excuse me. Can I talk to you for a minute?
- Yes, of course. Is something wrong?

Spelling

The spellings *ue, ew, ou* for the *oo* sound

CLIL: Science—Using fingerprints and footprints to solve crimes

The children find out about how the police catch thieves.

Competency Focus

The children will:

use critical thinking skills to identify clothes and accessories. (Lesson 1)	apply new grammar to previously learned vocabulary. (Lesson 2)	work in pairs to act out a dialogue. (Lesson 3)	personalize the story by thinking about their own experiences in similar situations. (Lesson 4)	develop cultural understanding by finding out about crime detection. (Lesson 7)
predict the content of a story. (Lesson 3)	make connections between events in the past. (Lesson 6)	present their thumbprint database to the class. (Lesson 8)	evaluate their own progress in the chapter. (Review)	
identify and talk about clues in a crime. (Lesson 5)				

Digital Overview

Teacher Presentation

Student eBook and Digital Activity Book

- Oral Storytelling Video 7.1: *Whodunit?*
- Interactive versions of AB activities
- Integrated audio and answer key for all activities

Teacher resources for planning, lesson delivery, and homework

Teacher Resource Center

- Class Planner Chapter 7
- Worksheets to print out (including notes and answers):
    - Grammar Worksheet 7A: What were you doing …? Was he wearing …?
    - Grammar Worksheet 7B: I was talking … when he took it.
    - Phonics Worksheet 7
    - Oral Storytelling Video Worksheet 7: *Whodunit?*
    - CLIL Graphic Organizer 7
    - Test Chapter 7
- Test Generator
- Literacy Handbook

Watch the Oral Storytelling Video

Children's resources for consolidation and practice at home

Student eBook and Reader eBook

- Oral Storytelling Video 7.1: *Whodunit?*

***The Inks* Student's App**

Vocabulary games: Clothes/accessories and clues/crimes

Vocabulary

Lesson objective: identify and talk about clothes and accessories
Key vocabulary: *belt, button, earring, gloves, handbag, necklace, scarf, tie*
Materials: Track 7.1

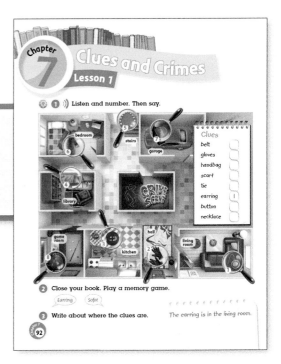

Warmer: Play "House A–Z"

Divide the class into teams. Write the alphabet vertically on the board for the teams to copy. Give them four minutes to write something in their house for every letter, e.g. *armchair, bedroom, closet,* etc. They swap lists with another team to check. Each correct answer wins one point. A correct answer that no other team has wins two. The team with the most points wins.

1))) 7.1 Listen and number. Then say.

- Have the children look at the online game and name the parts of the house. Pre-teach *accessory*.
- Play Track 7.1 twice. The children listen and point.
- Then they write the number of each accessory by the correct word. Elicit answers.
- Say the new words for the children to repeat.

Audioscript

Welcome to Who Stole the Jewels?—the online game where you are the detective. Last night, a thief took jewels from the Professor's house. You have to find out who took the jewels. Luckily, the thief left some clues …

Police found an earring in the living room. The earring was small and green. It was on the sofa. The red sofa. That's your first clue.

Police also found some gloves. They're small and black. They were
on the floor in the hall. Maybe the thief has small hands!

Now, we go into the kitchen. Look, a button on the table! Police think it came from the thief's coat. It's blue, so look for a blue coat.

The next clue is in the library. Look on the shelf. Can you see the green scarf? It's next to that brown book.

Now go up the stairs. The necklace is hanging on the stairs by the window. It's very beautiful. Who left it?

Now we go into the bedroom. The police found a belt in the bedroom. It's under the bed.

Next, look in the garage. Can you see a clue? It's in the car. That's right—it's a handbag.

Hm … A handbag, a necklace, an earring. Was the thief a woman?

But wait! What's this? The last clue is in the game room. Over there, on the pink chair. It's a man's tie!

These are your clues. Now you have to find the thief. Let's play Who Stole the Jewels? …

Answers

belt 6, gloves 2, handbag 7, scarf 4, tie 8, earring 1, button 3, necklace 5

2 Close your book. Play a memory game.

- Give the children 30 seconds to look at the picture and remember the position of the clues. Then have them close their books. Say the items (e.g. *earring*) to elicit the location (e.g. *sofa*).
- Divide the class into pairs. They take turns prompting with a clue for their friend to say where it is (without looking in their book).

3 Write about where the clues are.

- Read the example. Ask *Where's the belt?* to elicit the room. (*The belt is in the bedroom.*)
- Have the children write sentences about the clues in Activity 1 in their notebook. Elicit answers.

Answers

The earring is in the living room. The gloves are in the hall. The button is in the kitchen. The tie is in the game room. The scarf is in the library. The belt is in the bedroom. The necklace is on the stairs. The handbag is in the garage.

Optional activity: Crack the code

Write on the board: *Pira tepe testreasu reche sti sund ert heb igtr eei ti sfu llo fneckl acesa ndearri ngs.* Say *Solve the code to find the treasure.* Divide the class into pairs to figure out the message. If they are stuck, give them the first word (*Pirate*). Elicit the answer, asking children how they figured it out. (*Pirate Pete's treasure chest is under the big tree. It is full of necklaces and earrings.*—The words are split in the wrong place.)

1 Complete the words.

The children label the pictures. Elicit answers.

Answers

1 button **2** necklace **3** gloves **4** belt **5** scarf **6** tie

2 Complete the descriptions.

The children complete descriptions of the characters pictured using the words supplied. Elicit answers.

Answers

1 earrings, necklace **2** gloves, scarf **3** buttons, belt **4** tie **5** handbag

3 Choose and categorize the accessories in your notebook.

Elicit an example for each category listed. Ask *Which categories would you choose?* Elicit ideas, prompting children to give a reason for their choice. The children choose a pair of categories and list the words in their notebook, then compare with a friend.

Answers

Children's own answers.

Cooler: Play "Disappearing Words"

Play the game with *belt, button, earring, gloves, necklace, handbag, scarf, tie* (see Games Bank p. 19).

Competency Focus

Think! Critical Thinking

The children use critical thinking skills to understand the vocabulary by using visual clues and processing the written and spoken forms.

Digital Resources

Student eBook • Play "Kim's Game" with the new vocabulary. Display the SB page and point to the items pictured in Activity 1 to elicit each word. Use *Timer* to give the class one minute to memorize the items, then one minute to recall them. Repeat several times.

Grammar

Lesson objectives: ask and answer about what was happening at a specific time in the past

Key grammar: *What were you doing (at 2 o'clock yesterday)? I was working (in my classroom). Was he wearing (a tie)? No, he wasn't wearing (a tie).*

Secondary language: *office, principal, stole, suspect*

Materials: Track 7.2; Grammar Worksheet 7A [TRC printout] (optional); colored pencils/pens

Warmer: Play "The Shark Game"

Play the game with *necklace* and *earring* (see Games Bank p. 19).

1))) 7.2 Listen and read. Complete the detective's notes.

- Ask *Who's this man?* (*a police officer / a detective*) *Where is he?* (*in a classroom*) *What do you think the crime is?* Have the children read the notes. Pre-teach *office, principal, suspect.*

- Play Track 7.2. The children listen. Elicit the crime. (*Someone stole money from the school office.*)

- Play Track 7.2 again. The children listen and complete the detective's notes. Elicit answers.

- Ask *What did the man look like?* (*tall, thin, worried*) *What did the woman look like?* (*short, with curly brown hair, suspicious*)

Audioscript

Detective Notes: *Someone stole money from Sky View Elementary School yesterday. The money was in the school office. When the principal looked in the office, the money wasn't there. She called the police …*

Detective: *What were you doing at 2 o'clock yesterday?*

Girl: *I was working in my classroom.*

Detective: *Did you see anything unusual?*

Girl: *Yes, I did. I looked out of the window and I saw a man. He was walking very fast and he looked worried. He was tall and thin.*

Detective: *What was he wearing?*

Girl: *He was wearing black pants and a blue jacket. He was wearing a brown belt.*

Detective: *Was he wearing a tie?*

Girl: *No, he wasn't wearing a tie. But it was cold … He was wearing a scarf and black gloves.*

Detective: *What about you? What were you doing?*

Boy: *I was painting—it was my art class. I saw a suspicious-looking woman.*

Detective: *Did you? What did she look like?*

Boy: *She was short, and she had curly brown hair.*

Detective: *What was she wearing?*

Boy: *She was wearing a green skirt and a blue shirt with black buttons. And she was wearing a purple scarf.*

Detective: *Ah … was she wearing earrings?*

Boy: *No, she wasn't.*

Detective: *Was she wearing a necklace?*

Boy: *Yes, she was! It was very big and colorful!*

Teacher: *But that's the school secretary. She was taking the money to the bank!*

Answers

Man suspect—clothes: black pants, a blue jacket, a brown belt, a scarf, black gloves

Woman suspect—clothes: a green skirt, a blue shirt with black buttons, a purple scarf, big and colorful necklace

2))) 7.2 Listen again and circle.

- Play Track 7.2. The children listen and circle *was* or *wasn't* to complete the sentences about the story. Elicit answers.

Answers

1 was **2** wasn't **3** wasn't **4** was

Grammar Central

What were you doing at 2 o'clock yesterday? …

Elicit how the past progressive is formed (*was/were* + verb *–ing*) and used (*to talk about a past action or situation that lasted a long time*). Elicit other examples in the text.

For extra practice, try the **Grammar** section in the Student Book (p. 102)

Answers p. 102

Activity 1: **2** was working **3** was **4** wasn't running **5** was wearing **6** Were **7** weren't eating

Activity 2: **2** was watching **3** was **4** was walking **5** wasn't running **6** Was

Activity 3: Children's own answers.

3 Ask and answer with a friend.

- In pairs, the children take turns asking and answering.

Optional activity: Play "Consequences"

Play the game using *What were you doing at 4 o'clock? Who did you see? What was he/she wearing? What did he/she look like? Who was it?* (see Games Bank p. 19).

Children unscramble and write. Then color the man worksheet image.

1 Unscramble and write. Then color the man.

The children unscramble the questions. Elicit answers. Then they read the questions and answers, and color.

Answers

Who was talking during the movie? What was he wearing? Was he wearing a scarf?

The man in the back row, wearing hat colored as follows: blue jacket, black hat

2 Now look at the picture and complete the notes.

Children look at the picture and write.

Answers

Children's own answers.

3 Choose another person from Activity 1 and color. Then write.

The children choose another person in the picture in Activity 1 and color their clothes. Then they answer questions about the person.

Answers

Children's own answers.

Cooler: Play "The Chain Game"

Say *On Saturday morning, I was shopping at the mall.* Have a child repeat this and add (e.g.) *I was playing in the park.* Continue around the class.

Competency Focus

Learn

The children develop learning strategies by recognizing and applying language patterns. They show their understanding of previously acquired vocabulary and use it in a new context.

Digital Resources

Student eBook, Digital Activity Book • TIP As you monitor the children's progress, use *Add personal note* to keep a note of weaknesses in vocabulary, grammar, or pronunciation so you can review in later lessons.

Teacher Resource Center • For extra grammar practice, print out Grammar Worksheet 7A.

Reading: Story Extract

Lesson objectives: interrupt someone in a polite way; predict story content from title and pictures; read the extract from *Whodunit?* (beginning)
Functional language: *Excuse me, can I talk to you for a minute? Yes, of course. Is something wrong?*
Secondary language: *dig, escape, fur, kitten, maid, suit, to tiptoe*
Materials: Tracks 7.3 and 7.4

Warmer: Detective stories

Ask *Do you like detective stories? What was the last detective story you read / movie you saw? How do detectives find the criminals? What do they study?* Have children talk to the class about the detective stories or movies they read or saw.

Functional language

1))) **7.3   Listen and read. Then act out.**

- Have the children look at the pictures. Ask *Why is Cheng worried?* Elicit ideas.
- Play Track 7.3. The children listen and read along. Elicit other ideas for questions you could ask Felicity.
- Play Track 7.3 again, pausing for the children to repeat. Then they act out the dialogue in pairs. Encourage them to substitute different questions for *What should I get for my grandma's birthday?*

Before reading

2 Look at the story. Why do you think everyone's so busy?

- Explain the story title (*Whodunit?*) means *Who did it?* Have the children look at the pictures.
- Ask *Why is everyone so busy?* The children write their ideas. Elicit answers.

Answers

They're preparing for Grandma Agatha's birthday party.

3))) **7.4   Listen and read. Complete.**

- Play Track 7.4 twice. The children listen and read along.
- The children complete the sentences. Elicit answers.
- Ask *What were the maids doing?* (*cleaning*) *What were the cooks doing?* (*cooking*) *Why was Cousin Flo upset?* (*She couldn't find her fur hat.*)

Answers

1 Grandma Agatha **2** The gardeners **3** Peter **4** Cousin Flo
5 Tilly

4 What do you think happens next?

Have the children think and check one box. Elicit ideas including reasons but do not confirm. Say they will have to read the story to find out.

Answers

Children's own answers.

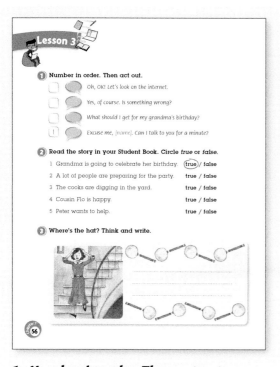

Divide the class into two teams. Start spelling a word (e.g. *button, gloves, necklace, handbag, earring*). When children think they know it, they raise their hand and say it and spell it. If they say and spell the correct word before you finish spelling it, they get one point. If they say the wrong word, they lose a point.

Competency Focus

Collaborate and Communicate

The children act out an authentic dialogue together, putting into practice the functional language.

Think! Critical Thinking

The children apply reading skills (exploiting pictures and text clues) to understand the story.

1 Number in order. Then act out.

Divide the class into pairs to number the lines of dialogue in order, then act it out. Have pairs act out for the class.

Answers

4, 2, 3, 1

2 Read the story in your Student Book. Circle *true* or *false*.

The children read the story extract again and circle true or false for each sentence. Elicit answers, including the correct versions of the false statements.

Answers

1 true **2** true **3** false **4** false **5** true

3 Where's the hat? Think and write.

Elicit ideas. The children write their answers. Elicit responses.

Answers

Children's own answers.

Digital Resources

Student eBook • Use *Highlighter* on *get for my grandma's birthday* and elicit the question with alternative endings.

• Show Picture 1 of the story extract. Ask the class to look at the picture. Elicit ideas on what is happening.

• TIP Store ideas in *Add personal note* for easy access during the lesson (here pictures of clothes and accessories).

Whodunit?

1

It was Grandma Agatha's birthday. Everyone was getting ready for the party. The cooks were cooking, the maids were cleaning, and the gardeners were digging. Peter was getting in everyone's way.

2

Cousin Flo ran down the stairs.

"My new fur hat!" she cried. "I was getting dressed and I saw it wasn't there."

"Hm, a crime," said Peter.

"I think Tilly the cook took it," said Cousin Flo. "She was trying it on."

3

Tilly the cook was making the cake. She didn't know where the hat was.

"I didn't take the hat. I'm very busy, Peter," she said, "and now someone's taken all my cream!"

4

Uncle Alistair was sleeping in the yard.

"Excuse me, Uncle Alistair. Can I talk to you for a minute?"

"Yes, of course," said Uncle Alistair.

"Have you seen Cousin Flo's hat?" asked Peter.

"No," said Uncle Alistair, "but my gloves are missing, too. I think Aunt Nora took them. She said they look silly."

5

Grandma Agatha was arranging flowers. She didn't know where the hat or the gloves were.

"You know, I can't find my handbag either," she said.

6

"Let's find out what's going on," said Peter. "Everyone meet in the living room in ten minutes. I'm going to be the detective."

7

Peter ran to his room. He changed into his suit. He found a belt, a tie, and a pair of glasses. He put on a hat. Now he looked like a real detective.

The cat came over.

"I need a clue, Kitty," said Peter.

8

The family was in the living room.

"Let's solve this crime," said Peter. "First, the hat."

"It was on my bed, then it wasn't there." Cousin Flo looked at Tilly the cook.

"I didn't take it," said Tilly. "I was cooking."

"What about the gloves?" asked Peter.

"Yes, Nora," said Uncle Alistair. "Give them back."

"I haven't seen your gloves. I was busy taking the cat to the vet."

9

"Hm, look, footprints!" said Peter. "Fur hat, handbag, gloves, and cream. A-ha! I think I know who stole these things. Come with me."

10

They went upstairs.

"Shh!" said Peter, "Be very quiet."

"Yes," said Uncle Alistair. "Don't let the thief escape."

Peter opened his bedroom door.

11

He tiptoed over to his dresser. The bottom drawer was open.

"Look inside," said Peter.

Inside, the cat was sleeping. Next to her were eight tiny kittens in a cozy nest made from a fur hat, some gloves, and a nice, soft handbag.

"There's your thief," said Peter. "Case closed."

Lesson objective: read and understand the modern detective story *Whodunit?* in the Reader
Materials: Track 7.5; Reader; Oral Storytelling Video Worksheet 7 [TRC printout] (optional)

Warmer: Review the story characters

Elicit the story characters from the extract in Lesson 3 and write them on the board (*Grandma Agatha, cooks, maids, gardeners, Peter, Cousin Flo, Tilly the cook*). Elicit what the children remember about the story.

Story Summary

Peter, a young boy, plays detective when items go missing from his family home. He follows the clues and discovers the thief is a cat!

Value: Don't take things that don't belong to you.

))) **7.5 While reading**

- Have the children look at the pictures in the Reader. Ask *What places can you see?*

- Read the story aloud or play Track 7.5. (See Story Time for suggestions.) The children listen and read along. Ask *Who was the thief?* (*the cat*)

- Play Track 7.5 again. Ask questions to check comprehension, e.g. *Whose birthday is it?* (*Grandma Agatha's*) *What things are missing?* (*Cousin Flo's fur hat, Tilly the cook's cream, Uncle Alistair's gloves, Grandma Agatha's handbag*) *Why did the cat take all the things?* (*to make a nest for her kittens*)

After reading: Reflect

- Ask questions to give the children the opportunity to think about the issues raised by the story, e.g. *Do you think Peter is smart? What is the most important clue? Is it right to accuse people without being sure? Have you ever accused someone of doing something they didn't do? Did you say "sorry" afterwards?*

Optional activity: What if …?

Divide the class into groups of four. Tell them *Imagine the cat did not take all those things. Who did it?* Have them think of a different ending for the story. Have children from each group tell their story to the class.

Story Time

"What happens next?"

With a mystery story like this, it works well to have the children sit around you and tell the story to them part by part. There is a lot of opportunity for prediction: *Do you think he/she took it? Why? Why not? Where do you think Peter will look for it now?* etc. This engages the children more in the story before they then sit and read/listen to the complete story for enjoyment.

Reading Strategy

Think–Pair–Share

Think–Pair–Share is a strategy that can be used before, while, and after reading. The children work individually, then in pairs or in groups of three, and then as a class. Ask questions related to the story which the children think about on their own, then discuss in pairs before sharing their ideas with the class.

For additional explanation and activities, see the Literacy Handbook on the Teacher's Resource Center.

Cooler: Play "Jump the Line"

Play the game using sentences about the story (see Games Bank p. 19).

Digital Resources

Reader eBook • Review the story extract in the Reader. Elicit predictions on what will happen before you read the whole story.

- Oral Storytelling Video 7.1 gives the story with a different ending. Watch it together at the end of the lesson, then discuss the differences.

Teacher Resource Center • Print out Oral Storytelling Video Worksheet 7 to help you get the most out of the video.

Student eBook • The children can watch Oral Storytelling Video 7.1 at home with their family.

Reading Comprehension and Critical Literacy

Lesson objectives: focus on *I* sentences; order the characters as they appear in the story; relate the story to personal experiences

Materials: Track 7.5; Reader; Oral Storytelling Video Worksheet 7 [TRC printout] (optional)

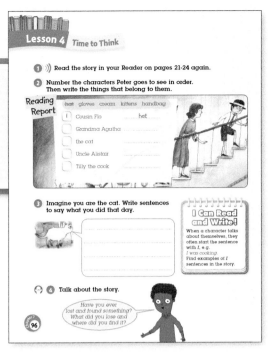

Note: Please ensure that your class has read the Reader story before you do this lesson.

Warmer: Play "Ready, Set, Draw!"

Play the game using *belt, button, earring, gloves, handbag, necklace, scarf, tie,* and other items of clothing (see Games Bank p. 19).

1))) 7.5　Read the story in your Reader.

- Have the children read the story. (Alternatively, play Track 7.5 and have them read along.) Elicit whether they were correct in their predictions in Lesson 3 Activity 4.
- Check comprehension by asking *Who was the thief?* (*the cat*) *Was Peter a good detective?*

2　Number the characters Peter goes to see in order. Then write the things that belong to them.

- Have the children number the characters in the order Peter goes to see them. Elicit answers.
- Then they write by each person the thing that belongs to them, using the words supplied. Elicit answers.

Answers

1 Cousin Flo—hat **2** Tilly the cook—cream
3 Uncle Alistair—gloves **4** Grandma Agatha—handbag
5 the cat—kittens

I Can Read and Write!

Have a child read the example (*I was cooking*). Elicit who said it. (*Tilly the cook*) Have the children find further examples in the story in pairs. Elicit answers.

3　Imagine you are the cat. Write sentences to say what you did that day.

- Have the children work in pairs telling the story from the point of view of the cat. Have children retell the story for class agreement. Do all the stories agree?

Answers

Children's own answers.

4　Talk about the story.

- Have the children read Jason's questions. Ask what they lost and how they found it.

Optional activity: Play "Disappearing Text"

Write a sentence on the board, e.g. *I think Aunt Nora took his gloves because they look silly.* Have the children read it out loud. Erase a word and have the children read the whole sentence again. Continue erasing words until children are saying the sentence without any prompts.

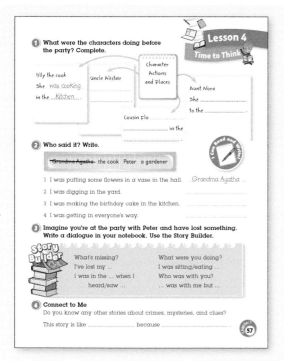

1 What were the characters doing before the party? Complete.

The children complete the notes about the suspects in the story. Elicit answers.

Answers

Tilly the cook: She was cooking in the kitchen.
Uncle Alistair: He was sleeping in the yard.
Cousin Flo: She was getting dressed in the bedroom.
Aunt Nora: She was taking the cat to the vet.

2 Who said it? Write.

The children practice the **I Can Read and Write!** feature by identifying which story character said each sentence. Elicit answers.

Answers

1 Grandma Agatha **2** a gardener **3** the cook **4** Peter

3 Imagine you're at the party with Peter and have lost something. Write a dialogue in your notebook. Use the Story Builder.

Use the **Story Builder** prompts to elicit ideas. The children write a dialogue in their notebook, then swap with a friend to check. Have children read out their dialogue for the class.

Answers

Children's own answers.

4 Connect to Me

Elicit ideas on mystery and crime stories (e.g. the Sherlock Holmes stories), before children write their own response. Elicit responses.

Answers

Children's own answers.

Cooler: Spot the mistakes

Read out the story to the children, but change some key words for a funny alternative, e.g. *Tilly the cook was making a hat.* Have the children shout *Stop!* and tell you what the correct word should be.

Competency Focus

Me: Critical Literacy
The children use critical literacy skills to reflect on the theme of the story and relate it to their personal experience.

Digital Resources

Reader eBook • Display the Reader on the board. Show Picture 4. Elicit what happened before and after this. Repeat with Pictures 7 and 10.

Student eBook, Digital Activity Book • TIP Use the forward and backward arrows to navigate to previous or later lessons.

Student eBook, Reader eBook • If you haven't already, show Oral Storytelling Video 7.1.

Teacher Resource Center • If you haven't already, print out Oral Storytelling Video Worksheet 7 to do the support activities.

Vocabulary, Song, and Spelling

Lesson objectives: identify and talk about clues and crimes; practice spellings of the *oo* sound: *ue, ew, ou*

Key vocabulary: *clue, crime, detective, fingerprint, footprint, thief, witness*

Secondary language: *ground, police chief*

Materials: Tracks 7.6 and 7.7; Phonics Worksheet 7 [TRC printout] (optional)

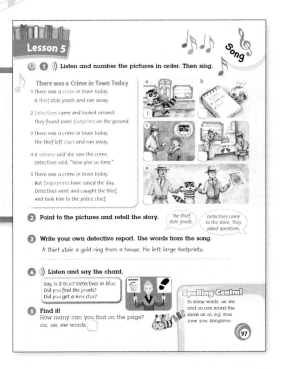

Warmer: Pre-teach vocabulary

Pre-teach the vocabulary using definitions, e.g. *crime— when someone does a bad thing, like steal something.* Then say the definitions to elicit the words.

---

1))) 7.6 Listen and number the pictures in order. Then sing.

- Play Track 7.6. The children listen and number the pictures in order. Elicit answers.
- Play Track 7.6 again for the children to sing along and point to the pictures.

Answers

1 a 2 d 3 b 4 c 5 e

2 Point to the pictures and retell the story.

- Have two children read the example. In pairs they continue the story, taking turns saying a sentence. Give support as necessary.
- Have pairs retell the story for the class.

3 Write your own detective report. Use words from the song.

- Read the example. Give the children time to write their reports, then compare them with a friend.
- Have children read their reports for the class.

Answers

Children's own answers.

Spelling Central

ue, ew, ou for the *oo* sound

Say the *ue, ew, ou* words for the children to repeat, exaggerating the *oo* sound. Have the children close their book. Write on the board *kangar____ , n____ , tr____ , y____* and ask children to complete the words with the correct spelling.

4))) 7.7 Listen and say the chant.

- Have the children look at the picture. Ask *What can you see?*
- Play Track 7.7. The children listen and read along. Elicit the words with *ue, ew, ou*.
- Play Track 7.7 again, pausing for the children to repeat.

5 Find it!

- Set a time limit for the children to find the *ou, ue*, and *ew* words on the page. Elicit answers.
- Elicit any other *ou, ue*, and *ew* words they know.

Answers

7—jewels, clues, true, blue, you, new, kangaroo

Optional activity: Sing and do

))) 7.6

Play the song again. The children listen and do actions for everything they can. Encourage them to be inventive!

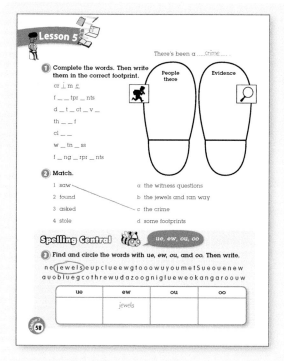

))) **7.6**

Play Track 7.6, pausing at random points in the song for the children to tell you how the song continues.

Competency Focus

Think! Critical Thinking

The children use critical thinking skills to identify written and spoken forms of new words, and match each word with its visual representation.

1 Complete the words. Then write them in the correct footprint.

Pre-teach *evidence*. The children complete the words by writing in the missing letters. Then they write them in the correct category—*People there* and *Evidence*. Elicit answers.

Answers

crime
People there: detective, thief, witness
Evidence: footprints, clue, fingerprints

2 Match.

The children match to make phrases. Elicit answers.
Answers

1 c **2** d **3** a **4** b

3 Find and circle the words with *ue, ew, ou,* and *oo.* Then write.

To practice the **Spelling Central** feature, the children circle the words and write them in the table. Check answers on the board.
Answers

ue: clue, Sue, blue, glue
ew: jewels, new, threw
ou: you
oo: too, zoo, kangaroo

Digital Resources

Student eBook • TIP Use *Timer* to set a time limit for SB Activity 5.

Teacher Resource Center • For phonics practice, print out Phonics Worksheet 7.

Student's App • Encourage the children to play the games on their smartphone/tablet. They could arrange to do this with a friend as a fun way to review the chapter vocabulary together. (*The Inks* Apps are free and available in the App Store and Google Play.)

Grammar and Reading

Lesson objective: talk about the past to solve a mystery
Key grammar: *I was talking (on the phone) when he took (it).*
Secondary language: *basketball, fixed, soccer*
Materials: Track 7.8; Grammar Worksheet 7B [TRC printout] (optional); prompt cards for "Charades" (Cooler)

Warmer: Verb listen and do

Ask the class to stand up. Say sentences featuring the simple past tense (e.g. *took, saw, stole*) or the past progressive (e.g. *was wearing, was doing, were hiding*) in random order. Have the children wave both arms in the air for the simple past and jump up and down for the past progressive.

1))) 7.8 Listen and read. Where was Jason's computer?

- Have the children look at the pictures. Ask *What are Felicity, Cheng, and Miguel doing in this story?* (*solving a crime/mystery*) *What's the mystery about?* (*Jason's computer*)
- Play Track 7.8. The children listen and read along. Ask *Where was Jason's computer?* (*James took it to fix it.*)
- Play Track 7.8 again and ask *Where was the computer when the man took it?* (*on Jason's desk*) *Who looks for footprints?* (*Cheng*) *Who looks for fingerprints?* (*Miguel*)

Optional activity: Play "The Telephone Game"

Play the game with *A lot of people were getting ready for the party.* and *The maids were cleaning and the cook was making a cake.* (see Games Bank p. 19).

Grammar Central

I was talking on the phone when he took it. ...

Have the children read the sentence. Ask *What continues happening?* (*I was talking*) *What happens and is finished?* (*he took it*) Elicit the tenses. (*past progressive* and *simple past*) Have the children find similar sentences in the story.

For extra practice, try the **Grammar Booster** section in the Student Book (pp. 103–105)

Answers p. 103

Activity 1: **2** took **3** was wearing **4** when **5** saw **6** were having **7** when **8** arrived

Activity 2: **2** was listening **3** when **4** were leaving **5** fell **6** was

Activity 3: Children's own answers.

p. 104

Activity 1: **2** Was **3** wasn't **4** doing **5** sleeping **6** jumped

Activity 2: **2** Mom was asking the neighbor for help when our dog started chasing the cat. **3** Were you helping your mom? **4** What was your dad doing all this time? **5** He was coughing and sneezing.

p. 105

Activity 1: **2** were sitting **3** have, looked **4** wasn't playing **5** was looking **6** was, doing **7** wasn't going **8** were, doing **9** was coming **10** saw **11** watch

Activity 2: **2** Ted looking for **3** Millie saw

2 Correct the mistakes.

- Ask *What was Cheng doing when he saw that Jason's computer was missing?* (*He was looking for Jason's soccer ball.*) *What was Cheng doing when he saw a man go to Jason's desk?* (*He was playing basketball.*) *What was Miguel doing when he saw a man leaving with the computer?* (*He was playing a video game.*)

- Have the children do the activity, then compare answers in pairs. Elicit answers.

Answers

1 Jason was talking **on the phone** when the man took the computer. **2** Miguel was **playing a video game** when the man left. **3** Cheng was **playing basketball** when the man went into the office.

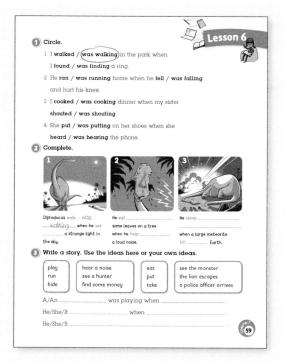

1 Circle.

The children circle the correct verb forms to complete the sentences. Elicit answers.

Answers

1 was walking, found **2** was running, fell
3 was cooking, shouted **4** was putting, heard

2 Complete.

The children write the correct verb form in each pair to complete the sentences. Elicit answers.

Answers

1 was walking, saw **2** was eating, heard
3 was sleeping, hit

3 Write a story. Use the ideas here or your own ideas.

Elicit ideas using the prompts supplied. The children write their stories. Ask them to tell their stories in small groups.

Answers

Children's own answers.

Cooler: Play "Charades"

Prepare prompt cards with sentences, e.g. *I was walking home when it started to rain. I was reading a book when the phone rang. I was eating an apple when I saw the worm.* Divide the class into two teams. Children take turns choosing a card and acting out the sentence for their team to guess. If they do not guess correctly, the other team tries to answer. A correct guess wins one point. The team with most points wins.

Competency Focus

Learn

The children develop learning strategies by recognizing and applying language patterns in different contexts.

Digital Resources

Student eBook, Digital Activity Book • TIP Give the children a lot of opportunities to use the digital resources—completing interactive activities, showing answers, writing and drawing on the board, etc. Make a point of encouraging less confident children to participate, because this will help them engage.

Teacher Resource Center • For extra grammar practice, print out Grammar Worksheet 7B.

CLIL: Science—Using fingerprints and footprints to solve crimes

Lesson objective: find out about clues the police use to catch thieves
Materials: CLIL Graphic Organizer 7 [TRC printout] (optional)

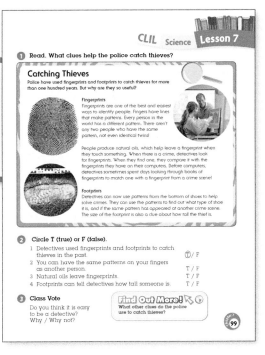

Warmer: Play "Missing Vowels"

Write on the board *Next to the cat were eight tiny kittens in a cozy nest made from a fur hat, some gloves, and a nice, soft handbag.*, omitting the vowels. Have children write in the vowels on the board. Repeat with *I haven't seen your gloves because I was busy taking the cat to the vet.*

1 Read. What clues help the police catch thieves?

- Ask *Do you know anyone who works for the police?* Elicit answers. Pre-teach *crime scene*.
- Have the children read the title and first sentence. Ask *What clues help the police catch thieves?* (*fingerprints and footprints*)
- The children read the rest of the text. Ask *What do fingers have?* (*lines that make patterns*) *Where do detectives today keep fingerprints?* (*in their computers*) *Why do the detectives look at the patterns in the footprints?* (*to find the type of shoe*)

2 Circle T (true) or F (false).

- Read the example. Have the children circle T (true) or F (false) for each sentence.
- Elicit answers, including the correct version of the false sentences.

Answers

1 T 2 F 3 T 4 T

3 Class Vote

- Have children discuss the question in small groups. Have them vote by showing a "thumbs up" for *easy* and a "thumbs down" for *difficult*. Count the votes.
- Elicit why being a detective is easy (e.g. *not much work to do, computers do the work,* etc.) and why it is difficult (e.g. *it's dangerous, you have to be very smart,* etc.).

Find Out More!

Ask the children to research other clues the police use to catch thieves, e.g. phone calls, clothes, hair/DNA, etc. Suggest appropriate resources, e.g. Internet, library books, etc. The children will need to complete this research before doing the follow-up activity in the Activity Book. (It could be set as homework.)

Optional activity: Detectives and Thieves

Explain the situation: *Someone stole a diamond. The police caught the thief but they haven't found the diamond.* Divide the class into pairs: one child is the detective, the other the thief. Have the pairs decide where the diamond was stolen from, and when. The detectives try to find out what the thieves did during that day. Give the "detectives" two minutes to think of the questions (e.g. *What were you doing yesterday / on Wednesday at … o'clock?*) while the "thieves" think about their alibis (e.g. *I was at the doctor's. I was watching television.*)

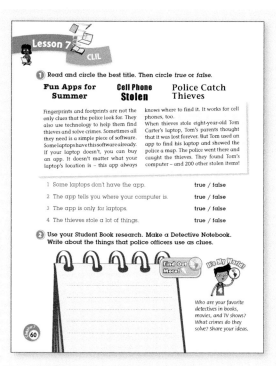

Play the game using *Why can you use fingerprints to identify people? What do detectives do when they find fingerprints? What does the size of a footprint tell?* (see Games Bank p. 19).

Competency Focus

Act

The children carry out research to find out more about clues the police use to catch thieves. This helps them expand their learning and relate it to their world, both inside and outside the classroom.

1 Read and circle the best title. Then circle *true* or *false*.

The children read the article once quickly and circle the best title. Elicit answers with reasons. (*Police Catch Thieves—The article talks about how the police use technology to catch thieves.*) Then they read the article again and circle true or false for each sentence. Elicit answers, including the correct versions of the false statements.

Answers

1 true **2** true **3** false **4** true

2 Use your Student Book research. Make a Detective Notebook. Write about the things that police officers use as clues.

Divide the class into groups of four. Have the children pool the information learned from their research in the Student Book and the Activity Book. They write about the clues police officers use individually. Have children talk about the clues to the class.

Answers

Children's own answers.

It's My World!

The children discuss in small groups their favorite detectives in books, in movies, and on TV. Elicit ideas. What crimes do they solve?

Digital Resources

Digital Activity Book • Extend AB Activity 1 by having children use *Highlighter* to identify the information for each answer in the text.

Student eBook • TIP Help children follow the text as you play the additional audio *available for SB Activity 1* or read the text aloud.

Teacher Resource Center • Print out CLIL Graphic Organizer 7 for the children to use in collating their Find Out More! research.

CLIL eBook • The children can use the CLIL eBook to expand their knowledge of the lesson topic.

Project

Lesson objectives: review language from Chapter 7; make a thumbprint database

Materials: soft lead pencils, construction paper, clear tape, pieces of white posterboard; two game pieces and a coin for each pair

Warmer: Play "Vocabulary Review"

Play the game with *belt, button, clue, crime, detective, earring, fingerprint, footprint, gloves, necklace, handbag, scarf, thief, tie, witness* (see Games Bank p. 19).

Prepare

1 Make a thumbprint database.

- Distribute the materials. Read through the instructions together and ensure the children are clear on what to do.

- Have the children follow the instructions. Display their fingerprints on the classroom wall.

Alternative craft activity

An easier project is for the children to look carefully at their fingers and draw a large fingerprint in their notebook. They compare their drawings, looking for similarities and differences. Encourage them to look for and copy the different patterns.

Showcase

2 Check the database!

- Have the children take a new fingerprint of the same thumb, write their name on the back of the paper, and swap with other children. Collect in the papers, shuffle them, and hand them out so each child has one paper.

- The children check the new fingerprint against the database (without looking at the name).

- Have children tell the class whose fingerprint it is using the **Ideas Box** for support. Have them check at the end by looking at the name on the back.

Optional activity: Play "Ready, Set, Draw!"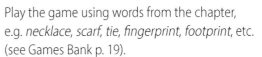

Play the game using words from the chapter, e.g. *necklace, scarf, tie, fingerprint, footprint*, etc. (see Games Bank p. 19).

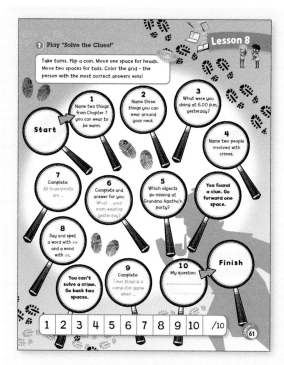

1 Play "Solve the Clues!"

See p. 43 for instructions on how to play the game.

Answers

1 gloves, scarf **2** scarf, tie, necklace **3** Children's own answer: I was –ing **4** *any two of:* thief, detective, witness **5** fur hat, cream, gloves, handbag **6** was; She was wearing … **7** different **8** *any one of:* jewels, new, threw + *any one of:* clue, Sue, blue, glue **9–10** Children's own answers.

Cooler: Play "Back to the Board"

Choose ten key words from Chapter 7. Divide the class into two teams. One child from each teams sits at the front, facing away from the board. Write one of the words on the board—they cannot look! Their teammates explain the word for the children to guess (using definitions, examples, mime, sound effects—anything except L1 or the word itself). Repeat with different children. A correct answer wins a point. The team with the most points wins.

Competency Focus

Collaborate and Communicate

By working together, the children consolidate their understanding of the language learned in a way which they will find fun and engaging. They also demonstrate their ability to work with friends and use interpersonal skills.

Digital Resources

Student eBook • Show the Prepare pictures, stage by stage, as you talk the class through the activity process.

• Choose from Chapters 4–7 to review a vocabulary topic from previous chapters. Have the children raise their hands to vote to select a topic. Then use *Timer* and give the class one minute to recall all the words in the topic. Repeat with a different topic if you have time.

Language Review

Lesson objective: review language from Chapter 7
Materials: Tracks 7.9 and AB 7.1; tray and accessories (Cooler)

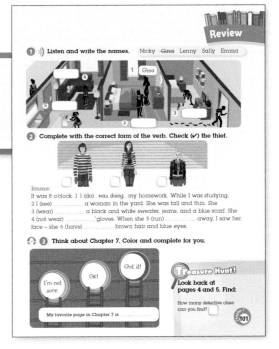

Warmer: Memory test

Have the children look back through the chapter and write three questions about the story, a picture, a word, etc. In pairs, the children test each other on what they can remember.

1))) 7.9 Listen and write the names.

- The children look at the picture. Ask *What happened?*
- Play Track 7.9 twice. The children listen and label the people pictured with the names supplied.
- Elicit answers.

Audioscript

Detective: *Good evening, Mrs. Brown. I'm Detective Watson. I'm here to solve the crime.*
Gina: *Good evening, Detective. Call me Gina, please. Yes, a thief has taken my necklace.*
Detective: *Hm … What time did they take it?*
Gina: *About 8 o'clock, I think. I was putting on my long dress and earrings, then I looked in the box, and it was gone!*
Detective: *And what was your family doing?*
Gina: *Well, Lenny was putting on his tie—we were going out to a restaurant. And our son Nicky was in his bedroom … he was looking for his belt.*
Detective: *And what about your daughter, Sally?*
Gina: *Sally was looking for her scarf in the living room.*
Sally: *Yes, that's right. I found it on the sofa.*
Detective: *And your other sister?*
Lenny: *Well, Emma was doing her homework in the kitchen. She couldn't come to the restaurant—she was studying for her math exam. But she saw a person outside. The person was looking through the window.*
Detective: *Well, I saw footprints in the yard. I think we're going to find the thief soon!*

Answers

1 Gina **2** Lenny **3** Nicky **4** Sally **5** Emma

2 Complete with the correct form of the verb. Check (✔) the thief.

- Children complete the statement.

Answers

1 was doing **2** saw **3** was wearing **4** wasn't wearing **5** ran **6** had ✔ by second suspect (tall, thin woman)

3 Think about Chapter 7. Color and complete for you.

- Children color the circle which represents how they feel about their own progress (self-evaluation).
- Have the children complete the sentence.

Treasure Hunt!

Have the children look at pp. 4–5 and count the detective clues. Elicit the answer. (*four—the tie, the scarf, the footprints, the gloves*)

Cooler: The thief has stolen …

Prepare a tray of items. Show it to the class. Then remove an item from the tray. Show them the tray again and say *Oh, no! The thief has stolen …* to elicit the missing item.

Competency Focus

Me: Self-evaluation
The children reflect on the chapter and express their opinions about their own progress.

Chapter 7 Exam Booster

1 Reading and Writing

Read the story. Choose a word from the box. Write the correct word next to numbers 1-4. There is one example.

Example

soccer	fingerprints	stole
footprints	belt	clue

On Friday, I was in the park with my friends. I was playing ......soccer......
when I saw a man running very fast. He was carrying a handbag – I think
he (1) .... it from a woman. He was wearing a dark coat with
a (2) .... and big buttons and he had black gloves.
The thief ran away. When I was talking to my friends, I saw there were
(3) .... under the trees by the gate. I called the police on
my cell phone. Then a detective arrived. He was looking for a
(4) .... when he found the empty handbag.

2 Now choose the best title for the story.

a A Helpful Man ☐   b The Lost Handbag ☐   c Helping the Police ☐

(96)

2 Listening

Listen to Jane talking about her friends and family. Why was each person busy last week? What were they doing? Listen and write a letter in each box. There is one example.

1 Jane   [F]   2 her brother   ☐

3 her mom   ☐   4 her dad   ☐

5 her grandma   ☐   6 her friend Eva   ☐

A	B	C	D
E	F	G	H

(97)

3 Reading and Writing

1 Read the story. Choose a word from the box. Write the correct word next to numbers 1–5. There is one example.

Last Saturday, I got a ...text message... that said "Meet me in town!" from
my friend Ben. I was waiting for him when I saw some strange people.
A man was wearing a long cloak and carrying a (1) ....
A woman was wearing a long dress and a (2) .... with jewels.
She was trying to (3) .... in a treasure chest.
I was watching them when an old man shouted "Cut!". I realized they were
filming a movie and the old man was the (4) .... It was an
action movie about a (5) .... who stole some treasure!

Example

text message	director	composer	hide
thief	sword	necklace	rub

2 Now choose the best name for the story.

a The Lost Treasure ☐   b Catching a Thief ☐   c Movie Magic ☐

Exam Tip
Look at the words before and after each gap to decide what kind of word fits.

(98)

1 Reading and Writing. Read the story. Choose a word from the box. Write the correct word next to numbers 1-4. There is one example.

The children complete the text using the words supplied.

Answers

1 stole **2** belt **3** footprints **4** clue **5** c

2))) AB 7.1 Listening. Listen to Jane talking about her friends and family. Why was each person busy last week? What were they doing? Listen and write a letter in each box.

Play AB Track 7.1 twice. The children listen and match.

Answers (Audioscript on p. 223)

Lines between: Monday—girl vacuuming; Wednesday—dad and girl at the vet with dog; Thursday—mom and girl baking Friday—girls walking in the park; Saturday—girl buying CD

3.1 Reading and writing. Read the story. Choose a word from the box. Write the correct word next to numbers 1-5. There is one example.

Children use the pictures to decide the correct word.

Answers

1 sword **2** necklace **3** hide **4** director **5** thief

3.2 Reading and writing. Now choose the best name for the story.

Children choose the best name.

Answers

b Catching a Thief

Digital Resources

Student eBook • Display the SB page. Open the Welcome page to give feedback on Treasure Hunt. Ask a child to find the detective clues.

Digital Activity Book • For the Exam Booster activities on the AB page, choose the audio button to access the recordings.

Teacher's Resource Center • Print out Test Chapter 7 to use at the end of this lesson. The Test Generator also allows you to create customized tests.

Chapter 8

Celebrations Overview

The children will:

- use critical thinking skills to identify features of celebrations and traditions.
- give extra information about people and things.
- read, understand, and act out a story.
- talk about celebrations.
- give extra information about places and events.
- find out about sky lanterns.
- make a world celebrations timeline.

Key Vocabulary

Celebrations and traditions: costume, decoration, dragon, feast, firework, gift, lantern, parade
Celebration verbs: bring, decorate, exchange, hang, invite, light, perform, visit

Key Grammar

- The person who (arrives first after midnight brings a special gift).
- The Chinese New Year is a festival that (is in January or February).
- That's the locker where (I put the cake).
- Birthdays are when (you invite friends and celebrate).

Reading Skills

Story: *Thor and the Stolen Hammer*
Genre: Norse myth

Literacy Development

- predict story content from title and pictures
- interpret and personalize the theme of the story
- identify how language is used for a particular effect

Functional Language

- You look happy.
- I got an A+ on my test!
- That's because you …
- Good job!

Spelling

The spellings *ea* and *ee* for the *ee* sound

CLIL: Social sciences—Sky lanterns

The children find out about sky lanterns.

Competency Focus

The children will:

use critical thinking skills to identify features of festivals. (Lesson 1) predict the content of a story. (Lesson 3) identify and talk about preparations for a celebration. (Lesson 5)	apply new grammar to previously learned vocabulary. (Lesson 2) give further information about places and events. (Lesson 6)	work in groups of four to act out a dialogue. (Lesson 3) present their research on world celebrations to the class. (Lesson 8)	personalize the story by choosing a superpower for themselves. (Lesson 4) evaluate their own progress in the chapter. (Review)	develop cultural understanding by finding out about light festivals. (Lesson 7)

Digital Overview

Teacher Presentation

Student eBook and Digital Activity Book

- Music Video 8.1 (8.2): *It's Time to Celebrate*
- Interactive versions of AB activities
- Integrated audio and answer key for all activities

Teacher resources for planning, lesson delivery, and homework

Teacher Resource Center

- Class Planner Chapter 8
- Worksheets to print out (including notes and answers):
  - Grammar Worksheet 8A: The person who arrives … It's a festival that …
  - Grammar Worksheet 8B: That's the locker where … Birthdays are when …
  - Phonics Worksheet 8
  - CLIL Graphic Organizer 8
  - Test Chapter 8
- Test Generator
- Literacy Handbook

Watch the Music Video

Children's resources for consolidation and practice at home

Student eBook

- Music Video 8.1 (8.2): *It's Time to Celebrate*

The Inks **Student's App**

Vocabulary games: Celebrations/traditions and celebration verbs

Chapter 8

Celebrations

Lesson 1

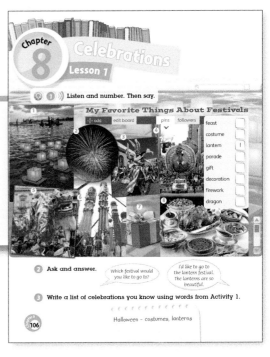

Vocabulary

Lesson objective: identify and talk about celebrations and traditions around the world

Key vocabulary: *costume, decoration, dragon, feast, firework, gift, lantern, parade*

Materials: Track 8.1

Warmer: How I celebrate

Ask *What celebrations do you have in your country? What are they about? What do people do? Do you know what people from other countries celebrate? What do they do?* Have a class discussion.

---

1))) 8.1 Listen and number. Then say.

- Have the children look at the blog and say what celebrations they recognize.
- Play Track 8.1 twice. The children listen and point.
- Then they write the number of each picture by the correct word. Elicit answers.
- Say the new words for the children to repeat.

Audioscript

Hi, I'm Simon. I love festivals. This is my display. Come and look at my pictures.

Look at the beautiful lanterns. There are a lot of lanterns floating on the water. They put small candles inside. It's the Lantern Festival in Hawaii.

Do you like my picture of fireworks in the sky? They look like stars. These red and green ones are my favorites. They made a loud bang. It was the Fourth of July in the United States.

I took this picture, too. I went to Carnivale in Brazil with my mom and dad. It was noisy and colorful. There were beautiful costumes. Can you see the woman with the hat of yellow feathers? She looks like a bird!

This was a Thanksgiving parade in the United States. There were hundreds of people walking through the streets. They were singing and dancing. Some people were wearing costumes, too. I love Chinese New Year. Look at this dragon. The dragons for Chinese New Year are always red and gold.

My cousin sent me this picture from Japan. There are beautiful decorations made of thin paper. These are pink, red, yellow, and green.

Here's a picture of one of my birthday gifts last year. Look at the red paper with gold ribbons. Can you guess what was inside? And last of all, look at this wonderful feast. It was Thanksgiving. My whole family was at our house. We ate turkey, potatoes, and vegetables. This is traditional for Thanksgiving. Delicious! Hm … I'm hungry …

Answers

feast 8, costume 3, lantern 1, parade 4, gift 7, decoration 6, firework 2, dragon 5

2 Ask and answer.

- Read the example and elicit a few more ideas. Have the children talk about which festival they would like to go to and why in pairs or small groups.

3 Write a list of celebrations you know using words from Activity 1.

- Brainstorm celebrations and write them on the board, e.g. *birthday, wedding, Halloween, Easter, Christmas, May Day*, etc.
- The children write their list in their notebook. They can do this individually or in pairs. Elicit ideas.

Optional activity: Write an acrostic

Divide the class into teams. Write *celebrations* vertically on the board and tell the teams to copy it on to a piece of paper. Give them three minutes to come up with words starting with each letter of *celebrations*. Explain that each correctly spelled word wins a point but if it is a word related to *celebrations* (e.g. *costume*), that wins two points. At the end, have teams swap and check each other's answers.

Divide the class into groups. Say *I like celebrating Thanksgiving. What about you?* Have a child answer and pose the question to another child in the group.

Competency Focus

Think! Critical Thinking

The children use critical thinking skills to deduce the relationship between the celebrations and their traditional elements by using visual clues and processing the written and spoken forms.

1 Look and complete the sentences. Then write the letters.

The children look at the picture and complete the sentences using the words supplied. They then write the letter for each picture detail by the correct sentence. Elicit answers.

Answers

1 decorations a 2 parade d 3 dragon g 4 Lanterns e 5 costumes h 6 fireworks f 7 feast c 8 gift b

2 Choose and categorize the celebration words in your notebook.

Elicit an example for each category listed. Ask *Which categories would you choose?* Elicit ideas, prompting children to give a reason for their choice. The children choose a pair of categories and list the words in their notebook, then compare with a friend.

Answers

Children's own answers.

Digital Resources

Student eBook, Digital Activity Book • TIP As you monitor the children's progress, use *Add personal note* to keep a note of weaknesses in vocabulary, grammar, or pronunciation so you can review in later lessons.

Grammar

Lesson objectives: talk about celebrations and give further information using *who* and *that*

Key grammar: *The person who (arrives first after midnight brings a special gift). The Chinese New Year is a festival that (is in January or February).*

Secondary language: *blossom, creature*

Materials: Track 8.2; Grammar Worksheet 8A [TRC printout] (optional)

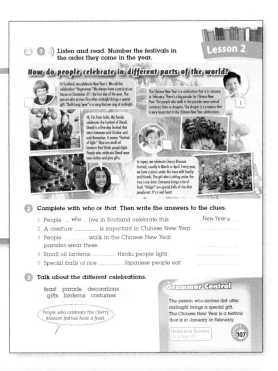

Warmer: Celebrations

Elicit celebrations in the children's country and discuss them to identify which is the most popular, and why.

1))) **8.2 Listen and read. Number the festivals in the order they come in the year.**

- Elicit what the children can see.
- Play Track 8.2 twice. The children listen and read along. They number the celebrations chronologically. Elicit answers.
- Ask *Which celebration is the most fun? Why?* Have the children discuss in pairs. Then elicit ideas.

Answers

1 Chinese New Year **2** Cherry Blossom Festival **3** Diwali
4 Hogmanay

2 Complete with *who* or *that*. Then write the answers to the clues.

- Read the example and remind children of when we use *who* and *that*. Pre-teach *creature* if necessary.
- The children complete the clues and then write the words on the lines. They check answers in pairs before reading them out to the class.

Answers

1 who—New Year's **2** that—the dragon
3 who—animal costumes **4** that—dipa **5** that—onigiri

Grammar Central

The person who arrives first after midnight brings a special gift. …

Have the children look at the patterns. *Ask Do we use* who *for a person or a thing?* (person) *And* that*?* (a thing) Point out that we use these words to give more information about someone or something.

For extra practice, try the **Grammar Booster** section in the Student Book (p. 116)

Answers p. 116

Activity 1: **2** who **3** who **4** that **5** that **6** that

Activity 2: **2** that **3** who **4** that **5** that **6** that **7** who **8** who

Activity 3: **2** who **3** that, Children's own answers

3 Talk about the different celebrations.

- Look at the words in the box and the example. Do another example with *that*, e.g. *The parade that they have in China for New Year's Eve is big.*
- Have the children talk about the celebrations in pairs using *who/that* and the words supplied. Elicit sentences.

Optional activity: Make a who chain

Ask the children to pick someone who means a lot to them. Brainstorm personality adjectives that could be used to describe these people. Write the adjectives on the board. Divide the class into groups of six. Say *My mom is a person who is always happy. What about your mom?* Have the first children in each group answer with a similar sentence about their moms, then turn to the next child on their left and ask the question, and so on. Other possibilities: *my dad, my best friend, my grandma,* etc.

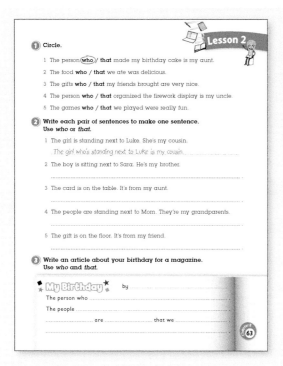

1 Circle.

The children circle *who* or *that* to complete the sentences. Elicit answers.

Answers

1 who **2** that **3** that **4** who **5** that

2 Write each pair of sentences to make one sentence. Use *who* or *that*.

The children write each pair of prompts as a single sentence, using *who* or *that*, as appropriate. Elicit answers.

Answers

1 The girl who's standing next to Luke is my cousin.

2 The boy who's sitting next to Sara is my brother.

3 The card that's on the table is from my aunt.

4 The people who are standing next to Mom are my grandparents.

5 The gift that's on the floor is from my friend.

3 Write an article about your birthday for a magazine. Use *who* and *that*.

Elicit ideas. The children complete the article. Invite children to read their articles to the class.

Answers

Children's own answers.

Cooler: Play "Disappearing Words"

Play the game with *costume, decoration, dragon, feast, firework, gift, lantern, parade* (see Games Bank p. 19).

Competency Focus

Learn

The children develop learning strategies by recognizing and applying language patterns. They show their understanding of previously acquired vocabulary and use it in a new context.

Digital Resources

Student eBook • Divide the class into teams. Teams answer in turn. Give prompts to elicit *who* or *that* (e.g. *the people, the book*). A child from the team answering writes *who* or *that*, as appropriate, using *Pen*. The other teams confirm. Each correct answer wins a point. The team with the most points wins.

Teacher Resource Center • For extra grammar practice, print out Grammar Worksheet 8A.

Reading: Story Extract

Lesson objectives: praise someone's hard work; predict story content from title and pictures; read the extract from *Thor and the Stolen Hammer* (beginning)

Functional language: *You look happy. I got an A+ on my test! That's because you … Good job!*

Secondary language: *dwarves, giant, smart, superhero*

Materials: Tracks 8.3 and 8.4

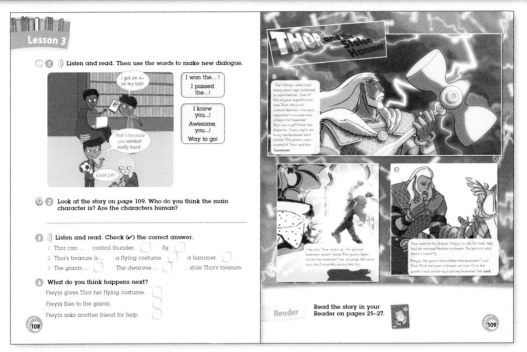

Warmer: The superhero Thor

Ask *Do you know who Thor is? Have you seen a movie about Thor? Do you like stories about Thor? What can Thor do?* Have children talk to the class about the stories about Thor or about other superheroes they like.

Functional language

1))) **8.3 Listen and read. Then act out.**

- Have the children look at the picture. Ask *What is Miguel showing the others?* (his test)
- Play Track 8.3. The children listen and read along. Ask *Why is Miguel happy?* (He got an A+.) *Are the others happy for him?* (yes)
- Play Track 8.3 again, pausing for the children to repeat. Divide the class into groups of four to act out the dialogue. Encourage them to think of different achievements to talk about.

Note: The **Reading Strategy** activity for this chapter is best done *before* you read the extract. See p. 187 and the Literacy Handbook for details.

Before reading

2 **Look at the story. Who do you think the main character is? Are they human?**

- Have the children read the story title and look at the pictures. They write their answers. Elicit ideas.

Answers

Children's own answers.

3))) **8.4 Listen and read. Check (✔) the correct answer.**

- Play Track 8.4. The children listen and read along.
- They read the sentences and check the answers.
- Play Track 8.4 again for them to check their answers. Elicit answers.

Answers

1 control thunder **2** a hammer **3** The giants

4 What do you think happens next?

- Have the children think about what is going to happen next and check one of the three sentences. Elicit ideas including reasons but do not confirm. Say they will have to read the story to find out.

Answers

Children's own answers.

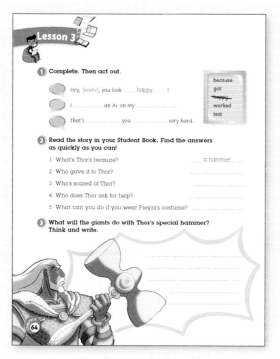

1 Complete. Then act out.

The children complete the dialogue in pairs using the words supplied, then act it out. Have pairs act out for the class.

Answers

happy; got, test; because, worked

2 Read the story in your Student Book. Find the answers as quickly as you can!

The children read the story extract again. They answer the questions as quickly as they can. Remind them of scanning techniques as necessary. Elicit answers.

Answers

1 a hammer 2 the dwarves 3 the giants 4 Freyja 5 fly

3 What will the giants do with Thor's special hammer? Think and write.

Elicit what the giants will do with the hammer. The children write their ideas. Elicit responses.

Answers

Children's own answers.

Cooler: Play "Finish the word"

Divide the class into two teams. Start spelling a word (e.g. *decoration, parade, lantern, costume, dragon, feast, firework, gift*). When children think they know it, they raise their hand and say it and spell it. If they say and spell the correct word before you finish spelling it, they get one point. If they say the wrong word, they lose a point.

Competency Focus

Collaborate and Communicate

The children act out an authentic dialogue together, putting into practice the functional language.

Think! Critical Thinking

The children apply reading skills (exploiting pictures and text clues) to understand the story.

Digital Resources

Student eBook • For support on SB activities 2–4, display the SB page. Ask children to use *Highlighter* to identify key words in the text that will help them understand the story's context and predict what is going to happen.

Digital Activity Book • Have children do the AB interactive digital activities or set them for homework.

THOR and the Stolen Hammer

1
The Vikings, who lived many years ago, believed in superheroes. One of the original superheroes was Thor. He could control thunder. His most important treasure was a beautiful hammer that was a gift from the dwarves. Every night, he hung the hammer next to him. The giants were scared of Thor and the hammer.

2
One day, Thor woke up. His special hammer wasn't there. "The giants have stolen the hammer.!" he shouted. His voice was like fireworks across the sky.

3
Thor went to his friend, Freyja, to ask for help. She had an unusual feather costume. The person who wore it could fly.
"Freyja, the giants have taken the hammer!" said Thor."Give me your costume, so I can fly to the giants' land and bring back my hammer," he said.

4
But Freyja thought someone who was smaller and smarter should try to get the hammer first. She gave her flying costume to their friend, Loki, who was very smart.

5
Loki flew to the giants' land. He could change shape, so he performed tricks for the giants.
"Give back the hammer that you stole," said Loki when he finished.
"I've hidden the hammer," said the giant king, Thrym. "Thor can have his hammer, but I want Freyja to live here with me. I want her flying costume, too."

6
Freyja didn't want to live with the giants or give them her flying costume. Smart Loki had an idea to trick the stupid giants.

7
Loki dressed Thor in the flying costume and jewels to make him look like Freyja. Then Loki dressed as Freyja's maid. They flew to the giants' land together.

8
The castle was decorated with lanterns. Thrym welcomed Freyja, who was really Thor in costume. They brought gifts for the giants.

9
There was a big feast. Thor put a lot of food on his plate. "What a woman! She can eat a whole ox!" Thrym said.
"That's because she's so happy to be here," said Loki.

10
Thrym was happy. "Bring the hammer," he said. "I can exchange it for Freyja."
His servant brought the hammer.

11
Thor grabbed the hammer and threw off the costume.
"Now I'm going to give you the gift that you deserve," shouted Thor. He smashed the giants' castle to pieces.

12
Thor was the first superhero. A day of the week is named after him. Thursday was first named Thor's Day.

Lesson objective: read and understand the Norse myth
Thor and the Stolen Hammer in the Reader
Materials: Track 8.5; Reader

Warmer: Clap and stamp

Have the class stand up. Say true/false sentences about the story extract, e.g. *Thor is a superhero.* (T) *Freyja isn't Thor's friend.* (F) If the sentence is true, the children clap their hands; if false, they stamp their feet. Children who make a mistake sit down. The last child standing wins.

Story Summary

Thor, a superhero in Viking times, can control thunder. When his precious hammer is stolen by the giants, he tries to find it with the help of his friends, Loki and Freyja. Thor tricks the giant king, Thrym, by disguising himself and he manages to get his hammer back.

Value: Work together

))) **8.5 While reading**

- Have the children look at the pictures in the Reader. Ask *Who puts on the magic costume?* (*Loki and Thor*)

- Play Track 8.5. The children listen and read along. Ask *Does Thor get his hammer back?* (*yes*)

- Play Track 8.5 again. Ask questions to check comprehension, e.g. *Where did Thor fly?* (*to the land of the giants*) *Who did the giants think he was?* (*Freyja*) *What did Thor do when he recovered his hammer?* (*He destroyed the giants' castle.*)

After reading: Reflect

- Ask questions to give the children the opportunity to think about the issues raised by the story, e.g. *Why did the giants steal Thor's hammer? Was Loki's idea to dress up Thor as Freyja smart? Is it OK to trick people? Was Thor right to destroy the giants' castle?*

Optional activity: I'm a superhero!

Have the children discuss in pairs which of the characters in the story they would most like to be and why. Elicit responses.

Story Time

Keeping focus

It is sometimes easy for children's attention to wander during a long reading/listening of a story. When you play the CD, tell the children you will stop the CD sometimes and they have to finish off the phrase. This helps them keep focused on the story, and also lets them play a part in the storytelling.

Reading Strategy

Visual Imagery

Visual Imagery is a very important strategy that good readers should apply while reading and listening to a story. It helps them personalize the story by building their own mental pictures as they read. It also offers good comprehension support.

For additional explanation and activities, see the Literacy Handbook on the Teacher's Resource Center.

Cooler: Play "Monkey"

Divide the class into two teams (A and B), who stand up facing each other. Have the first child in Team A begin reading the story. When you shout *Monkey!*, the reading switches over to the first child on Team B. Continue in this way, shouting *Monkey!* at random points for the reading to switch.

Digital Resources

Reader eBook • Show the Reader story, one picture at a time and elicit what is going to happen next.

- Have children use *Highlighter* to identify in the story where they find the information for the questions you ask in the While reading section.

Reading Comprehension and Critical Literacy

Lesson objectives: identify how language is used for a particular effect; relate the story to personal experiences

Materials: Track 8.5; Reader

Lesson 4 Time to Think

1.))) Read the story in your Reader on pages 25–27.
2. Circle T (true) or F (false).

Reading Report

1 The giants stole Thor's hammer. T / F
2 Freyja's costume makes people fly. T / F
3 Freyja wanted to live with the giants. T / F
4 Freyja gave her costume to Thor. T / F
5 Loki can change shape. T / F
6 Loki dressed Thor to look like Freyja. T / F
7 The giants kept Thor's hammer. T / F

3. Write about your favorite thing. Why is it special to you?

My favorite thing is ....

I Can Read and Write!

How do we know that Thor's hammer is special? Find places in the story that tell the reader how important the hammer is.

4. Talk about the story.

What special power would you choose?

110

Note: Please ensure that your class has read the Reader story before you do this lesson.

Warmer: Search the pictures

Have the children look at the story. Name four key objects, people, or actions shown in the pictures to elicit the number of the picture they appear in. Then invite children to prompt for the class.

1.))) **8.5 Read the story in your Reader.**
   - Have the children read the story. (Alternatively, play Track 8.5 and have them read along.) Elicit whether they were correct in their predictions in Lesson 3 Activity 4.
   - Check comprehension by asking *Why is Thor angry at the beginning of the story?* (*The giants have stolen his hammer.*) *What does he do in the end?* (*He smashes the giants' castle to pieces.*)

2. **Circle T (true) or F (false).**
   - Have the children circle T (true) or F (false) for each sentence. Elicit answers, including the correct version of the false sentences.

   Answers

   1 T 2 T 3 F 4 F 5 T 6 T 7 F

I Can Read and Write!

Have the children scan the story and find the words that tell why Thor's hammer is important. Elicit answers.

3. **Write about your favorite thing. Why is it special to you?**
   - Elicit the children's favorite objects (toys, CDs, books, etc.). Elicit an adjective or two about each object that makes it special.
   - Have the children write about their favorite thing. They swap with a friend.
   - Elicit responses.

   Answers

   Children's own answers.

4. **Talk about the story.**
   - Have the children read Jason's question. Ask *What special power would you choose?* Elicit options and have the children choose and compare in pairs. Elicit ideas.

   Optional activity: Who said that?

   Read out dialogue from the story to elicit who said it.

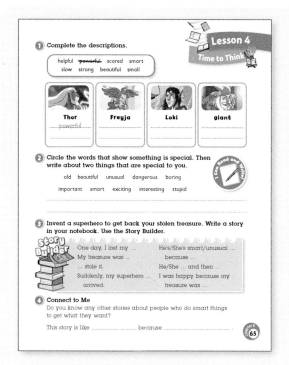

1 Complete the descriptions.

The children complete the descriptions of the story characters using the words supplied. Elicit answers.

Answers (suggested)

Thor: powerful, strong
Freyja: helpful, beautiful
Loki: smart, small
giant: scared, slow

2 Circle the words that show something is special. Then write about two things that are special to you.

The children practice the **I Can Read and Write!** feature by circling the adjectives that indicate something is special. Elicit answers. Then they write about two special things for them. Have children discuss their special things in small groups.

Answers

beautiful, unusual, important, smart, exciting, interesting + children's own answers

3 Invent a superhero to get back your stolen treasure. Write a story in your notebook. Use the Story Builder.

Use the **Story Builder** prompts to elicit ideas. The children write a story in their notebook, then swap with a friend to check. Have children read their story for the class.

Answers

Children's own answers.

4 Connect to Me

Elicit ideas on stories about smart people (e.g. Iron Man, Spiderman, Ulysses, etc.) before the children write their own response. Elicit responses.

Answers

Children's own answers.

Cooler: Play "Jump the Line"

Play the game with *Freyja flew to the giants' land first.* (F) *Loki dressed Thor in the costume to make him look like Freyja.* (T) *Thor did not eat a lot at the feast.* (F) *Thor smashed the giants' castle to pieces.* (T) *Thor was the first superhero.* (T) *Tuesday is named after him.* (F) (see Games Bank p. 19).

Competency Focus

Me: Critical Literacy

The children use critical literacy skills to reflect on the theme of the story and relate it to their personal experience.

Digital Resources

Reader eBook • Display the Reader on the board. Have children act out one of the pictures in the story (on their own or in pairs) for the class to guess.

Student eBook • To give feedback on SB Activity 3, display the SB and have children use *Pen* to write about their favorite thing on the board.

Student eBook, Digital Activity Book • TIP With the answer key, you can show the answers all at once or one by one to customize feedback.

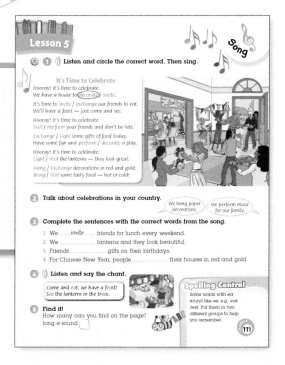

Vocabulary, Song, and Spelling

Lesson objectives: talk about celebrations in detail; practice spelling words with *ee* and *ea*

Key vocabulary: *bring, decorate, exchange, hang, invite, light, perform, visit*

Secondary language: *celebrate, feast, tasty*

Materials: Tracks 8.6 and 8.7; Phonics Worksheet 8 [TRC printout] (optional)

Warmer: Pre-teach vocabulary

Pre-teach the vocabulary using definitions, e.g. *Invite—ask someone to come to your party.* Then say the definitions to elicit the words.

1))) 8.6 Listen and circle the correct word. Then sing.

- Have the children look at the picture and count the people. (*14*)
- Play Track 8.6. The children listen and circle the correct option in each pair. Elicit answers.
- Play Track 8.6 again for the children to sing along and mime.

Answers

decorate, invite, Visit, Exchange, perform, Light, Hang, Bring

2 Talk about celebrations in your country.

- Have two children read the example dialogue.
- Divide the class into pairs. They talk about different celebrations at home or school. Elicit ideas.

3 Complete the sentences with the correct words from the song.

- Have the children complete the sentences using key vocabulary from the song.
- Elicit answers.

Answers

1 invite **2** light **3** exchange **4** decorate

Spelling Central

ea and *ee* for the *ee* sound

Say *eat* and *feet* for the children to repeat. Point out the pronunciation of *ea* and *ee* is the same. Have the children create two sections in their notebook: *ea* and *ee*. Ask them to note down the words by section and keep updating them.

4))) 8.7 Listen and say the chant.

- Have the children look at the picture. Ask *What can you see?*
- Play Track 8.7. The children listen and read along. Elicit the words with *ee* and *ea*.
- Play Track 8.7 again, pausing for the children to repeat.

5 Find it!

- Set a time limit for the children to find *ee* and *ea* words on the page. Elicit answers. Point out as necessary that *great* does not have a long *ee* sound.
- Elicit any other *ee* /*ea* words they know.

Answers

6—eat, feast, see, weekend, trees, feet

Optional activity: Play "The Yes/No Game"

Have a child stand up. Say *On your birthday, do you decorate the house?* Have the child answer truthfully without using *yes* or *no*, but *I/we do.* or *I/we don't.* If the child answers *yes* or *no*, they are out, and another child takes their place. If within a minute the child has not said *yes* or *no*, they win.

Have the children respond with different actions when they hear words with *ee* or *ea*, e.g. clap for *ee* and snap their fingers for *ea*. Say words in random order for the children to react.

Competency Focus

Think! Critical Thinking

The children use critical thinking skills to identify written and spoken forms of new words and complete the activity.

1 Unscramble and write. Then write the letters.

The children unscramble and write the word. They then write the label for each picture detail by the correct word. Elicit answers.

Answers

1 visit d **2** invite h **3** decorate f **4** light b **5** bring e
6 hang c **7** perform a **8** exchange g

2 Think of celebrations. Ask and answer.

Elicit celebrations. Write them on the board. Divide the class into pairs. They ask and answer the questions about celebrations. Elicit responses.

3 Circle and complete the words with *ea* or *ee*.

To practice the **Spelling Central** feature, the children circle and complete the words. Elicit answers.

Answers

seem, eat, feast, please, sleep, teach, trees, easy, queen, knee

Digital Resources

Student eBook • Choose the karaoke version of Music Video 8.1 (8.2) and encourage the children to dance and sing along, using the lyrics on screen. Associating movements with words makes them more memorable. Pause the video for the children to continue dancing and singing.

Teacher Resource Center • For phonics practice, print out Phonics Worksheet 8.

Grammar and Reading

Lesson objective: practice using the relative pronouns *where* and *when*

Key grammar: *That's the locker where (I put the cake). Birthdays are when (you invite friends and celebrate).*

Secondary language: *birthday card, locker, share, smart*

Materials: Track 8.8; Grammar Worksheet 8B [TRC printout] (optional); two sets of cards for matching game (optional)

Warmer: Board race

Divide the class into two teams and give each team a board pen. The children on each team take turns running to the board to write a name, place, object, or activity from the song. Teams check each other's answers. Then elicit sentences using some of the key words on the board.

1))) **8.8** **Listen and read. What special day is it today?**

- Have the children look at the pictures and ask *What is Felicity doing in Picture 3?* (*hanging decorations*)
- Play Track 8.8. The children listen and read along. Ask *What special day is it today?* (*Cheng's birthday*)
- Play Track 8.8 again. Ask *Where does Felicity put the cake?* (*in a locker*) *Where does she put the birthday gift and card?* (*on a shelf*) *Why?* (*It's a surprise party.*)

2 Complete.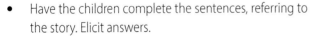

- Have the children complete the sentences, referring to the story. Elicit answers.

Answers

1 where you put backpacks
2 where you put books
3 when you do homework
4 when you invite friends and celebrate with them

Grammar Central

That's the locker where I put the cake. . . .

Have the children look at the patterns. Ask *Do we use* where *to give more information about a place or a time/event?* (*place*) *And* when? (*a time/event*)

For extra practice, try the **Grammar Booster** section in the Student Book (pp. 117–119)

Answers p. 117

Activity 1: **2** where **3** where **4** when **5** when **6** when

Activity 2: **2** a **3** d **4** e **5** b

Activity 3: Children's own answers.

p. 118

Activity 1: **2** where **3** when **4** who **5** who **6** that **7** where

Activity 2: **2** that **3** when **4** where **5** who

p. 119

Activity 1: **2** when **3** who **4** ago **5** where **6** that **7** who **8** yet **9** where **10** who **11** that **12** where

Activity 2: **1** that **2** who, Children's own answers.

Optional activity: Play a matching game

Prepare cards with sentence beginnings and endings, e.g. *A locker is a place / where you put your backpack. A birthday is a day / when you invite friends to a party. Diwali is a festival / that lasts five days. The dragon and the lion are creatures / that are very important for Chinese people. The people who are singing / are my friends.* Put the beginning cards face down on your desk in a pile; lay out the ending cards face up. Divide the class into two teams. Have a child from each team come to the front, turn over a sentence beginning, and memorize it. They go back to their team. The team listens to the sentence half, and sends another child to find the sentence ending.

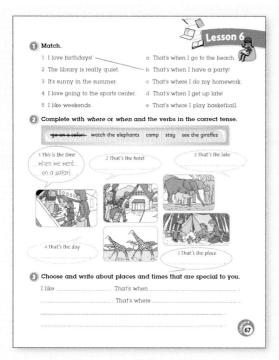

1 Match.

The children match the sentences. Elicit answers, asking them to say if they agree/disagree with the sentences.
Answers

1 b 2 c 3 a 4 e 5 d

2 Complete with *where* or *when* and the verbs in the correct tense.

The children complete the sentences using *where* or *when* and the words supplied. Elicit answers.
Answers

1 when we went on a safari
2 where we stayed

3 where we watched the elephants
4 when we saw giraffes
5 where we camped

3 Choose and write about places and times that are special to you.

Elicit ideas. The children write about places and times special to them. They compare with a friend. Have children read their texts to the class.
Answers

Children's own answers.

Cooler: Unscramble the sentences

Write a sentence on the board, scrambling the order of the words: *Birthdays are when you invite friends and celebrate with them.* Have children work in pairs to figure out the sentence. Repeat with *The place where we put our clothes is called a wardrobe.*

Competency Focus

Learn

The children develop learning strategies by recognizing and applying language patterns in different contexts.

Digital Resources

Student eBook • For extra grammar practice in class, divide the class into teams. Teams answer in turn. Give prompts to elicit *where* or *when* (e.g. *the house, July*). A child from the team answering writes *where* or *when*, as appropriate, using *Pen*. The other teams confirm. Each correct answer wins a point. The team with the most points wins.

Teacher Resource Center • For extra grammar practice, print out Grammar Worksheet 8B.

CLIL: Social science—Sky lanterns

Lesson objective: find out about sky lanterns
Materials: CLIL Graphic Organizer 8 [TRC printout] (optional)

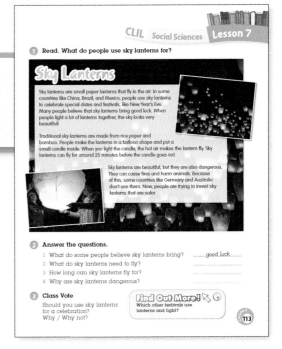

1 Read. What do people use sky lanterns for?

Sky Lanterns

Sky lanterns are small paper lanterns that fly in the air. In some countries like China, Brazil, and Mexico, people use sky lanterns to celebrate special dates and festivals, like New Year's Eve. Many people believe that sky lanterns bring good luck. When people light a lot of lanterns together, the sky looks very beautiful!

Traditional sky lanterns are made from rice paper and bamboo. People make the lanterns in a balloon shape and put a small candle inside. When you light the candle, the hot air makes the lantern fly. Sky lanterns can fly for around 25 minutes before the candle goes out.

Sky lanterns are beautiful, but they are also dangerous. They can cause fires and harm animals. Because of this, some countries like Germany and Australia don't use them. Now, people are trying to invent sky lanterns that are safer.

2 Answer the questions.
1 What do some people believe sky lanterns bring? ....good luck....
2 What do sky lanterns need to fly?
3 How long can sky lanterns fly for?
4 Why are sky lanterns dangerous?

3 Class Vote
Should you use sky lanterns for a celebration? Why / Why not?

Find Out More! Which other festivals use lanterns and light?

113

Warmer: Play "Missing Vowels"

Write on the board *The traditional Thanksgiving dinner is turkey, potatoes, and vegetables.*, omitting the vowels. Have children write in the vowels on the board. Repeat with *Dipa are small oil lanterns that Hindu people who celebrate Diwali light up.*

1 Read. What do people use sky lanterns for?

- Ask *What are these?* (*sky lanterns*) *Have you ever made/ seen one?*

- Have the children read the first paragraph. Ask *What do people use sky lanterns for?* (*to celebrate special dates and festivals / because they believe they bring good luck*)

- The children read the rest of the text. Ask *What are sky lanterns made of?* (*rice paper and bamboo*) *What do people put inside?* (*a small candle*) *What makes the lantern fly?* (*the hot air from the candle*)

2 Answer the questions.

- Read the example question and answer. Have the children answer the questions, referring to the text.

- Elicit answers.

Answers

1 good luck **2** hot air **3** around 25 minutes
4 They can cause fires and harm animals.

3 Class Vote

- Give the children time to think about the question. Have them vote yes by raising an imaginary lantern to the sky, and no by staying still with arms folded. Count the votes.

- Elicit ideas on why you should use sky lanterns (e.g. *they're pretty, easy to make*) and should not (e.g. *fire risk, harms animals, create trash*).

Find Out More!

Ask the children to research which other festivals use lanterns and light. Suggest appropriate resources, e.g. Internet, library books, etc. The children will need to complete this research before doing the follow-up activity in the Activity Book. (It could be set as homework.)

Optional activity: Make sentences around the class

Explain you are going to make sentences as a class about sky lanterns. Give the children a minute to look at the text again. Start the first sentence: *People …* The children take turns adding a word, e.g. *use … sky … lanterns …* When a sentence is complete, start another.

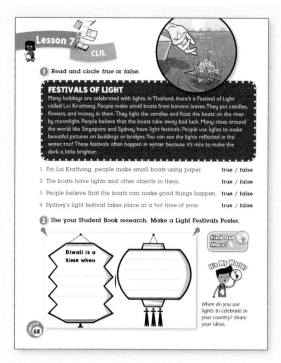

Play the game using *Name four countries where people use sky lanterns. What are sky lanterns made from? How long can sky lanterns fly? Why don't Germany and Australia use sky lanterns?* (see Games Bank p. 19).

Competency Focus

Act

The children carry out research to find out more about festivals which use light. This helps them expand their learning and relate it to their world, both inside and outside the classroom.

1 Read and circle *true* or *false*.

The children read the article. They circle true or false for each sentence. Elicit answers, including the correct versions of the false sentences.

Answers

1 false **2** true **3** true **4** false

2 Use your Student Book research. Make a Light Festivals Poster.

Divide the class into groups of four. Have the children pool the information learned from their research in the Student Book and the Activity Book. They write about light festivals to make their poster individually. Have children talk about their posters to the class.

Answers

Children's own answers.

It's My World!

Have the children discuss in small groups when they use lights in their country to celebrate. Elicit ideas.

Digital Resources

Student eBook • Show the SB picture. Ask *Have you seen these before? Where?* Elicit what the children know about sky lanterns.

• Have children use *Highlighter* to identify key words in the text to help them understand it.

Teacher Resource Center • Print out CLIL Graphic Organizer 8 for the children to use in collating their Find Out More! research.

CLIL eBook • The children can use the CLIL eBook to expand their knowledge of the lesson topic.

Project

Lesson objectives: review language from Chapter 8; make a world celebrations timeline; talk about a celebration

Materials: clothesline, index cards, colored pencils/markers, magazines or pictures, pegs; two game pieces and a coin for each pair

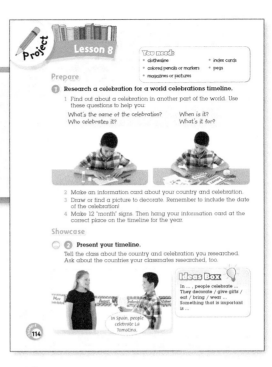

Warmer: Play "The Telephone Game"

Play the game with *The Vikings named a day of the week after Thor, because he was their first superhero.* and *In some countries like China and Brazil people use sky lanterns to celebrate special dates and festivals.* (see Games Bank p. 19).

Prepare

1 Research a celebration for a world celebrations timeline.

- Distribute the materials. Read through the instructions together and ensure the children are clear on what to do. Hang the clothesline at children's height in an accessible place in the classroom.

- Have the children do research to find a celebration in another part of the world and information about it. Make sure they do not all choose the same.

- Choose 12 children to make months signs. Hang these up on the clothesline.

- Have the children fill in their information cards and hang them by the correct month.

Alternative craft activity

An easier project is for the children to research a celebration and design a poster for it.

Showcase

2 Present your timeline.

- The children present their celebration to the class, using the **Ideas Box** for support. Encourage them to ask each other questions.

Optional activity: Play "Change Seats"

Elicit from each child the celebration they researched for the project. Then say *Change seats if you are Hogmanay!* Children who researched that stand up and change seats. While the children are moving around, take away one chair. The child who does not find a chair is out. The winner is the last child sitting down.

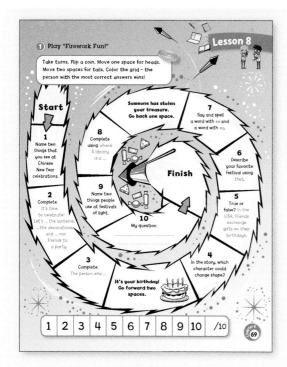

1 Play "Firework Fun!"

See p. 43 for instructions on how to play the game.

Answers

1 *any two of:* dragon, costumes, parade, feast, lanterns, decorations, fireworks **2** light, hang, invite **3** Children's own answer. **4** Loki **5** true **6** Children's own answer. **7** *any word with* ee, e.g. see + *any word with* ea, e.g. feast **8** A library is a place where you study/take out books. etc. **9** *any two of:* sky lanterns, banana boat, candles, etc. **10** Children's own answer.

Cooler: Play "Word Steps"

Write *dragon* on the board. Have the children use the last letter to start a new word and form steps, e.g. *dragon—new—window*. Play as a class or in groups, starting with a new word from Chapter 8.

Competency Focus

Collaborate and Communicate

By working together, the children consolidate their understanding of the language learned in a way which they will find fun and engaging. They also demonstrate their ability to work with friends and use interpersonal skills.

Digital Resources

Student eBook • Before the lesson, you could research celebrations in different parts of the world on the Internet and store ideas in *Add personal note*, to show the children and give them ideas for their timelines.

• Show the Prepare pictures, stage by stage, as you talk the class through the activity process.

Language Review

Lesson objective: review language from Chapter 8
Materials: Tracks 8.9, AB 8.1 and AB 8.2

Warmer: Play "Vocabulary Review"

Play the game with *bring, exchange, hang, invite, light, perform, visit, costume, decoration, dragon, feast, firework, gift, lantern, parade* (see Games Bank p. 19).

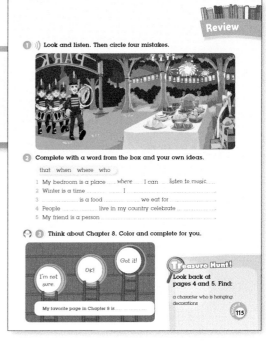

1))) **8.9 Look and listen. Then circle four mistakes.**

- Play Track 8.9 twice. The children listen and circle the details which are different from the track. Elicit answers.

Audioscript

Mia: Hi, Charlie, what are you doing?
Charlie: I'm getting ready for the summer festival.
Mia: What's that?
Charlie: Well, it's a festival that happens in our town every summer. I'm performing this year.
Mia: Is it a festival that celebrates summer?
Charlie: Yes. Look, this is my costume for the parade. I'm playing the drums in the band.
Mia: Great. Can I help you with anything?
Charlie: Well, you can come to the school—it's where the parade finishes. I'm going to help with the decorations. We hang lanterns in the trees.
Mia: What about candles?
Charlie: No, we don't hang candles in the trees—it's too dangerous!
Mia: OK. What happens then?
Charlie: Well, tonight after the parade, there are going to be people who perform, and then a lot of fireworks.
Mia: Can I come, too?
Charlie: Of course, and you can invite all of your family and friends!
Mia: Should I bring a gift?
Charlie: No, we don't exchange gifts at the summer party, but we always have a big feast!
Mia: Cool! It sounds great!

Answers

tambourine (should be drums), candles (no candles), park (should be school), gifts (no gifts)

2 Complete with a word from the box and your own ideas.

- The children complete the sentences with the words supplied and their own ideas. Elicit responses.

Answers

1 where, listen to music **2** when **3** that **4** who **5** who and children's own answers

3 Think about Chapter 8. Color and complete for you. 🎧

- Have the children look back at Chapter 8. Elicit their favorite parts. The children then color the circle which represents how they feel about their own progress (self-evaluation). Have the children complete the sentence about their favorite page. Elicit responses.

Treasure Hunt!

Have the children look at pp. 4–5, and find a character who is hanging decorations. Have the children hold up their Student Book and point to the right place on the page.

Cooler: Play a spelling game

Divide the class into teams. Give them two minutes to write two lists: words with *ea* and words with *ee*. Ask the team with the most words to read them out. Elicit any other words not covered.

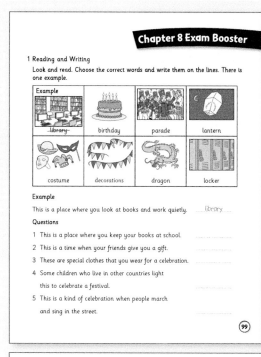

firework—purple, cake—brown, gift—yellow

Written on banner: Happy Summer

3))) AB 8.2 Listening. Listen and color and write. There is one example.

Play Track AB 8.2 twice. The children listen and color and write according to the recording.

Answers (Audioscript on p. 224)

Picture colored as follows: lamp - yellow, belt - brown, tie - blue, dragon on lamp - green. *Written on banner:* Parade

Competency Focus

Me: Self-evaluation

The children reflect on the chapter and express their opinions about their own progress.

Digital Resources

Teacher Resource Center • Print out Test Chapter 8 to use at the end of this lesson. The Test Generator also allows you to create customized tests.

• For the Exam Booster activities on the AB page, choose the audio buttons to access the recordings.

Student's App • Encourage the children to play the games on their smartphone/tablet. Ask them to record their scores to compare in the next lesson. (*The Inks* Apps are free and available on the App Store and Google Play.)

1 Reading and Writing. Look and read. Choose the correct words and write them on the lines. There is one example.

The children write the items described.

Answers

1 locker **2** birthday **3** costume **4** lantern **5** parade

2))) AB 8.1 Listening. Listen and color and write. There is one example.

Play Track AB 8.1 twice. Children listen and color and write.

Answers (Audioscript on p. 224)

Picture colored as follows: lantern—orange,

Chapter 9 — My Achievements Overview

The children will:

- use critical thinking skills to identify personal achievements.
- ask and answer about life experiences.
- read, understand, and act out a story.
- talk about life experiences they want to achieve.
- talk about experiences they have not had and explain why.
- find out how to calculate percentages.
- make an accordion scrap book.

Key Vocabulary

Personal achievements: build a den, catch a fish, climb a tree, fly a kite, go stargazing, make a snowman, swim in the ocean, watch the sunrise

Wider-world achievements: climb a mountain, eat foreign food, fly in a helicopter, hit a home run, ride a camel, run a marathon, sail the ocean, travel abroad

Key Grammar

- Have you ever climbed (a tree)? Yes, I have.
- Have you ever caught (a fish)? No, I haven't.
- I've never run (a marathon), but I'd like to.
- I've never flown (in a helicopter). I'm too scared!

Reading Skills

Story: *Kakapo Adventure*
Genre: modern adventure story

Literacy Development

- predict story content from title and pictures
- interpret and personalize the theme of the story
- find sequencing words in the story

Functional Language

- Have you thought about …ing … ?
- Yes, I'd love to. I'm really interested in …
- Me, too!

Spelling

Words with difficult spelling

CLIL: Math—Calculating percentages

The children find out about the percentages of people who have had certain experiences.

Competency Focus

The children will:

use critical thinking skills to identify personal achievements. (Lesson 1)

predict the content of a story. (Lesson 3)

talk about different life experiences. (Lesson 5) | apply new grammar to previously learned vocabulary. (Lesson 2)

talk about experiences they have never had and give reasons why. (Lesson 6) | work in pairs to act out a dialogue. (Lesson 3)

present their accordion scrap book to the class. (Lesson 8) | personalize the story by talking about their own camping experience. (Lesson 4)

evaluate their own progress in the chapter. (Review) | develop understanding of their community by finding out about pet ownership. (Lesson 7) |

Digital Overview

Teacher Presentation

Student eBook and Digital Activity Book

- Oral Storytelling Video 9.1: *Kakapo Adventure*
- Interactive versions of AB activities
- Integrated audio and answer key for all activities

Teacher resources for planning, lesson delivery, and homework

Teacher Resource Center

- Class Planner Chapter 9
- Worksheets to print out (including notes and answers):
  - Grammar Worksheet 9A: Have you ever climbed …?
  - Grammar Worksheet 9B: I've never run a marathon, but I'd like to.
  - Oral Storytelling Video Worksheet 9: *Kakapo Adventure*
  - Phonics Worksheet 9
  - CLIL Graphic Organizer 9
  - Test Chapter 9 and End-of-year Test
- Test Generator
- Speaking Assessment: Cambridge English Young Learners Exams

Watch the Oral Storytelling Video

- Literacy Handbook

Children's resources for consolidation and practice at home

Student eBook and Reader eBook

- Oral Storytelling Video 9.1: *Kakapo Adventure*

The Inks Student's App

Vocabulary games: Personal achievements and wider-world achievements

My Achievements

Lesson 1

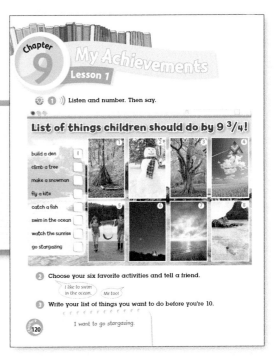

Vocabulary

Lesson objective: identify and talk about personal life experiences and achievements

Key vocabulary: *build a den, catch a fish, climb a tree, fly a kite, go stargazing, make a snowman, swim in the ocean, watch the sunrise*

Materials: Track 9.1

Warmer: Visualization

Have the children close their eyes and think about their last vacation. Ask *What did you do that was special? Did you play a special game / visit a special place / do something unusual? Were you alone when this happened? Who was with you? How did you feel?* Have them open their eyes and write down words that describe their experience. Have the children work in pairs to talk about their ideas. Elicit responses.

1))) 9.1 Listen and number. Then say.

- Read out the blog heading *List of things children should do by 9¾!* Explain that *by 9¾* means "just before they turn 10 years old." Ask *When is your birthday?* around the class and find out who will turn 10 first.
- Play Track 9.1 twice. The children listen and point.
- Then they write the number of each picture by the correct phrase. Elicit answers.
- Say the new phrases for the children to repeat.

Audioscript

Girl: What are you doing?
Boy: I'm making a list of things I want to do in the next year before I'm 9¾!
Girl: Why?
Boy: Because I read about a girl who's doing the same thing on the Internet ... and it sounded fun!
Girl: Oh, wow! Look at her blog ...
Boy: I'd really like to build a den. Look at the den—it has very

long sticks. I'd like to make a fire and camp there for the night.
Look at that big tree. She wants to climb a tree.
I love climbing trees!
And can you see the snowman? It has a long scarf and a black hat. She wants to build a snowman, and I do, too.
Girl: Look at this picture of a windy day. There's a colorful kite in the sky. I'd like to fly a kite.
Boy: I'd like to fly a kite, too.
Girl: Look at this picture of the stars at night. We can go stargazing ...
Boy: Mm, but I really love the ocean. Look at that picture—the water looks warm. I'd like to swim in the ocean.
Girl: I like the ocean too, but I don't want to swim in the ocean. It's very deep! I'd like to catch a fish though. Look at that big gray fish.
Boy: We can camp on the beach. Then in the morning we can watch the sunrise. Look at the orange sky over the ocean ...

Answers

build a den 1, climb a tree 3, make a snowman 2, fly a kite 4, catch a fish 5, swim in the ocean 8, watch the sunrise 7, go stargazing 6

2 Choose your six favorite activities and tell a friend.

- Read the example and elicit answers, *Me, too!* or *I don't.* Have the children in pairs take turns talking about their favorite activities.
- Invite children to say what they like to do for the whole class to respond.

3 Write your list of things you want to do before you're 10.

- Have a child read the example. Ask *What would you like to do before your next birthday?* Elicit answers.

- Have the children write their list in their notebook. They can write as many things as they wish.

- Have children share their wishes, with the rest of the class raising their hand if they agree.

  Answers

  Children's own answers.

Optional activity: I like to … with … in …

Divide the class into small groups. Say *I like to go stargazing. I do this with my friends in the mountains!* to the first child in each group. They have to say a similar sentence about an activity they like to the second child, and so on.

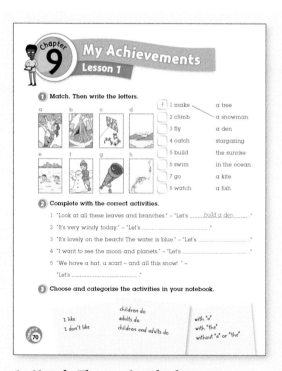

1 Match. Then write the letters.

The children match words to make phrases and then match the phrases to the pictures, writing the correct letters. Elicit answers.

Answers

1 make a snowman f **2** climb a tree a **3** fly a kite c
4 catch a fish h **5** build a den b **6** swim in the ocean e
7 go stargazing g **8** watch the sunrise d

2 Complete with the correct activities.

The children read the mini-dialogues and complete the responses with phrases from Activity 1.

Answers

1 build a den **2** fly a kite **3** swim in the ocean
4 go stargazing **5** make a snowman

3 Choose and categorize the activities in your notebook.

Elicit an example for each category listed. Ask *Which categories would you choose?* Elicit ideas, prompting children to give a reason for their choice. The children choose a pair of categories and list the words in their notebook, then compare with a friend.

Answers

Children's own answers.

Cooler: Play "Activity Ping-Pong"

Divide the class into two teams. You "serve" the first word, e.g. *catch*. The first team completes the phrase, e.g. *a fish*. The teams continue taking turns starting and completing the key vocabulary phrases. Each correct answer gets a point. The team with the most points wins.

Competency Focus

Think! Critical Thinking

The children use critical thinking skills to understand the vocabulary by using visual clues and processing the written and spoken forms.

Digital Resources

Student eBook • Play "Kim's Game" with the new vocabulary. Show the items pictured in SB Activity 1 and elicit each activity. Use *Timer* to give the class one minute to memorize the items, then one minute to recall them. Repeat several times.

Grammar

Lesson objective: talk about what they have done

Key grammar: *Have you ever climbed (a tree)? Yes, I have.*
Have you ever caught (a fish)? No, I haven't.

Secondary language: *It sounds fun, though!, yard*

Materials: Track 9.2; Grammar Worksheet 9A [TRC printout] (optional)

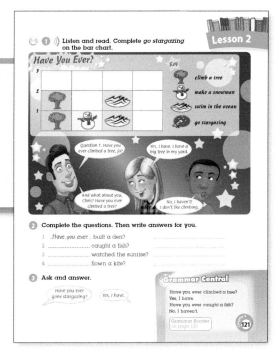

Warmer: Play "Disappearing Words"

Play the game with Lesson 1 key vocabulary (see Games Bank p. 19).

1))) **9.2   Listen and read. Complete *go stargazing* on the bar chart.**

- Explain that the two trees in the bar chart mean that two people have climbed a tree.
- Play Track 9.2. The children listen and read along. They complete the bar chart for *go stargazing*. Elicit answers.

Audioscript

Teacher: *Question 1. Have you ever climbed a tree, Jo?*
Jo: *Yes, I have. I have a big tree in my yard.*
Teacher: *And Jen, have you ever climbed a tree?*
Jen: *Yes, I have, too. It was very tall. I was a little scared!*
Teacher: *And what about you, Chris? Have you ever climbed a tree?*
Chris: *No, I haven't! I don't like climbing.*
Teacher: *OK, two people have climbed trees.*
And question 2. Jo, have you ever built a snowman?
Jo: *No, I haven't. I live in Spain. It's too hot for snow!*
Teacher: *OK! And Jen, have you ever built a snowman?*
Jen: *Yes, I have. I built a snowman with my sister in Canada. We gave him my long scarf, and potatoes for eyes.*
Teacher: *And you, Chris. Have you ever made a snowman?*
Chris: *No, I haven't. I don't like snow!*
Teacher: *OK! Next question. This is question 3. Jo, have you ever swum in the ocean?*

Jo: *Yes, I have. I swim in the ocean every weekend.*
Teacher: *You are lucky! Have you ever swum in the ocean, Jen?*
Jen: *Yes, on vacation last year. The ocean wasn't very warm though.*
Teacher: *And Chris, what about you?*
Chris: *No! I can't swim!*
Teacher: *Now, this is question 4. Have you ever gone stargazing, Jo?*
Jo: *No, I haven't. I go to bed early.*
Teacher: *What about you, Jen?*
Jen: *No, I haven't. It sounds fun, though.*
Teacher: *And Chris, have you ever gone stargazing?*
Chris: *Yes, I have! I love stargazing. I go every weekend with my dad. I know the names of all the stars . . .*

Answers

go stargazing: one

Grammar Central

Have you ever climbed a tree? . . .

Explain we use *Have you ever . . . ?* to ask what a person has/has not done yet (but might do in the future).

For extra practice, try the **Grammar Booster** section in the Student Book (p. 130)

Answers p. 130

Activity 1: **2** have **3** Have, ever flown **4** have **5** Have, ever made **6** haven't **7** Have, ever caught **8** haven't

Activity 2: **2** Have you ever, Yes I have. / No, I haven't. **3** Have you ever, Yes I have / No, I haven't. **4** Have you ever, Yes I have / No, I haven't.

Activity 3: Children's own answers.

2 Complete the questions. Then write answers for you.

- Have the children complete the questions and write short answers for themselves. Elicit answers.

Answers

1–4 Have you ever; children's own answers

3 Ask and answer.

- In pairs, the children take turns asking and answering questions about their life experiences.
- Invite pairs to ask and answer a question for the class.

Optional activity: Play "Verb Ping-Pong"

Divide the class into two teams. The teams take turns saying a verb in the present tense and responding with the present perfect. If they repeat a verb, get it wrong, or take longer than five seconds, the other team wins a point. The team with the most points wins.

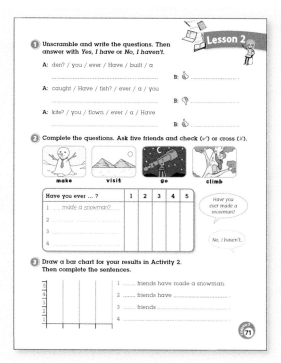

1 Unscramble and write the questions. Then answer with *Yes, I have* or *No, I haven't.*

The children unscramble the questions and write answers using the prompts. Elicit responses.

Answers

1 Have you ever built a den? Yes, I have.

2 Have you ever caught a fish? No, I haven't.

3 Have you ever flown a kite? Yes, I have.

2 Complete the questions. Ask five friends and check (✔) or cross (✘).

The children complete the questions. Elicit questions. They work in groups to ask and answer the questions, and complete the table. Elicit feedback.

Answers

1 made a snowman **2** visited the Pyramids
3 gone stargazing **4** climbed a tree
Children's own answers.

3 Draw a bar chart for your results in Activity 2. Then complete the sentences.

Draw an example bar chart on the board. Help children draw their own, referring to the grid in Activity 2. Then they complete the sentences.

Answers

Children's own answers.

Cooler: Mime time

In pairs, the children take turns prompting, asking *Have you ever . . . ?* and miming an activity from Lesson 1. Their friend responds by identifying the activity and saying *Yes, I have.* or *No, I haven't.*

Competency Focus

Learn

The children develop learning strategies by recognizing and applying language patterns. They show their understanding of previously acquired vocabulary and use it in a new context.

Digital Resources

Student eBook, Digital Activity Book • TIP Use *Add personal note* to note weaknesses in the children's vocabulary, grammar, or pronunciation so you can revisit in later lessons.

Teacher Resource Center • For extra grammar practice, print out Grammar Worksheet 9A.

Reading: Story Extract

Lesson objectives: talk about what they would like to do; predict story content from title and pictures; read the extract from *Kakapo Adventure* (middle)

Functional language: *Have you thought about …ing … ? Yes, I'd love to. I'm really interested in … Me, too!*

Secondary language: *bush, exciting, (park) ranger*

Materials: Tracks 9.3 and 9.4

Warmer: Play "The Shark Game"

Play the game using *Have you ever swum in the ocean?* and *Chris goes stargazing every weekend with his dad.* Draw a line for each word and explain the sentence is about the children in the last lesson (see Games Bank p. 19).

Functional language

1))) **9.3** **Listen and read. Then act out.**

- Have the children look at the picture. Ask *What's Jason showing Felicity?* (*a picture on his laptop*)

- Play Track 9.3. The children listen and read along. Ask *What are they talking about?* (*an adventure trip*) *Do they agree with each other?* (*yes*)

- Play Track 9.3 again, pausing for the children to repeat. Then they act out the dialogue in pairs. Encourage them to talk about different ideas.

Before reading

2 **Look at the story. What do you think the characters are doing?**

- Elicit the story title. Have the children guess what a *kakapo* is.

- Then ask them to look at the pictures and write what they think the characters are doing. Elicit ideas.

Answer

Children's own answers.

3))) **9.4** **Listen and read. Circle T (true) or F (false).**

- Play Track 9.4. The children listen and read along.

- Give them time to read the sentences and circle true or false.

- Play Track 9.4 again for the children to check answers in pairs. Elicit answers, including the correct version of the false sentences.

Answers

1 F 2 T 3 F 4 F

4 What do you think happens next?

- Have the children think and check their answer. Elicit ideas including reasons but do not confirm. Say they will have to read the story to find out.

Answers

Children's own answers.

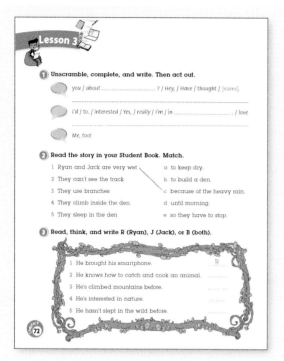

1 Unscramble, complete, and write. Then act out.

Divide the class into pairs to unscramble and complete the dialogue, then act it out. Have pairs act out for the class.

Answers

Hey, [name]. Have you thought about + [children's own answer]?

Yes, I'd love to. I'm really interested in + [children's own answer].

2 Read the story in your Student Book. Match.

The children read the story extract again. They match the sentence halves. Elicit answers.

Answers

1 c 2 e 3 b 4 a 5 d

3 Read, think, and write R (Ryan), J (Jack), or B (both).

The children identify who is described in each sentence, writing R for Ryan, J for Jack, or B for both. Elicit answers.

Answers

1 R 2 J 3 J 4 B 5 R

Cooler: Play "Story A–Z"

Write the alphabet vertically on the board for the children to copy. Divide the class into teams. Give the class four minutes to write something from the story extract for every letter, e.g. *adventure, branch,* etc. They swap lists with another team to check. Each correct answer wins one point. A correct answer that no other team has wins two. The team with the most points wins.

Competency Focus

Collaborate and Communicate

The children act out an authentic dialogue together, putting into practice the functional languages.

Think! Critical Thinking

The children apply reading skills (exploiting pictures and text clues) to understand the story.

Digital Resources

Student eBook • For support on SB activities 2–4, display the SB page and ask children to use *Highlighter* to identify key words in the text that will help them understand the story's context and predict what is going to happen.

Student eBook, Digital Activity Book • TIP Choose an assistant! Ask a child to be responsible for choosing the relevant buttons (e.g. to go to the next activity or answer key).

KAKAPO ADVENTURE

1

Ryan was visiting his Uncle Jack, a park ranger. Jack was searching for a rare parrot in the New Zealand bush. Ryan was interested in nature and was going to help.

Jack: Have you ever flown in a helicopter?

Ryan: No, I've never done anything that exciting before.

2

The helicopter took them to an island. Jack and his team were camping on the beach.

Jack: Have you ever climbed a mountain?

Ryan: No, I haven't, but I'd like to.

Jack: We're going to climb that big one tomorrow.

3

First, they cooked their dinner over the fire. Then, they did some stargazing.

Jack: What are you doing with that thing?

Ryan: Trying to text Mom.

Jack: Those city toys don't work out here. We have to set off early tomorrow so we can get back before dark.

4

The next morning, Ryan watched the sunrise. After that, they packed warm clothes, food, and water.

Jack: We have to be prepared.

5

They followed the track, watching for birds.

Jack: Those clouds look bad.

Ryan: Should we go back?

6

They reached the top of the mountain. Suddenly, heavy rain started to fall. They couldn't see the track.

Jack: We can't go on. Have you ever built a den before?

Ryan: No, I haven't.

7

Jack and Ryan leaned branches against a tree.

Jack: We need more branches.

8

Soon, they had a shelter. They climbed inside to keep warm. The rain continued, but they were dry inside the den.

Jack: We have to stay here until morning.

Ryan: I didn't expect to sleep out here!

9

That night, they ate chocolate for dinner and slept in the den. In the middle of the night, there was a strange, deep booming sound. Ryan was scared, but Uncle Jack was very excited.

Ryan: I've never heard anything like that before!

Jack: It's a kakapo. A night parrot. They are very rare.

10

The kakapo was sitting in a hole in front of the den.

Jack: Don't move. We shouldn't disturb him, he's calling a female. The others aren't going to believe this.

Ryan: Yes, they are. I can video him with my smartphone.

11

Back at camp, the others were excited.

Jack: Have you ever seen one in the wild before?

Researcher: No. What amazing footage.

Ryan: I've tracked his location with my phone.

Jack: He'll come back to his hole again.

12

For Ryan, it was time to go home. He was sailing back with the supply boat.

Ryan: I've never had such an exciting vacation. I've flown in a helicopter, climbed a mountain, and built a den.

Jack: And filmed one of the world's rarest birds. Have you thought about working with us next summer?

Ryan: That would be great!

Jack: And bring that smartphone.

Lesson objective: read and understand the modern adventure story *Kakapo Adventure* in the Reader

Materials: Track 9.5; Reader; Oral Storytelling Video Worksheet 9 [TRC printout] (optional)

Warmer: Review the story extract

Write on the board *Jack, Ryan, mountain, track, rain, den*. Have children retell the story extract, using the words as cues. Prompt with questions as necessary.

Story Summary

Ryan visits his Uncle Jack, a ranger in the New Zealand bush, and tries out many things for the first time. The highlight of his adventure is seeing a kakapo, a night parrot, which he videos with his smartphone.

Value: Have new experiences

))) **9.5 While reading**

- Have the children look at the pictures in the Reader. Ask *Does Ryan's adventure look fun?*

- Play Track 9.5. The children listen and read along. Ask *Was Ryan's phone useful?* (yes)

- Play Track 9.5 again. Ask questions to check comprehension, e.g. *Why is Ryan in New Zealand?* (He's visiting his Uncle Jack.) *What does Jack do?* (He's a park ranger.) *What is Jack searching for?* (a rare parrot) *Has Ryan ever climbed a mountain / flown in a helicopter?* (no) *What did Ryan video?* (the kakapo) *Is Ryan going to come back next summer?* (yes)

After reading: Reflect

- Ask questions to give the children the opportunity to think about the issues raised by the story, e.g. *Why didn't Jack think it was a good idea to take a smartphone on the trip? Do you think it was a good idea? Did Ryan enjoy his vacation?*

Optional activity: Play "The Chain Game"

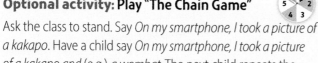

Ask the class to stand. Say *On my smartphone, I took a picture of a kakapo.* Have a child say *On my smartphone, I took a picture of a kakapo and* (e.g.) *a wombat.* The next child repeats the whole sequence, then adds a new animal. If a child makes a mistake or cannot add a detail, they sit down and the chain starts again. The last child standing wins.

Story Time

Exploiting illustrations

Interesting artwork provides opportunity for discussion and enhancing understanding. Engage the children further by pointing to pictures and asking questions, e.g. *Are their bags heavy? Have you ever gotten this wet in the rain? Are they comfortable in the den? What do you think of the kakapo?*

Reading Strategy

Jigsaw

The Jigsaw strategy is a collaborative way of reading. The children read only part of the story or text, then share the information with other readers. Piecing the information together so they can retell the story as a group helps children develop a range of reading and communication skills.

For additional explanation and activities, see the Literacy Handbook on the Teacher's Resource Center.

Cooler: An interview

In groups of three, the children imagine they are a journalist interviewing Jack and Ryan about the kakapo. Have the groups act out their interviews for the class.

Digital Resources

Reader eBook • Show Pictures 9–12. Elicit what the children can see and ask for revised story predictions.

- Oral Storytelling Video 9.1 gives the story with a different ending. Watch it together at the end of the lesson, then discuss the differences.

Teacher Resource Center • Print out Oral Storytelling Video Worksheet 9 to help you get the most out of the video.

Student eBook • The children can watch Oral Storytelling Video 9.1 at home with their family.

Reading Comprehension and Critical Literacy

Lesson objectives: learn about and use sequencing words; relate the story to personal experiences

Materials: Track 9.5; Reader; Oral Storytelling Video Worksheet 9 [TRC printout] (optional)

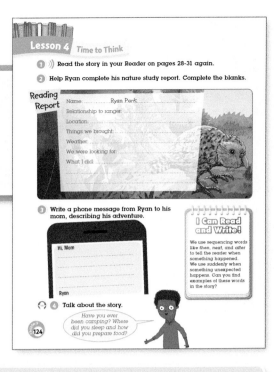

Note: Please ensure that your class has read the Reader story before you do this lesson.

Warmer: Play "Simon Says"

Play the game with (*Simon says . . .*) *build a den / fly a kite / fly on a helicopter / make a snowman*, etc. (see Games Bank p. 19.)

1))) 9.5   Read the story in your Reader.

- Have the children read the story. (Alternatively, play Track 9.5 and have them read along.) Elicit whether they were correct in their predictions in Lesson 3 Activity 4.

- Check comprehension by asking *Was the trip going well at the beginning?* (no) *What difficulties did they find on the way?* (heavy rain / bad weather)

2   Help Ryan complete his nature study report. Complete the blanks.

- Read the headings in the report. Have the children complete the information. Elicit answers.

Answers

Ryan Park; nephew; New Zealand; warm clothes, food; water, and a smartphone; heavy rain; parrots; videoed the kakapo with my smartphone

I Can Read and Write!

Write on the board *then, next, after, suddenly*. Ask *When do you use these words?* (*at the start of a sentence*) Explain that *then, next, after* show the order things happen and that *suddenly* is used when something unexpected happens. Have the children scan the story to find sequencing words. Elicit answers.

3   Write a smartphone message from Ryan to his mom, describing his adventure.

- Elicit what Ryan would want to say to his mom, e.g. *I'm having fun. I'm OK.*, etc.

- Have the children write the message. Elicit messages.

Answers

Children's own answers.

4   Talk about the story.

- Have the children read Jason's questions and answer them. Have children talk about their camping experiences. Ask *Did you have fun? Why? Why not? Would you enjoy a vacation like Ryan's?*

Optional activity: Play "Consequences"

Play the game using *Last summer, I went camping with . . . / We . . . / Then, . . . / Next . . . / I was . . . / And suddenly, . . . / We realized that . . .* (see Games Bank p. 19).

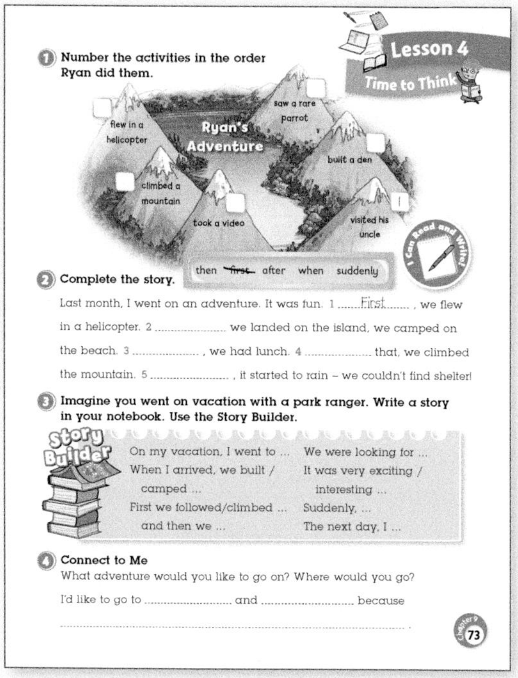

The worksheet page (page 73) is shown at the top left:

> ① **Number the activities in the order Ryan did them.**
>
> Lesson 4
> Time to Think
>
> Ryan's Adventure
> flew in a helicopter
> saw a rare parrot
> built a den
> climbed a mountain
> took a video
> visited his uncle
>
> I Can Read and Write!
>
> ② **Complete the story.**
>
> then ~~first~~ after when suddenly
>
> Last month, I went on an adventure. It was fun. 1 ___First___ , we flew in a helicopter. 2 _____ we landed on the island, we camped on the beach. 3 _____ , we had lunch. 4 _____ that, we climbed the mountain. 5 _____ , it started to rain – we couldn't find shelter!
>
> ③ **Imagine you went on vacation with a park ranger. Write a story in your notebook. Use the Story Builder.**
>
> Story Builder
> On my vacation, I went to ...
> When I arrived, we built / camped ...
> First we followed/climbed ... and then we ...
> We were looking for ...
> It was very exciting / interesting ...
> Suddenly, ...
> The next day, I ...
>
> ④ **Connect to Me**
> What adventure would you like to go on? Where would you go?
> I'd like to go to _____ and _____ because _____
>
> 73

1 Number the activities in the order Ryan did them.

The children number the activities in the order Ryan did them in the story. Elicit answers.

Answers

flew in a helicopter—2; climbed a mountain—3; took a video—6; visited his uncle—1; built a den—4; saw a rare parrot—5

2 Complete the story.

The children practice the **I Can Read and Write!** feature by completing the story using the words supplied. Invite children to read out parts of the story.

Answers

1 First **2** When **3** Then **4** After **5** Suddenly

3 Imagine you went on vacation with a park ranger. Write a story in your notebook. Use the Story Builder.

Use the **Story Builder** prompts to elicit ideas. The children write a story in their notebook, then swap with a friend to check. Have children read their story for the class.

Answers

Children's own answers.

4 Connect to Me

Elicit ideas on places and adventures (e.g. *Africa, look for giraffes because they're my favorite animal*, etc.) before the children write their own response. Elicit responses.

Answers

Children's own answers.

Cooler: Play "Monkey"

Divide the class into two teams (A and B), who stand up facing each other. Have the first child in Team A begin reading the story. When you shout *Monkey!*, the reading switches over to the first child on Team B. Continue in this way, shouting *Monkey!* at random points for the reading to switch.

Competency Focus

Me: Critical Literacy

The children use critical literacy skills to reflect on the theme of the story and relate it to their personal experience.

Digital Resources

Reader eBook • Show the Reader story, picture by picture. Minimize the screen and use *Timer* to give the children two minutes to recall the main events of the story in pairs. Elicit answers, showing the story pictures to confirm.

• Have children use *Highlighter* to identify the time phrases in the Reader story.

Student eBook, Reader eBook • If you haven't already, show Oral Storytelling Video 9.1.

Teacher Resource Center • If you haven't already, print out Oral Storytelling Video Worksheet 9 to do the support activities.

Vocabulary, Song, and Spelling

Lesson objectives: identify and talk about life experiences they want to achieve; practice words that are difficult to spell

Key vocabulary: *climb a mountain, eat foreign food, fly in a helicopter, hit a home run, ride a camel, run a marathon, sail the ocean, travel abroad*

Secondary language: *go horseback riding*

Materials: Tracks 9.6 and 9.7; Phonics Worksheet 5 [TRC printout] (optional)

Warmer: Pre-teach vocabulary

Pre-teach the phrases using mimes for the children to copy. Then write the present and present perfect pairings on the board (e.g. *ride—have ridden*). Prompt with the present perfect to elicit the present.

1))) 9.6 Read and circle the words for the blanks. Then listen, complete, and sing.

- Say each verb for the children to repeat.
- Play Track 9.6. The children listen and complete the song using the verbs supplied. Elicit answers.
- Play Track 9.6 again for the children to sing along and mime the activities.

Answers

ridden, sailed, climbed, eaten, flown, hit, traveled, run

2 Ask and answer.

- Read the example dialogue with a child.
- Divide the class into pairs. They take turns asking and answering questions about their life experiences. Ask pairs to ask and answer a question for the class.

3 Choose verbs and write another verse for the song.

- The children write another verse in pairs.
- Elicit new verses.

Answers

Children's own answers.

Spelling Central

Words with difficult spelling

Read the **Spelling Central** box. Ask *Do you find these words difficult to spell?* Elicit ideas to remember the spelling, e.g. copy them a few times, write them on pieces of paper and look at them every day, etc.

4))) 9.7 Listen and say the chant.

- Have the children look at the picture. Ask *What can you see?*
- Play Track 9.7. The children listen and read along. Elicit the words with difficult spelling.
- Play Track 9.7 again, pausing for the children to repeat.

5 Find it!

- Set a time limit for the children to find difficult words to spell on the page. Point out that they will come up with different answers. Elicit ideas.
- Elicit any other difficult words they know.

Answers

Children's own answers.

Optional activity: Find more difficult words

Have the children scan the previous pages of their Student Book for words which are difficult to spell. Ask them to say the words and to write them on the board.

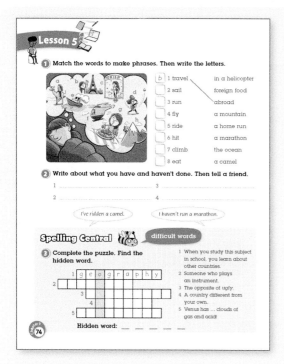

Cooler: Sing a line

))) **9.6**

Play Track 9.6 for the children to sing along. Then divide the class into two groups. Have a child in each group sing a line of the song—child 1 sings *Have you ever ridden a camel?*; child 2 sings *Or sailed the ocean blue?*, and so on. Continue the song around the circle, until it is finished.

Competency Focus

Think! Critical Thinking

The children use critical thinking skills to identify written and spoken forms of new words and complete the activity.

1 Match the words to make phrases. Then write the letters.

The children match the phrases. They then write the letter for each picture detail by the correct phrase. Elicit answers.

Answers

1 travel abroad b
2 sail the ocean e
3 run a marathon c
4 fly in a helicopter f
5 ride a camel a
6 hit a home run d
7 climb a mountain h
8 eat foreign food g

2 Write about what you have and haven't done. Then tell a friend.

Elicit ideas. The children write about their experiences, then discuss them in pairs. Have pairs tell the class about themselves. Do they have many experiences in common?

Answers

Children's own answers.

3 Complete the puzzle. Find the hidden word.

To practice the **Spelling Central** feature, the children use the clues to solve the puzzle and write the hidden word. Elicit answers.

Answers

1 geography **2** musician **3** beautiful **4** abroad **5** dangerous

Hidden word: ocean

Digital Resources

Student eBook • TIP Display the SB for "heads-up" singing. This will enable you to check all the children are participating and identify any who are struggling.

• TIP Use *Timer* to set a time limit for SB Activity 5.

Teacher Resource Center • For phonics practice, print out Phonics Worksheet 9.

Student's App • Encourage the children to play the games on their smartphone/tablet. They could do this with a friend as a fun way to review the chapter vocabulary together. (*The Inks* Apps are free and available on the App Store and Google Play.)

Grammar and Reading

Lesson objective: talk about personal experiences using the present perfect and *never*

Key grammar: *I've never run (a marathon), but I'd like to. I've never flown (in a helicopter). I'm too scared!*

Secondary language: *booked*

Materials: Tracks 9.6 and 9.8; Grammar Worksheet 9B [TRC printout] (optional)

Warmer: What was the last word?

))) **9.6**

Divide the class into two teams. Give one child from each team a board pen. Play Track 9.6, pausing after key vocabulary (words in red). (Alternatively, read the text aloud.) The children run to the board and write the last word. Continue in this way, with a different child responding each time.

1))) **9.8   Listen and read. What has Felicity never done?**

- The children look at the pictures. Ask *What are they looking at?* (*magazines*)

- Play Track 9.8. The children listen and read along. Ask *What has Felicity never done?* (*traveled abroad*)

- Play Track 9.8 again. Ask *What are Cheng and Miguel doing?* (*cutting magazine pictures to make lists*) *Has Miguel ever flown in a helicopter?* (*No, but he would like to.*) *Does Felicity want to fly in a helicopter?* (*No, she's too scared.*) *Has Cheng ever run a marathon?* (*no*) *What has Felicity's mom done?* (*She's booked a vacation to Egypt.*)

Grammar Central

I've never run a marathon, but I'd like to. …

Have the children look at the patterns. Point out the position of *never* with the present perfect. (*between* have/ has *and the verb*) Explain that in English, we do not use *never* with a negative (double negative). Elicit from the class things they've never done but would like to; and things they've never done and wouldn't like to. Encourage them to explain why.

For extra practice, try the **Grammar Booster** section in the Student Book (pp. 131–133)

Answers p. 131

Activity 1: **2** 've never eaten **3** 've never ran **4** 've never jumped **5** 've never visited

Activity 2: **2** been, d **3** driven, a **4** climbed, c

Activity 3: Children's own answers.

p. 132

Activity 1: **2** haven't **3** never been **4** ever been **5** have **6** never fallen **7** have

Activity 2: **2** Yes, she has. **3** Yes, she has. **4** No, she hasn't. **5** Children's own answers. **6** Children's own answers.

p. 133

Activity 1: **2** thought **3** ever seen **4** haven't **5** heard **6** ever **7** walking **8** liked **9** brought **10** never felt

Activity 2: **1** Have you ever … (Children's own answers.) **2** Children's own answers.

2 Write three things you've never done, but would like to.

- Have the children complete the sentences. Give support as necessary.
- They compare answers in pairs. Invite children to read a sentence to the class.

Answers

Children's own answers.

Optional activity: Play "Disappearing Text"

Write on the board *I've never visited a pyramid, but I'd like to. I've never swum with dolphins. I'm too scared!* Have the children read it aloud. Erase a word and have the children read the whole text again. Continue erasing words until children are saying it without any prompts.

---

3 Look and write.

The children use the picture prompts to complete the sentences. Elicit answers.

Answers

I've never climbed a mountain, but I'd like to.
I've never eaten fried snake. I don't like foreign food.
I've never ridden an elephant, but I'd like to.
I've never walked in the jungle. I + children's own answer

Cooler: Have you ever …?

Write prompts on the board, e.g. *been to the moon, run a marathon, played ice hockey, flown a plane, ridden a kangaroo, driven a car*, etc. Divide the class into groups of six. Ask *Have you ever been to Japan?* Have the first child in each group answer *No, I've never been to Japan.* or *Yes, I've been to Japan.* That child asks the next child a different *Have you ever …?* question, and so on around the group.

Competency Focus

Learn

The children develop learning strategies by recognizing and applying language patterns in different contexts.

---

1 Complete the email.

The children complete the email using the words supplied. Elicit answers.

Answers

1 I've **2** never **3** like **4** to **5** I'd **6** but

2 Unscramble and write.

The children unscramble and write the sentences. Elicit answers.

Answers

1 I've never traveled abroad, but I'd like to.
2 I've never sailed the ocean, but I'd like to.
3 I've never watched for whales. I'm too scared!

Digital Resources

Student eBook • Display the SB page. Read through the story one picture at a time. Ask questions to check comprehension as you go.

Student eBook, Digital Activity Book • TIP With the answer key you can reveal the answers all at once or one by one, so you can customize feedback.

Teacher Resource Center • For extra grammar practice, print out Grammar Worksheet 9B.

CLIL: Math—Calculating percentages

Lesson objectives: figure out percentages and talk about life experiences
Materials: CLIL Graphic Organizer 9 [TRC printout] (optional); cards for "Board Pelmanism" (optional)

CLIL Math Lesson 7

1 Read. What percentage of people from the USA have traveled abroad?

Life Experiences

The USA is a very big country. It has a population of over 310 million people. Around 110 million of those people have traveled abroad. This is around 35% of the population. Look:

110 ÷ 310 = 0.35 x 100 = 35

This means around 1 in 3 people have traveled to a different country!

2 Talk to your classmates and make a bar chart.

Have you ever ... flown in a helicopter?

flown in a helicopter   eaten foreign food   traveled abroad

3 Calculate percentages.

1   number of classmates who have flown in helicopter
    ÷
    total number of classmates   X 100 = ...

2   number of classmates who have eaten foreign food
    ÷
    total number of classmates   X 100 = ...

3   number of classmates who have traveled abroad
    ÷
    total number of classmates   X 100 = ...

4 Class Vote
Do you need a lot of money to have interesting life experiences? Why / Why not?

Find Out More!
Find out which pets your classmates have owned.

127

Warmer: Vocabulary math

Draw a grid of nine squares on the board. In each square write a vocabulary item and a value, e.g.:

the Sun = 1, popcorn = 2, handbag = 3, etc.

Teach *plus* and *minus*. Have the children do simple math with the words/numbers: *What's the Sun plus popcorn?* (*handbag*) *What's handbag minus the Sun?* (*popcorn*)

1 Read. What percentage of people from the USA have traveled abroad?

- Write 20% on the board. Explain that this is a percentage and it means 20 out of 100. Read the question and elicit ideas.

- Have the children read the text. Ask *What percentage of people from the USA have traveled abroad?* (35%) Copy the equation on the board and explain it.

- Have the children read the text again. Ask *What's the population of the USA?* (*310 million people*) *How many of those people have traveled abroad?* (*110 million people*)

2 Talk to your classmates and make a bar chart.

- Elicit the questions to ask. Then the children mingle and ask their friends the questions, drawing lines in the bar chart for the yes answers.

- Divide the class intro small groups to compare their results. Elicit answers and show them how to draw the bar chart on the board.

3 Calculate percentages.

- Do an example with the class, e.g. *2 classmates (have flown in helicopter) ÷ (e.g.) 25 classmates x 100 = 8%.*

- Have the children figure out the percentages individually or in pairs. Elicit answers.

Answers

Children's own answers.

4 Class Vote

- Ask *Do you need a lot of money to have interesting life experiences? Why?* (*Things like travel can be expensive.*) / *Why not?* (*You can do things for free like meet new people and explore the outdoors.*) Have the class think about their answer and the reason for it, then vote. Count the votes. Discuss reasons as a class.

Find Out More!

Have a class discussion about pets, using e.g. *Have you had a pet? What type? What pet would you like to have?* Have the children do a class survey to find out what pets their friends have owned. They will need to complete this research before doing the follow-up activity in the Activity Book. (It could be set as homework.)

Optional activity: Play "Board Pelmanism"

Prepare cards using *climb / a mountain, eat / foreign food,* etc. Put the cards face down on the board. Have children turn over the cards to try and make a pair.

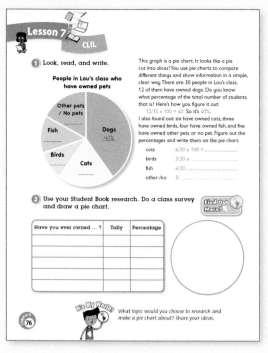

Cooler: Play "Tic-Tac-Toe"

Play the game using *communicate, stargazing, ocean, Germany, crutches, romance, astronaut, fantasy, alphabet* (see Games Bank p. 19). To win a square, a child has to say a sentence using the word.

Competency Focus

Act

The children carry out research to find out more about how many pets their friends have owned. This helps them expand their learning and relate it to their world, both inside and outside the classroom.

1 Look, read, and write.

The children calculate the percentages and complete the pie chart. Elicit answers.

Answers

Dogs 40%, Cats 20%, Birds 10%, Fish 13%, Other pets / No pets 17%

2 Use your Student Book research. Do a class survey and draw a pie chart.

Divide the class into groups of four. Have the children pool the information they learned from their research in the Student Book and the Activity Book. They complete the questions in the table individually, either using the pets in the text in Activity 1 or choosing their own options. They mingle to ask the questions, counting the responses and noting them in the Tally column. They calculate the percentages and draw their pie chart. Have children show their pie charts and present the percentages to the class.

Answers

Children's own answers.

It's My World!

The children discuss in small groups what topic they would choose to research and make a pie chart about. Elicit ideas.

Digital Resources

Student eBook • TIP Use *Add personal note* to log the results of the class vote. Involve the children in tallying the results and writing the scores on the board.

Teacher Resource Center • Print out CLIL Graphic Organizer 9 for the children to use in collating their Find Out More! research.

CLIL eBook • The children can use the CLIL eBook to expand their knowledge of the lesson topic.

Project

Lesson objectives: review language from Chapter 9; make an accordion scrap book; talk about their achievements

Materials: paper, scissors, glue, construction paper, pictures, magazines, colored pencils/markers, ribbon; two game pieces and a coin for each pair

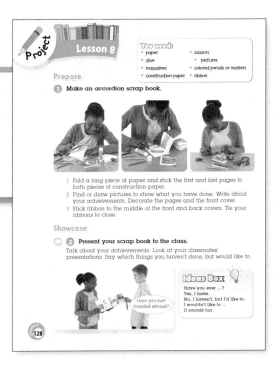

Warmer: Play "Vocabulary Review"

Play the game with ten words from Chapters 1–9, e.g. *Arabic, roller coaster, bandage, receive, hieroglyphics, earring, perform, reply, stargazing, receive* (see Games Bank p. 19).

Prepare

1 Make an accordion scrap book.

- Distribute the materials. Read through the instructions together and ensure the children are clear on what to do.

- The children follow the instructions to make their scrap books. Give support as necessary.

Alternative craft activity

An easier project is to give the children a large sheet of paper for them to design a poster to show what they have learned and achieved during the year.

Showcase

2 Present your scrap book to the class.

- Explain to the children they will present their scrap books to the class, using the **Ideas Box** for support. Given them time to practice in pairs.

- Have the children present their scrapbook to the class.

Optional activity: Scrap book vote

Take a vote on the best scrap book presented to the class.

Chapter 9 — My Achievements — Lesson 1

1 Match. Then write the letters.

a	b	c	d
e	f	g	h

f	1 make	a tree
	2 climb	a snowman
	3 fly	a den
	4 catch	stargazing
	5 build	the sunrise
	6 swim	in the ocean
	7 go	a kite
	8 watch	a fish

2 Complete with the correct activities.

1 "Look at all these leaves and branches." – "Let's ....build a den......."

2 "It's very windy today." – "Let's ...."

3 "It's lovely on the beach! The water is blue." – "Let's ...."

4 "I want to see the moon and planets." – "Let's ...."

5 "We have a hat, a scarf – and all this snow!" –
"Let's ...."

3 Choose and categorize the activities in your notebook.

70

I like	children do	with "a"
I don't like	adults do	with "the"
	children and adults do	without "a" or "the"

Competency Focus

Collaborate and Communicate

By working on this project together, the children consolidate their understanding of the language learned in a way which they will find fun and engaging. They also demonstrate their ability to work with friends and use interpersonal skills.

1 Play "Run a Marathon!"

See p. 43 for instructions on how to play the game.

Answers

1 den, fish, marathon **2** Have you ever swum in the ocean? No, I haven't, but I'd like to. **3** ride a camel, sail the ocean, travel abroad **4** beautiful **5** a pie chart **6** a kakapo **7–8** Children's own answers. **9** Yes, I have. / No, I haven't. **10** Children's own answers.

Cooler: Phrase building

Have the class stand. Model the activity. Say a verb, e.g. *I've made* … The first child responds by adding a noun, e.g. *I've made a snowman*. They then prompt with a new verb, e.g. *I've built* … for the next child to complete. Continue around the class or in groups. If a child makes a mistake or cannot add a new verb, they are out and sit down. The last person standing wins.

Digital Resources

Student eBook • Show the pictures, stage by stage, as you talk the class through the activity process.

• The children choose one topic from Chapters 1–9. They review the vocabulary at home in preparation for a quiz that you can have in your next class.

Language Review

Lesson objective: review language from Chapter 9
Materials: Tracks 9.9 and AB 9.1, AB 9.2 and AB 9.3

Warmer: Story Review

Use Lesson 6 in all chapters. Say things that Story Central characters have done to elicit the character name.

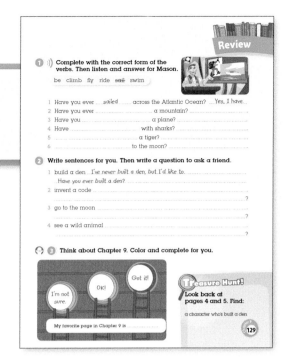

1)) **9.9** **Complete with the correct form of the verbs. Then listen and answer for Mason.**

- Play Track 9.9 twice. The children listen and complete.
- The children write their answers. Elicit responses.

Audioscript

Interviewer: Good afternoon, Mason Jackson, and thank you for coming on the show.

MJ: My pleasure.

Interviewer: Now, Mason, you've done some incredible things in your life, haven't you? Have you ever been in danger?

MJ: Well, yes, Mike, I have. I've done a lot of dangerous things. I've sailed across the Atlantic Ocean, I've climbed Mount Everest, and I've swum across fast rivers.

Interviewer: And have you ever flown a plane?

MJ: No, I haven't. I've never flown a plane, but I'd like to. I have flown in a helicopter.

Interviewer: Have you ever met any dangerous animals?

MJ: Well, I haven't swum with any sharks or whales. But I've seen snakes in the jungle . . . and I've ridden a tiger.

Interviewer: Wow! And is there anything you've never done, but would like to?

MJ: Well, yes, Mike. I've never been to the moon, but I'd like to go!

Interviewer: Now that really is dangerous! Thank you very much for talking to us.

Answers

1 sailed—Yes, I have. **2** climbed—Yes, I have. **3** ever flown—No, I haven't. **4** you ever swum—No, I haven't. **5** Have you ever ridden—Yes, I have. **6** Have you ever been—No, I haven't.

2 **Write sentences for you. Then write a question to ask a friend.**

- Children write sentences and questions.

- In pairs, they take turns asking and answering questions.

Answers

Children's own answers. **1** Have you ever built a den? **2** Have you ever invented a code? **3** Have you ever been to the moon? **4** Have you ever seen a wild animal?

3 **Think about Chapter 9. Color and complete for you.**

- Children color the circle which represents how they feel about their own progress (self-evaluation).
- Have the children complete the sentence.

Treasure Hunt!

Have the children look at pp. 4–5, and find a character who has built a den.

Cooler: Reader review

Give the children several minutes to look back at all the Reader stories and remember which ones they liked best.

Competency Focus

Me: Self-evaluation

The children reflect on the chapter and express their opinions about their own progress.

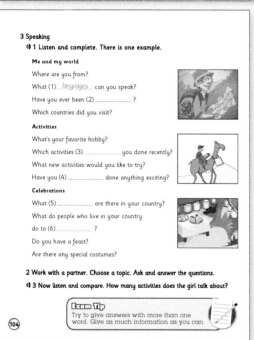

1 Reading and Writing. Read the story. Choose a word from the box. Write the correct word next to numbers 1–4. There is one example.

Children complete the text using the words supplied.

Answers

1 sticks 2 stargazing 3 dolphins 4 abroad 5 b

2))) AB 9.1 Listening. Listen and tick (✔) the box. There is one example.

Play Track AB 9.1 twice. They listen and check the correct picture in each section.

Answers (Audioscript on p. 224)

1 b 2 a 3 c

3.1))) AB 9.2 Speaking. Listen and complete. There is one example.

Play Track AB 9.2 twice. The children listen and write the correct word for each sentence. Check answers.
(Audioscript on p. 224)

3.2 Speaking. Work with a partner. Choose a topic. Ask and answer the questions.

Children work in pairs to ask and answer the questions in activity one. Listen to check answers.

3.3))) AB 9.3 Speaking. Now listen and compare. How many activities does the girl talk about?

Play Track 9.3 twice. The children listen and compare how many activities the girl talks about. Check answers.
(Audioscript on p. 224)

Digital Resources

Teacher Resource Center • Print out Test Chapter 9 and End-of-year Test to use at the end of this lesson. The Test Generator also allows you to create customized tests.

• For the Cambridge English Young Learners Exam activities, there are speaking prompts available for this chapter.

Exam Booster Audioscripts

)) AB 1.1
N: Example.
M: Hi, W. Did you read a book about a different country?
G 1: Yes, I did. I read this one—it's about a French G from Paris.
M: Was it good?
G 1: Yes, it was. I learned a lot about France.
N: Can you see the line? This is an example. Now you listen and draw lines.
N: One.
M: Hi, B. Is that your book?
B: Yes, I finished the story yesterday.
M: Which country was it about?
B: It was about Egypt and an Egyptian B. He lived near the Pyramids. Look— you can see his house.
M: That's really interesting, B.
N: Two.
M: Hello, Vicky. What's that book you've got there?
G: Well, I think it's about houses and life in Mexico.
M: You think?
G: Yes, but it's in Spanish—and I don't speak Spanish.
M: Well, you have to learn!
N: Three.
B 1: Hi, Dave. Can you help me?
B 2: Hi, Paul. What's the problem?
B 1: I need to find out about Canada for my project.
B 2: Well, they speak English and French there—so you can find books in both languages.
B 1: That's great. I can speak French, too!
N: Four.
G: Hello, Dave.
B: Hello, Lucy.
G: Are there any books about Japan?
B: Yes, here's one. It's about Japanese food but it's in English.
G: Good—I don't speak Japanese. Oh, this looks fun—what delicious food! Thanks, Dave.
N: Five.
M: Hello, Tom. What's your book about?
B: It's about GerMy. I want to learn about the country before I visit my friend Hans.
M: So Hans is GerM?
B: Yes, but he speaks really good English, too.

)) AB 2.1
N: One
W 1: Good morning. Can I help you?
M 1: Yes, it's Mr. Brown. I have a bad headache and a fever. I need to see the doctor.
W 1: OK, Mr. Brown. Hmm ... Yes, you can see the doctor on Tuesday, at 10 a.m. You should stay in bed today, and rest quietly.
M 1: Thank you.
N: Can you see the letter E? Now you listen and write a letter in each box.
N: Two
W 2: Hello, it's Mrs. Robson. Can I see the

doctor, please?
W 1: What's the problem?
W 2: I have a bad stomach ache.
W 1: Oh dear. Did you eat anything different?
W 2: No, but I ate too much cake!
W 1: Well, you can see the doctor on Monday at 5 p.m. ... And you shouldn't eat anything — just drink some tea.
N: Three
W 1: Good afternoon.
W 3: Oh, hello. Is the doctor there?
W 1: Yes, but he's busy today. What's wrong?
W 3: It's Johnny. He has a very bad cough. He went swimming in the river yesterday.
W 1: You should give him some cough medicine.
W 3: Yes, I did, but he's still coughing.
W 1: OK, you can see the doctor on Friday at 2 p.m.
W 3: That's fine. Thank you.
N: Four
W 1: Good morning.
M 2: Hello. This is Mr. Davis.
W 1: You don't sound good. Do you have a sore throat?
M 2: Yes. It's very bad. I don't know what to do.
W 1: Well you should try not to eat or speak. You can come at 10:30 tomorrow morning.
M 2: Thank you.
N: Five
W 1: Good morning. Can I help you?
W 4: It's my little G Julie — she has an earache.
W 1: Oh dear. Well, she shouldn't go to school today — she should stay in bed and keep her ear warm.
W 4: OK.
W 1: And if she's not better, call again tomorrow.
W 4: Thank you.
N: Six
W 1: Good afternoon.
M 3: This is Mr. Smith. My son Paul broke his leg.
W 1: What happened?
M 3: Well, he played soccer this morning and he fell over. Then he couldn't walk.
W 1: Well, it's Saturday today. Paul can see the emergency doctor — or you can go to the hospital.
M 3: OK. Thank you.

)) AB 2.2
N: One
W: Hello, B. How are you?
B: Not so good today.
W: Why? What's the matter?
B: I was on my skateboard in the park. There were a lot of people and I fell off. I couldn't walk. I got a big cut on my knee.
W: Oh dear. Well, you should stay home and rest.
N: Can you see the letter C? Now you listen and write a letter in each box.
N: Two
W: Hi W, what happened to you?

W: Well, it was my Mom's birthday this weekend. There was a party and I wanted to make a cake.
W: But you aren't very good at cooking!
W: I know. Well, first I got a cut on my finger. Then I got a burn on my hand.
W: So that's why you have two bandages!
N: Three
W: Hello M. Are you okay?
M: Hmm. I'm fine now but I had a bad stomach ache last week. I couldn't eat anything.
W: Did you go to the doctor's?
M: Yes, I did. She gave me some medicine.
W: And what did she say?
M: She said I shouldn't eat cake every day and I should try to eat more healthy foods like fruits.
N: Four
W: Hi, G. You look tired. What did you do last week?
G: Well, I went to visit my uncle. He lives near the ocean.
W: Cool!
G: Yes, I went water-skiing all week. But on the last day it was chilly and a bit foggy and I fell off.
W: Is your leg broken?
G: No, it isn't. But I have to walk with crutches for a few days.
N: Five
W: Hi Peter. What's the matter?
B: It was Sports day yesterday. It was terrible.
W: Why? Which sports did you play?
B: I threw the javelin. Now my arm hurts. I couldn't write or do my homework last night.
W: Is it broken?
B: No, it isn't.
W: Well, you should go to the doctor's tomorrow.
B: Yes, I will.
N: Six
W: Hello W. How are you?
W: Hello W. I'm having a bad day.
W: Why? What's wrong?
W: Well first I wanted to clean the kitchen floor but I couldn't use the vacuum cleaner. It doesn't work.
W: Oh dear.
W: So I used the broom — but it takes a long time.
W: Yes.
W: And when I finished I wanted a sandwich but there wasn't any bread.
W: Oh. Let's go to the café then.
W: Good idea!

)) AB 3.1
W: Hello, Buzz. Come in, please.
M: Hello, Control. I can hear you now.
W: Hi, Buzz—how My planets can you see in the new galaxy?
M: I'm looking through the big window now. I can see three ... no, four planets ... one is much farther away.
W: That's great, Buzz—four planets to study.

N: Can you see the answer? Now you listen and write.
N: One
W: What about the first planet, Buzz?
M: It's more interesting than the others.
W: Why, Buzz? What can you see?
M: It has rings around it!
W: What color are the rings?
M: Red and orange.
W: Red and orange! Wow! Fantastic!
N: Two
W: How about the second planet?
M: Well, that one is farther away. But it's different from the others.
W: Why?
M: Well, it has a lot of moons. I can see nine moons in orbit around the planet.
W: OK, Buzz, let me log that information. Nine moons.
N: Three
M: Come in, Control. There's something traveling fast in the sky.
W: Buzz, can you identify it? Is it a planet?
M: No, it's going too fast. I think it's a rock ... yes, it's a meteor.
W: Oh, no. Meteors are more dangerous than planets.
M: Hold on ... the computer says it's about eight meters across.
W: Okay ... eight meters ... So, it isn't an asteroid. You're OK, then.
N: Four
M: Now I'm looking at the third planet.
W: What's it like?
M: Well, that's the one most similar to Mars. I traveled to Mars in 2012. It was icy and cold and this planet is cold, too.
W: Oh, yes, 2012 ... that was the most interesting trip before this.
N: Five
W: Buzz, what can you tell us about the fourth planet?
M: Yes, it's the farthest away from our rocket, so it's difficult to see.
W: I think you can name that planet ... You discovered it!
M: OK. I name the fourth planet ... BUZZO!
W: Ha, ha! How can I write that in the log?
M: B-U-Z-Z-O.
W: OK. I name this Planet Buzzo. I won't forget that name.

)) AB 3.2
B: The mountain is different. It's not in space.
G: Yes, the meteor, the astronaut and the rocket all travel in space. The mountain is different — it's on Earth.

)) AB 3.3
N: One
B: The restaurant is different. It's not a ride.
G: Yes, the carousel, the Ferris wheel, and the slide are rides at the amusement park. The restaurant is different. You can't ride it.

N: Two
B: This is different. The B can play soccer. It isn't an injury.
G: Yes, here he can't walk. Here he can't eat, and here he can't do his homework. This is different — he can play soccer.
N: Three
G: This planet is different. It's the biggest planet. These are smaller.
B: Yes, this one is different. I think it's Saturn. This one has rings but these planets don't have rings. It's the most beautiful planet.

))) AB 4.1

N: Which type of movie does W like best?
B 1: Which movies do you like, W?
G 1: Well, I like science fiction—I've seen a few of those movies.
B 1: How about horror movies?
G 1: No, I haven't seen any horror movies. I don't like them.
B 1: So what are your favorite movies?
G 1: Animations—they're great.
N: Can you see the tick? Now you listen and tick the box.
N: One
N: Which kind of movie hasn't Jon seen?
G 2: Hi Jon. Have you seen the new action movie at the movie theater?
B 2: Yes, it was cool. And I've seen the new comedy movie, too.
G 2: Oh, yes. I haven't seen it yet. Was it good?
B 2: Yes, really funny.
G 2: Have you seen that new musical?
B 2: No, I haven't seen it and I'm not going to! I really hate musicals.
N: Two
N: What hasn't Jenny done yet?
W: Jenny, have you finished your homework yet? It's dinner time.
G 3: Yes, Mom. I've done my math and my history.
W: And have you cleaned up your room?
G 3: Yes, Mom. It's all done.
W: Come on, then—let's eat!
N: Three. What has Rob done?
G 2: Oh, look, there's a play on at the theater. Have you seen it, Rob?
B 1: No, I haven't—I've never been to the theater. I prefer movies.
G 2: Well, there's a new fantasy movie on at the movie theater. Have you seen that already?
B 1: Yes, I have. I love fantasy movies. My cousin went to visit the studio where they make those movies. She said it was cool. It's Katy's birthday party on Saturday.

))) AB 5.1

B: Hello, this is Dave.
W: Oh, hello, Dave. This is Katy's mom.
B: Oh, hi, Mrs. Jones.
W: I'm calling about the party.
B: A party—oh, yes. It's Katy's birthday party on Saturday.
W: Can you see the answer? Now you listen and write.
N: One
B: Is Lucy there?
W: No, I'm sorry, I haven't seen her today. I think she's at her piano lesson.

W: Well, can I leave a message for Lucy from Katy?
B: Yes, of course. Hang on—I'll write it down.
N: Two
W: Can you tell her the day of the party has changed?
B: Okay. It isn't on Saturday, then?
W: No, we moved it to Sunday, October 25th.
B: Sunday, October 25th.
N: Three
W: And can you tell her that we've had to change where the party is, too. We've invited so My people… there's not enough space at home.
B: OK, so where is it now?
W: It's at the Kingsley Center at 3 o'clock.
B: How do you spell that?
W: K-I-N-G-S-L-E-Y.
B: OK—is that the one on the other side of town?
W: Yes, that's right.
N: Four
W: Once Lucy knows about the changes, she needs to tell Katy if she can still come to the party.
B: OK.
W: Can you ask her to send Katy an email?
B: Yes. Write an email to Katy about the party …
W: Did you get all that, Dave?
B: Yes, I've written it all down.
N: Five
W: Oh, Dave, one more thing. Can you tell Lucy to bring her sneakers? We've organized some sports and games for the party, too.
B: Yes … OK … sneakers. She bought some new ones a week ago.
W: Thanks, Dave.
B: You're welcome, Mrs. Jones.

))) AB 5.2

W: Hello B. I'm calling about the museum visit.
B: Hello, W. Have you sent me a text message?
W: No, I haven't. I've sent you an e-mail with all the information.
B: I haven't received it yet.
W: Well, I sent it to your mom two days ago.
B: Oh yes. She says she's already received it.
N: Can you see the answer? Now you listen and write.
N: One
B: I've already looked at the message. Which museum is it?
W: It's the museum in Lakestone.
B: Lakestone? How do you spell that?
W: L-A-K-E-S-T-O-N-E
B: Lakestone. Great! I haven't been there yet.
N: Two
W: It's a very interesting museum.
B: Is it more interesting than our town museum?
W: Oh yes. There are a lot of different things to see.
B: Are there any machines?
W: Yes, there's a Morse code machine. And there's an old radio. You can listen to it!

B: That sounds fun.
N: Three
W: Oh, B. You should see the space gallery, too.
B: Yes. I've already seen some photos of it. It looks great!
W: There's an astronaut suit. And there's a map of the planets and how they move in the solar system.
B: Wow!
N: Four
B: What's the oldest thing in the museum?
W: Well, there are some very old Egyptian objects.
B: Cool!
W: Yes, they have symbols on them called hieroglyphics. People used them to communicate about 5,000 years ago.
B: That's amazing.
N: Five
B: Is there anything I should bring with me?
W: Well, you should bring your cell phone to take a few photos.
B: Anything else?
W: You should bring a notebook. Then you can make notes about the most unusual objects in the museum.
N: Now listen again.

))) AB 6.1

W: Look, Jenny, isn't that your hat under the chair?
G 1: No, it isn't mine. It's yours, Daisy, isn't it?
G 2: Does it have a picture of a bird on it?
W: Yes, it does.
G 2: Yes, that hat is mine.
N: Can you see the line? This is an example. Now you listen and draw lines
N: One
W: And whose bag is this, between the box and the chair?
G 1: Oh, give that to Mike—I think it's his.
B 1: Are you sure it's mine? What's inside?
G 1: There's a math book with a name … Mike Thomson.
B 1: Ha, ha! It's mine then.
N: Two
W: What about these gloves next to the box? Whose are these?
G 1 & G 2: They aren't ours.
G 1: They're Bs' gloves. Aren't they yours, Pete?
B 2: Yes, they're mine. Oh! There are three of them!
N: Three
W: Whose umbrella is this on the table?
G 1: Is it really big?
W: Yes!
G 1: Does it have a hole in it?
W: Yes!
G 1: It's Tim's. I don't think it keeps him very dry!
N: Four
W: What did you lose, Jenny?
G 1: I lost my Bet, Miss.
W: There's a Bet on the chair. Look—it's beside the book.
G 1: That's mine. Thank you!
N: Five
W: What's wrong, Sue?

G 3: I lost my boots.
W: Has anyone seen Sue's boots? What about these boots in the box?
B 1 & B 2: Those are our soccer boots!
G 3: Oh, look, those boots are mine! The ones in front of the box.

))) AB 6.2

N: Picture A. Today Paul played soccer. Afterward, he felt very tired. He has already finished reading his book. Now he is sleeping.

))) AB 6.3

N: Picture B. Now Paul is dreaming. He is in a dark cave. He is wearing a cloak and a big hat and he has a sword. He has found a treasure chest with a lot of jewels and a ring. Paul thinks the treasure is his.
N: Picture C. Paul has put on the ring with the big jewel. It's a magic ring. Paul starts to disappear. His feet have already disappeared.
N: Picture D. Paul is back in his bedroom. He has fallen out of bed. The story book is on the floor. His sister is laughing. But there is a ring with a jewel under t he bed.

))) AB 7.1

N: One
M: Hi, W. Did you all have a busy week? I didn't see you or your family.
W: Yes, we did. My cousin Emma is visiting soon so I was getting ready.
M: Did you have to clean the house?
W: Well I cleaned the living room.
M: Did you sweep the floor?
W: No, I used the vacuum cleaner. The living room looked much nicer when I finished!
N: Can you see the letter F? Now you listen and write a letter in each box.
N: Two
M: And what else did you do to help your mom?
W: Well I cleaned my bedroom.
M: That was hard work!
W: Yes, it was. But my brother was great. He helped me clean my bedroom.
M: That was kind.
N: Three
M: Why was your mom busy? What was she doing?
W: Well, my mom was cooking food for everyone. She made a lot of food!
M: What did she make?
W: On Thursday she made a big chocolate cake and a really big pizza.
M: mm … my favorite!
N: Four
M: What about your dad? Why was he so busy?
W: Well, he was working a lot.
M: I called on Wednesday but there was no answer.
W: Oh, yes. On Wednesday, my dad and I took the dog to the vet.
M: Is your dog OK?
W: Yes, he's better now.
N: Five
M: Did you have to do a lot of shopping?

W: Oh, yes. On Saturday I went to the mall with my grandma. We bought a lot of things.
M: Was it fun?
W: Not really. Grandma was wearing a necklace but she lost it somewhere.
M: Oh dear!
N: Six
M: What a busy week! Did you relax at all?
W: On Friday, I went to the park with my friend Eva.
M: That was nice.
W: Well, yes … but a W was walking near us when a M ran up and stole her handbag. I had to describe the thief to the police!

))) AB 8.1
W: Look, it's a party for Midsummer night. It's the time when we celebrate the longest day in the year.
B: What do you do?
W: We celebrate in the yard. Can you see the decorations?
B: The decorations that are on the house?
W: Yes. Color it blue.
B: OK, that looks good.
N: Can you see the blue decorations? This is an example. Now you listen and color and write.
N: One
W: It's a beautiful evening. Can you see the lantern?
B: The lantern that's hanging in the tree?
W: Yes, that's it. Can you color it?
B: What color?
W: You choose.
B: OK. I'm making it orange …
N: Two
W: Can you see the children who are watching the fireworks?
B: Yes, they're next to the house.
W: Look at the sky … can you see the firework?
B: Yes. It's beautiful.
W: Can you color it purple?
B: Yes, that looks great.
N: Three
W: Are you hungry?
B: Yes, I am.
W: Can you see a table at the back of the yard?
B: Yes.
W: That's the place where they're serving the food.
B: Oh, yes! What a feast! I can see a cake.
W: Yes. It's chocolate. Can you color the cake brown?
B: Yes, OK … yummy!
N: Four
W: Can you see the sign on the stage?
B: Yes.
W: Can you write some words on the sign?
B: OK.
W: Write the words Happy Summer.
B: OK … there … Happy … Summer.
N: Five
W: That G is celebrating something else … It's her birthday.
B: Yes … look … her mom is holding a gift.

W: Can you color the gift yellow?
B: Yes, that's a good color. I wonder what it is!
W: It's a surprise!

))) AB 8.2
W: Would you like to color this picture now?
G: Yes, please. These children are wearing costumes for a celebration, I think.
W: Yes. Can you see the G who is wearing a cloak?
G: Yes. She's a queen. What color is her cloak?
W: You can color it purple.
G: Okay.
N: Can you see the purple cloak? This is an example. Now you listen and color and write.
N: One
W: Now, I'd like you to color something else. Can you see the B with the magic lamp?
G: Yes, he's next to the pirate.
W: That's right! Can you color the lamp?
G: Sure. Can I color it orange?
W: No, it's yellow.
G: All right.
N: Two
W: Can you see the other G in the picture?
G: The G who is wearing the pirate costume?
W: Yes. Color the belt brown.
G: Okay.
W: Have you finished coloring yet?
G: Yes.
N: Three
W: Can you see the B who is dressed as a detective?
G: Yes, he's between the queen and the B with the magic lamp.
W: That's right. He's wearing a tie.
G: Can I color it blue?
W: That's a nice color but I'd like you to color it red, please.
G: Okay.
N: Four
W: Can you see the place where the M is standing?
G: Yes. The M who is hanging the last lantern? Next to the tree?
W: That's right. Can you see the dragon on the lantern?
G: Yes. Is it red?
W: No, it isn't. You can color it green.
G: Great!
N: Five
W: Now I'd like you to write something. Can you see the sign?
G: Yes, it's on the left.
W: Can you write the word Parade?
G: Where? On the sign?
W: Yes.
G: Okay. We have a parade to celebrate the end of school. It's fun!
W: Okay. You've finished. Thank you.

))) AB 9.1
N: What has Julie done?
M: So, tell me about the outdoor activities you've done.
G 1: Well, when I visited the Nature Park, I went fishing.
M: Did you catch a fish?

G 1: No, I didn't, and I didn't swim in the river. But I climbed a mountain!
M: That's great!
N: Can you see the tick? Now you listen and tick the box.
N: One. How has Pete traveled?
M: Have you ever been on an exciting trip, Pete?
B 1: Well, I've never sailed across the ocean. But I've been on vacation to other countries.
M: Did you fly in a plane?
B 1: No, I traveled by train. It was a long trip!
N: Two. What hasn't W done?
M: W, what have you done?
G 2: Well, I've been to Canada to visit my cousin.
M: Wow, that was exciting! Did you go skiing?
G 2: No, I haven't learned to ski yet. But I'm going to.
M: What did you do with your cousin?
G 2: We built a big snowM.
N: Three. What has Tom won?
M: Has anyone ever won a sports prize?
B 2: Well, I've run three races—but I've never won!
M: But you've won the 100m race, haven't you, Tom?
B 2: No, I haven't. But I've won a prize with my baseball team—we're fantastic!

))) AB 9.2
W: Hello. Let's talk about you and your world. Where are you from?
B: I'm from Spain.
W: What languages can you speak?
B: Spanish, English, and French.
W: And have you ever been abroad?
B: Yes, I have. I've been to France.
W: And now let's talk about your favorite activities. Which activities have you done recently?
B: I've built a den.
W: Great! And have you ever done anything really exciting?
B: Yes, I have. I've swum in the ocean and I've seen a dolphin.
W: Wow!
W: And finally, let's talk about celebrations. What festivals are there in your country?
B: Well, in Spain we have a lot of festivals. I like the New Year festival.
W: And what do people who live in your country do to celebrate?
B: After New Year we have a parade. It's fun.
W: Great! Thank you.

))) AB 9.3
M: Now let's talk about your hobbies and activities.
G: Okay.
M: What's your favorite hobby?
G: I like swimming and water sports. I've swum in the ocean.
M: And which activities have you done recently?
G: I've flown my kite in the park. It's fun!
M: And what new activities would you like to try?

G: Well, I've never run a marathon, but I'd like to.
M: Have you ever done something exciting?
G: Well, I've ridden a camel and I've eaten foreign food. That was really exciting!
M: Great! Thanks.